Entrance Gates to the Old Part of the Burying Ground
Erected by Faith Trumbull Chapter, D. A. R.

INSCRIPTIONS

FROM GRAVESTONES IN THE OLD BURYING GROUND

Norwich Town, Connecticut

*with
Illustrations from Original Photographs*

George S. Porter

HERITAGE BOOKS
2012

HERITAGE BOOKS
AN IMPRINT OF HERITAGE BOOKS, INC.

Books, CDs, and more—Worldwide

For our listing of thousands of titles see our website
at
www.HeritageBooks.com

A Facsimile Reprint
Published 2012 by
HERITAGE BOOKS, INC.
Publishing Division
100 Railroad Ave. #104
Westminster, Maryland 21157

Originally published by
The Society of the Founders
of Norwich, Connecticut

The Bulletin Press, Norwich, Connecticut
1933

These inscriptions were purchased of Mr. Porter's estate in 1913, by the Society of Founders of Norwich, Conn., and 250 copies are now published by the society in March, 1933

— Publisher's Notice —
In reprints such as this, it is often not possible to remove blemishes from the original. We feel the contents of this book warrant its reissue despite these blemishes and hope you will agree and read it with pleasure.

International Standard Book Numbers
Paperbound: 978-0-7884-0479-5
Clothbound: 978-0-7884-9235-8

INSCRIPTIONS

Index to Illustrations

1. Entrance Gates, Cemetery Lane - - - - - - - - - Frontispiece
2. Twenty French Soldiers - - - - - - - - - - Page 9
3. Mr. John Post, Sergt. Thomas Waterman, Deacon Simon & Mrs. Mary Huntington — Page 32
4. Deacon Thomas & Mrs. Mary Adgate, Mr. Stephen & Mrs. Hannah Gifford - - Page 56
5. Mr. Thomas & Mrs. Mary Leffingwell Dr. Solomon Tracy & Ebenezer Backus, Esq. - - - - - - - - - - - Page 80
6. Deacon Christopher Huntington - - - - - - - - - Page 104
7. The Generals Huntington - - - - - - - - - - Page 128
8. Samuel Huntington, Esq., Rev. Benjamin Lord - - - - - - Page 152
9. Memorial Gates, East Town Street - - - - - - - - Page 169

The Old Burying Ground at Norwich Town

Address Delivered by George S. Porter at the Dedication of the Hubbard Gates July 4, 1903.

The members of Faith Trumbull Chapter, Daughters of the American Revolution, deemed it fitting that on this occasion be presented a brief sketch of the sacred spot affectionately known as the Old Burying Ground. Although the successor of that at Bean Hill both are in a sense one, and a history of either would be incomplete without that of its fellow.

That death respects neither age nor person was proven in the infant plantation of Norwich, when in March, 1661, twenty-one months subsequent to its purchase from the Indians, Mary Andrews, the wife of Thomas Post, was taken. There being then no place of public sepulture in the town her remains were interred in the home lot of her husband at Bean Hill. Nine months thereafter this place of burial was secured by the town, the record being as follows: "December 16, 1661. The Towne hath purchased a burying place of Thomas Post at the Reare of his lott: he is to allow a highway of six foot broad through his lott unto the said burying place. The said Thomas Post hath been satisfied by the Town as on record appears."

Additional land was subsequently secured from the adjoining lot of John Gager, when the names of these original owners naturally attached themselves to the Bean Hill burying ground. In January, 1693, the boundaries of the whole tract were recorded, and in 1697 Samuel Gager was granted by the town "twelve acres of land on Connecticut Plains," in consideration of that taken from his father's home lot.

The historian of Norwich informs us that Connecticut Plains was within the bounds of the Nine-Miles-Square on what was then called the path to Connecticut, *i. e.*, the old road extending through Colchester to Hartford. It may here be explained that this path was so called because for many years after the settlement of the colony the three towns of Windsor, Wethersfield and Hartford were collectively and distinctively known as Connecticut.

Miss Caulkins wrote: "In very few instances are the graves of the first generation of our settlers distinguished by cœval monuments. The men of that age, encompassed with labors and privations, exhausted in laying the foundations of society, had no leisure to cultivate the monumental arts and rear tombs and columns over their fallen companions. But the more favored inhabitants of a later day, the prosperous sons of these laborious fathers, have a debt of grateful reverence to pay which should lead them to preserve the sacred dust from dishonor and cherish with reverent awe the sepulchres of the fathers."

We will add that if any of the early graves in this hallowed spot were ever marked by memorial tributes of love, respect and veneration, all evidence long since disappeared. There exists today not a single vestige to visibly indicate the last resting-places of those of Norwich who passed away prior to the year 1700. After that date the interments in these grounds were few and may have been confined to members of the Gager family.

Several of the original proprietors of Norwich removed to newly founded towns in the vicinity, but of those who remained, who died prior to 1700 and who were undoubtedly interred in this, the oldest place of burial in the town, numbering as nearly as can be determined, fifteen, were the following: William Backus, Sr., Thomas Bliss, John Bradford, Deacon Hugh Calkins, Richard Edgerton, John Gager, Lieut. Francis Griswold, Christopher Huntington, William Hyde, Major John Mason, Dr. John Olmsted, Jonathan Royce, Nehemiah Smith, Lieut. Thomas Tracy and Robert Wade.

The peculiar, indescribable charm of Norwich, as evidenced by the filial affection of its sons and daughters, as well as by the devotion to its interests by those of adoption, has been productive of natural and permanent results. Of these we cannot at this time speak in detail, but may be permitted to mention the Mason monument now standing near the old Post and Gager burying place at Bean Hill.

During the bi-centennial anniversary of the signing of the town's purchase deed which was celebrated in Norwich, in September, 1859, the corner stone of the monument to be erected in honor of Major John Mason, the conqueror of the Pequots and the foremost of the original proprietors of the town, was reverently laid in our beautiful Yantic cemetery. It was subsequently decided, however, that a more appropriate site for so historical a memorial would be the attractive elevation near Bean Hill, in the vicinity of the spot in which the remains of the hero and those of the early settlers were interred, and which served our forefathers as a place of sepulture for forty years.

At the session of the general assembly of May, 1871, the Mason Monument association was granted corporate existence, the Act being approved June 15th following.

The incorporators, all of whom have passed away, were Jedidiah Huntington, Hiram P. Arms, La Fayette S. Foster, John T. Wait, John L. Devotion, James M. Meech, Charles A. Converse, John Dunham, William A. Buckingham, William A. Brewer, Amos W. Prentice, James S. Carew, James Lloyd Greene, Lorenzo Blackstone and James A. Hovey.

The monument was erected in 1871 at a cost of $650.00, and on its four sides were lettered the names of the following thirty-seven early residents of Norwich: Major John Mason, Rev. James Fitch, John Pease, John Tracy, John Baldwin, Jonathan Royce, John Post, Thomas Bingham, Thomas Waterman, Robert Allyn, Sergeant Thomas Leffingwell, Richard Wallis, Thomas Adgate, John Olmstead, Stephen Backus, Thomas Bliss, John Reynolds, Josiah Reed, Richard Hendys, Christopher Huntington, Ensign William Backus, Francis Griswold, Nehemiah Smith, Thomas Howard, John Calkins, Richard Edgerton, Thomas Post, John Gager, Samuel Hide, William Hide, Lieut. Thomas Tracy, Morgan Bowers, Robert Wade, John Birchard, Simon Huntington, Stephen Gifford and John Bradford.

If, in this list, we should substitute the name of William Backus, Sr., for that of his son, Stephen, to it add the name of Deacon Hugh Calkins and from it eliminate the names of Richard Wallis, Stephen Gifford and Richard Hendys, we should have the list of the thirty-five original proprietors of Norwich, as carefully compiled and adopted by the Society of the Founders of Norwich.

After all expenses had been paid the Association had about $150.00 remaining. This unexpended money was deposited in the Norwich Savings Society, a portion of which was to be used for necessary repairs and the balance, with its accumulations, to be utilized in 1959 in the erection of a more imposing memorial on the Norwich Town Green. January 1st of the present year, this fund amounted to $743.24.

February 12, 1872, Lyman W. Lee of Norwich, in consideration of $20.00 deeded to the Mason Monument association a certain piece of land fifteen feet square, in which the Mason monument then stood, adjacent to the former burying ground, together with a right of way to the deeded premises, by the existing traveled path, in and over the land of the grantor, which way was to extend from the Main street leading from the First Congregational meeting house to Bean Hill, for all persons to pass and repass freely and without hindrance, but on foot only.

An amendment to the original charter, approved March 22, 1882, created the treasurer of the town the treasurer of the association, he to have charge of, hold, invest and reinvest its funds; the town clerk was made its secretary, and the mayor and the two senior aldermen of the city of Norwich and the selectmen of the town, during their terms of office, were created directors of the association.

With an increased and an increasing population the necessity for additional ground for interment purposes became imperative. At this time, or January 4, 1699-1700, Lieut. Samuel Huntington of Norwich, in consideration of £90, deeded to "m^r John Tracy, Sarg^t Caleb Abell, Joshua Abell, Daniel Tracy and Richard Bushnell of the same Norwich, in behalf of the s^d Town" "for the use, benefit and behoofe of the s^d Town of Norwich," his home lot estimated to contain about five acres, together with all the buildings, &c., thereon. This property lay east of the green and extended "from the home lot of Simon Huntington, 2d, to the southern line of" what is now "the burying ground lane, covering a frontage of 37½ rods." The major portion was intended for the use of Rev. John Woodward, who was expected soon to officiate "in the work of the ministry among us." An acre and a half, however, was reserved for purposes of public interment as is evidenced by the contract with Mr. Woodward, which bore date August 15, 1699, a portion of which is here quoted:

"And also we do propose and promise to give to you y^{tt} home lott together with the dwelling house and barn and all other appurtenances thereunto belonging which ware major Fitches which sd Lott house and barn shall be att the Dispose of yourselfe heirs and assignes att and after the day of your ordination nevertheless and it is so to be understood that we do reserve to o^r selves and sett apart one acre and halfe of sd lott for a burying place lying at the lower corner of the sd lott next to the land in the present ten ^{or} of the Rev. nd mr. Fitch."

The "One acre & an halfe" was subsequently surveyed and the record entered on the town book January 20, 1714-15.

In 1734 it was decided that "the Burying Place adjoining to the Lott that was Mr. Gookins, shall be laid open to the common from and after the 1st of September next."

In time it became necessary to secure additional land, and July 12, 1796, Azariah Lathrop "for the consideration of twenty-seven pounds five shillings lawfull money received to my full satisfaction of Samuel Woodbridge, Gardner Carpenter and Mundator Tracy all of said Norwich as they are the standing committee of the first society in said Norwich" deeded "unto them in their said capacity and the rest of the inhabitants of said society and their successors all that my piece or parcel of land lying in the said society adjoining the publick burying ground" "containing One hundred and nine rods of land."

March 27, 1819, Luther Spalding "for Divers good Causes and Considerations moving me hereunto and Especially for the Consideration of Four hundred Sixty nine dollars and seventy one cents" conveyed unto John H. Townsend a lot of land "with a dwelling house and Barn standing thereon" adjoining "the publick burying ground." On the same day Mr. Townsend sold "unto said first Ecclesiastical Society" the above mentioned land, the consideration being $524.50.

April 13, 1819, "Erastus Huntington, Girard Carpenter and Joseph C. Huntington of the first Ecclesiastical Society of the Town of Norwich aforesaid" "Being thereunto authorized by a Vote of said Society" and in consideration of $325.00 conveyed a portion of the same property to Lyman Roath. On the same date the last named deeded to the First Ecclesiastical society certain land adjoining the public burying ground, the consideration being $225.00. In this deed the entrance from the old Town street is thus described:

"The Lane is at the main street one rod wide, and at the southend of the Lane at thirteen rods and nine and a half links from said Main street it is thirty links wide."

Fault is frequently found that entrance to the interesting Huntington lot is prohibited by the enclosing picket fence. The legal right of the family to protect this property is evidenced by a deed bearing date April 3, 1789, in which Azariah Lathrop "for the consideration of forty shillings lawfull money rec^d to my full satisfaction of Jedidiah Huntington, Andrew Huntington & Joshua Huntington of said Norwich," deeded to them "one Rod of Land North of, and adjoining to, the common Burying Ground in the first Society of said Norwich for the purpose of Building a Tomb; said Rod of land buts Southerly on said common burying ground and extends Northerly from said common burying ground one Rod, and from the Center of said Tomb Easterly & westerly eight feet and a quarter each way, containing in the whole one square rod of land." Some adjoining property was subsequently acquired by the family.

Although the old burying ground experienced an active career of one hundred and fifty years, during which period perhaps thousands were interred within its limits, there are to-day but about thirteen hundred headstones to visibly remind us of the generations which are gone.

This old place of sepulture was neglected for many years. Numerous memorial stones which indicated the last resting-places of sacred dust fell to earth, and many others, tottering in their places, strove to prolong a usefulness which was unappreciated by the living world about them. Some of the tombs, resultant of the passage of time and the action of the elements were in a sad state of dilapidation and decay, their gaping wounds exposing to public view the whitened bones once so reverently laid to rest. The fences, broken and fallen, offered no opposition to the stray cattle that roamed at will through the neglected grounds causing needless damage and destruction. Coarse, rank and poisonous weeds abounded, and altogether a repulsive atmosphere of neglect, decay and ruin pervaded the place.

The Norwich Rural association was organized April 4, 1869, its objects being "to improve and ornament the streets and public grounds of the town of Norwich by planting and cultivating trees, cleaning and repairing the sidewalks and doing such other work as shall tend to beautify and improve said walks, streets and grounds, and also to repair and keep in order the old burying ground."

Of the good work accomplished by this society during the past third of a century it is within the province of this paper to refer only to that portion which soon became apparent in our second city of the dead. The work of reclamation was at once begun, willing hands and open purses demonstrating the interest so universally felt. During the second year of the association's life additional financial aid was readily obtained which, with kindly acts and appreciative words, greatly encouraged those who had the work in charge. By the close of the year 1870, a substantial stone wall had replaced the forlorn and broken fences, numerous gravestones had been carefully righted and reset, the tombs had been properly repaired, and unsightly weeds had been uprooted and grass seed sown. In 1877 rustic gates of red cedar, designed by the late George Allen Rudd, placed at the entrances, had succeeded their useless and dilapidated predecessors.

In the General Statutes of Connecticut may now be found the following:

"In any town in which exist public burial grounds or cemeteries, not under the control or management of any cemetery association, which have been neglected and allowed to grow up to weeds, briars and bushes, and the fences about the same allowed to become broken, decayed or dilapidated, it shall be the duty of the selectmen of such town, upon the petition of twenty legal voters who are taxpayers of such town, to annually cause such burial grounds to be cleaned from weeds, bushes and briars, and to repair and put in orderly and decent condition the fences or walls about the same; provided, that in no one year shall the expenditure by said selectmen for said purposes, in any one burial ground or cemetery, exceed in the whole the sum of one hundred dollars."

This legislative action relieved the Rural Association in a measure of its self-imposed supervision, yet its interest has never abated. At its annual meeting held May 4, 1885, it was stated that in accordance with the above Act, the selectmen had expended sixty dollars on the grounds during the preceding year. At a similar meeting, held May 5, 1899, a committee consisting of Messrs. Henry W. Kent and Albie L. Hale and Miss Carolyn A. Sterry was appointed to draft a petition to the selectmen praying for the improvement of the old burying ground. The following resulted:

"To the selectmen of the Town of Norwich:

"We, the undersigned, legal voters and taxpayers of said town, respectfully represent that the burial grounds situated at Norwich Town in the said town of Norwich, the same not being under the control and management of any cemetery association, have been neglected and allowed to grow up to weeds, briars and bushes, and the fences about said grounds allowed to become broken, decayed and dilapidated, and therefore petition

"That you may cause said burial grounds to be cleaned from weeds, bushes and briars and the fences or walls about said grounds put in orderly and decent condition; that the sum of $600.00 be appropriated for such purpose, and that the question of such appropriation be presented to the next annual town meeting to be held in and for said Town of Norwich on the first Monday of October, 1899."

This petition bore one hundred and sixteen signatures. To preserve the list of signers, which otherwise would be lost in the archives of the City Hall, the names are here recorded:

William A. Aiken, A. A. Adam, Leonard B. Almy, Willis Austin, Frank S. Avery, Frances A. Bacheler, Cynthia M. Backus, Eunice J. Backus, J. H. Bailey, Charles Bard, David N. Billings, C. E. Blackman, Albie L. Hale, Herbert W. Hale, Philo Hard, Edward Harland, J. A. Hoffman, Charles L. Hubbard, Harriet A. Huntington, Mary Ann Huntington, by C. A. S., M. D. Huntington, Sarah L. Huntington, Lewis A. Hyde, Burrill W. Hyde, William Alfred Jones, D. R. Kinney, W. S. C. Perkins, Moses Pierce, G. G. Pitcher, Mrs. C. A. Potter, Lewellyn Pratt, Charles H. Preston, George C. Raymond, Harriet C. Robinson, N. D. Robinson, Alice A. Rudd, by M. St. J. R., Mary St. John Rudd, John P. Ryan, L. H. Saxton, J. A. Brady, F. T. Brown, J. C. Bushnell, Charles R. Butts, H. L. Butts, J. H. Carpenter, S. B. Case, A. H. Chase, C. P. Cogswell, George D. Coit, J. Connell, John P. Conners, C. N. Congdon, Thomas H. Cranston & Co., A. A. DeWitt, Aron W. Dickey, William G. Ely, Lucius A. Fenton, William H. Fitch, J. T. Frazier, John A. Gager, N. G. Gilbert, S. A. Gilbert, Maria P. Gilman and sisters, A. P. Gleason, Mary S. Gulliver, Mrs. H. A. LaPierre, B. W. Lathrop, J. S. Lathrop, William B. Lathrop, Bela P. Learned, Lyman W. Lee, Costello Lippitt, S. K. Lovett, Louis J. Lynch, W. E. Manning, H. H. McKenna, James McNally, Stephen B. Meech, William F. Bailey, H. H. McGlone, John Mitchell, John Mullen, Frederic L. Osgood, William G. Palmer, William S. Palmer, Anne R. S. Park, A. Peck, Anthony Peck, Ira L. Peck, Sarah H. Perkins, L. J. Saxton, Frederick T. Sayles, D. P. Scribner, Frank D. Sevin, N. Douglass Sevin, Elizabeth T. Sherman, W. H. Shields, A. D. Smith, A. J. Smith, O. S. Smith, Welcome A. Smith, Henry Steiner, Carolyn A. Sterry, John A. Sterry, John Stott, William R. Stott, Caroline L. Thomas, by M. P. G., Jonathan Trumbull, Francis Valler, Emily P. Wattles, Mary E. Wattles, Eliza P. Weir, James H. Welles, George E. Williams, Hugh H. Osgood and Herbert L. Yerrington.

The petition was favorably acted upon in the town meeting held on the evening of October 17th, when the sum asked was appropriated. Under the supervision of First Selectman Archibald S. Spalding and his successor, Arthur D. Lathrop, the grounds were cleared of undergrowth, the old stone walls were repaired and new ones constructed to replace the old and broken wooden fences. Soon thereafter many of the gravestones were reset by families, individuals and the Rural Association, the last-named contributing ten dollars from its slender treasury.

Two years ago to-day, Faith Trumbull Chapter, Daughters of the American Revolution, unveiled the boulder and bronze tablet, which indicate the graves of the French soldiers—our Revolutionary allies—who died in Norwich and were buried within these grounds in 1778. It has been asserted of late that these men were never in the town and consequently could not have sickened, died and been buried here; yet it is averred by an elderly gentleman that in his boyhood days the spot was indicated to him by several old men who had witnessed the interments and were familiar with the circumstances as subsequently recorded by the historian of Norwich.

The memorial stones of four of the original proprietors of the town still stand within the limits of these grounds. That bearing the oldest date records that Deacon Simon Huntington passed away June 28, 1706. Deacon Thomas Adgate died July 21, 1707, and was followed by Sergeant Thomas Waterman June 1, 1708, and by John Post November 27, 1710. Their companions, who were doubtless buried here, but whose graves are unmarked, were Morgan Bowers, who "departed this life" in 1701, or soon thereafter; Thomas Post September 5, 1701; John Reynolds, June 25, 1702; John Calkins, January 8, 1702-3; Lieut. Thomas Leffingwell about 1714 and Lieut. William Backus about 1721.

Enriching the Old Burying Ground is the dust of officers and men who fought in the various wars of colony and nation, including forty-six who actively participated in our struggle for independence and whose graves have been permanently marked by the Sons of the American Revolution. We have here a signer of the Declaration of Independence and the eighteenth governor of Connecticut; statesmen, legislators, lawyers and judges; two clergymen of the First church, deacons, tythingmen and other ecclesiastical officials; physicians, editors and publishers, as well as a few Tories and the hundreds who acquired no personal distinction and quietly passed away.

On the brow of the elevation which descends toward the old "dolorous swamp" stands the headstone of Boston Trow Trow, one of the negro governors of Connecticut, who died May 28, 1772, at the age of sixty-six years. These sham officials existed in many Connecticut towns prior to the Revolution and in some of them subsequently, the last in Norwich being (as Miss Perkins informs us), Ira Tosset, whom some present will recall.

Of these "governors" Miss Calkins wrote:

"In former times the ceremony of a mock election of a negro governor created no little excitement in their ranks. The servants for the time being assumed the relative rank and condition of their masters, and were allowed to use the horses and many of the military trappings of their owners. Provisions, decorations, fruits and liquors were liberally surrendered to them. Great electioneering prevailed, parties often ran high, stump harangues were made, and a vast deal of ceremony expended in counting the votes, proclaiming the result, and inducting the candidate into office—the whole too often terminating in a drunken frolic, if not in a fight.

"After the death of Boston Trow Trow, Sam Hun'ton was annually elected to this mock dignity for a much greater number of years than his honorable namesake and master, Samuel Huntington, Esq., filled the gubernatorial chair. It was amusing to see this sham dignitary after his election, riding through the town on one of his master's horses, adorned with plaited gear, his aids on each side, *a la militaire*, himself puffing and swelling with pomposity, sitting bolt upright and moving with a slow, majestic pace, as if the universe were looking on. When he mounted or dismounted his aids flew to his assistance, holding his bridle, putting his feet into the stirrips, and bowing to the ground before him. The Great Mogul, in a triumphal procession, never assumed an air of more perfect self-importance than the negro governor at such a time."

It is unfortunate that our early records are so nearly silent regarding the wives, mothers and daughters of other days. The "new woman," however, was then unknown, and the virtues and self-sacrifices of her predecessors, known in the family circle and in the communities in which they dwelt, have not been revealed to us in the detail we might wish.

Firm and erect stands the headstone of John Trumbull, editor and publisher of the "Norwich Packet," as though keeping "watch and ward" over another in the vicinity, which is deeply imbedded in the earth as though sunken from a sense of shame and sorrow. The latter marks the grave of Amy Huntington, the wife of James Robertson, one of Mr. Trumbull's partners. It may be that the sensitive patriotism of this daughter of the Huntingtons, shocked at the Tory proclivities of her husband, sank beneath a condition she could not change, as she passed away June 15, 1776, in her 31st year.

Not far distant stands a stone which indicates the last resting-place of one who, had she lived, might have preserved in its purity a now blotted page of American history. She died in Norwich August 15, 1758, and the pure influence of this gentle mother was lost upon her brilliant soldier son, the traitor of the Revolution.

The records of other wives, mothers and daughters who sleep within these hallowed grounds might be recalled with profit did time permit, but for the present we must content ourselves with breathing an atmosphere permeated with the influence of deeds well done.

In individual lives it is not only the duty but the pleasure to care for the young, the aged and the helpless; in our community life it is our duty, as it should be our pleasure, to give the best of care to our

OLD BURYING GROUND.

GEO. S. PORTER.

3 Washington Place,
Norwich, Conn.

INSCRIPTIONS

TWENTY FRENCH SOLDIERS, 1778
SEE PAGE 5

Mr. Porter added genealogical data to accompany many of the inscriptions, and in order to identify the persons, he referred to early settlers to whom he gave the following numbers: 1 Mary (Andrews) Post; 2 William Backus, Sr.; 3 Lt. Francis Griswold; 4 Major John Mason; 5 Capt. John Mason; 6 John Bradford; 7 Samuel Hyde; 8 Thomas Bliss, Jr.; 9 William Hyde; 10 Lt. Thomas Tracy; 11 Nehemiah Smith; 12 Dr. John Olmstead; 13 John Elderkin; 14 Thomas Bliss, Sr.; 15 Jonathan Royce; 16 Hugh Calkins; 17 Christopher Huntington; 18 John Baldwin, 1st; 19 Richard Edgerton; 20 John Gager; 21 Samuel Gager; 22 Rev. James Fitch; 23 John Pease; 24 John Tracy; 25 Thomas Bingham; 26 Robert Allyn; 27 Lieut. Thomas Leffingwell; 28 Richard Wallis; 29 Stephen Backus; 30 John Reynolds; 31 Josiah Read; 32 Richard Hendy; 33 Lt. William Backus; 34 Thomas Howard; 35 John Calkins; 36 Thomas Post; 37 Morgan Bowers; 38 Robert Wade; 39 John Birchard. Most of these were buried in the First Burying Ground of Norwich.

He then begins with No. 40, The Woodbridge Tomb, of which he writes: "This was erected after 1774 by several connected families and known as the Woodbridge Tomb. Who and how many were received within its gloomy walls, it is now impossible to determine, but that it was the recipient of the bodies of numerous former residents of Norwich, was subsequently evidenced when, resultant of long years of neglect the dilapitated structure exposed its open ghastly wounds to public view.

Its condition gradually deteriorated, no kindly hand was extended to save, and at last, unable to continue an unaided existence, it fell confusedly to mother earth, an unsightly mass.

About the year 1865, the bones, bricks and mortar were buried, the ground was smoothed over and all trace of this habitation of the dead was obliterated.

"In the old burying ground at Norwich Town, on the hillside between two maple trees, and immediately in the rear of the residence of the late Hon. John Turner Wait, there was yesterday, June 24, 1907, placed a marble stone bearing the following inscription:

No. 41

COL.
ZABDIAL
ROGERS
20 CT. MIL.
REV. WAR.
MAY 20, 1737
MARCH 13, 1808

This stone marks the site of the old Woodbridge Tomb within which the body of Col. Rogers was buried."

42.
Mrs. Lydia Rogers
died Feb. 21, 1814.
aged 69 years.
and her former husband
Mr. Edward Conoy
died April 12, 1791,
aged 44 years.

(footstone)
L. R.
E. C.

43.
Abiah
Cleveland

44.
In memory of Mr.
Afa Cady who died
April 8th 1794, in ye
56th Year of his age.

Death is a debt
to nature due
Which I have paid
& fo muft you.

45.
Hannah
Pitcher

46. Two small granite stones—much sunken.

47. Small granite stone—much sunken.

48. In memory of
Mrs Abigail confort
of Mr. Eben^r Reeve
who died Feb^ry 21^ft
1799 in the 53^d year
of her age.

(footstone)
M^rs
Abigail
Reeve

49. In memory of
Mrs Bethiah wife
to Mr Ebenezer
Reeve who died
Jan^r 19th 1786
in ye 29th year
of her age

(footstone)
M^rs
Bethiah
Reeve

50. In Memory of
Hannah the
wife of Elisha
Clark fhe died
May the 15th
AD 1781 in
4th year of
her age.

51. In Memory of
Mrs Lydia Clark
relict of
Mr Elifha Clark
who died Jan 11th
1814 aged 75 years.

(footstone)
L. C.

52. In memory of
Hannah Harland.
She died October
the 28th 1803
in the 19th year
of her age.

(footstone)
Hannah
Harland

53. Inter'd beneath
lie the remains
of
Abiah
late the valu'd wife and friend
of
Aaron Cleveland
who died Aug^ft 23^d 1788
in ye 39th Year of her age.
ef'
I am the referection
and the life. Because I
live ye fhall live alfo.
Jefus Chrift.

(footstone)

54. In Memory of
Sarah
Daughter of
Mr Aaron &
Abiah Cleveland
who died nov
27 1779
Aged 3 years
& 11 months

55. In memory of
Aaron Porter
fon of
Aaron & Abiah
Cleveland who died
July 11th 1780
Aged 2 years.

(footstone)
Aaron Porter
Cleveland

(footstone)
56. MRS.
HANNAH
SMITH
1753

57. In memory of
Gurdon fon to
Mr Eleazer & M^rs
unice Kingsley
ho died March
th 1787 in his
2^d year.

58. In Memory of M^rs
Judith Bill wife
to Mr Beriah Bill
who died July 5th
AD. 1783 in ye 48th
year of her age
The ſweet remem
of the Juſt

59. In memory of
John Cunningham
Potts ſon of M^r
Chriſtopher & M^rs Su
ſannah Potts, who was
Drownded July 13th
1775. Aged 4 years
6 months & 12 days.

When ſpring appears
& Vilots blow
& ſheds a rich perfume
How ſoon the fragrant
breath is lost
How short lived is ye bloom

60. In memory of Samuel
ſon to Mr Samuel & M^rs
Marcy Cleveland he di
ed Octr 5th 1784 in
ye 4th year of his age

Sleep my babe
thy work is done
Chriſt is thy Savior
Heaven thy home.

61. In memory of
David ſon to M^r
John and Mrs Jeru
ſha Cleaveland
who died march
30th 1791, in his
4th Year.
(footstone)

62. In memory of Walter
hous Cleaveland ſon
to Mr John Cleaveland
& Eunice his Wife
he died Nov^br 18th
1776 in his 3^d year

(footstone)
Walter
Cleaveland

63. In Memory of Mrs.
Lydia wife of M^r
Ezekiel Huntley, ſhe
died Octr 3^d 1787 in y^e
28th year of her age
My lover friend familiar all

Removed from light & out of call
To dark Oblivion is retir'd
Death or to me at leaſt expir'd.

64. MR
STEPHEN GIFF
ORD DIED NOV^R
27 1724 AGED
83 YEARS

65. Here Lies Interred
the Body of Mr John
Gifford Jn^r Born
Appral the 26th AD
1710 and died in the
33 year of his age

(footstone)
M^r
John
Gifford
Jn^r

66. Here lies intered
the body of Mr
John Gifford
Born Apriel AD
1673 and died
in the 76th year
of his age

67. MR^s
HANAH GIFF
ORD DYED JAN^y
20 1724+AGED
79 YERS

68. Here Lies Buried
the Body of Mr
Joſhua Woodword
of Gloceſter in the
State of Maſſachu
ſetts, deceased 4th
of Oct^br 1781 in
ye 19th year of
his Age

69. In memory of William
fon to Mr John & Mrs
Mary Nutter he Died
fep 6th: 1782 in his
2d year
at his left hand lies
two infant Brothers.

Sleep fweet babes
& take thy reft
God calls the home
he faw it beft.

70. LUCRETIA TRACY.
died
March 28, 1825,
aged 77.

(footstone)
L. T.

71. In memory of Mrs
Hannah wife to Mr.
William Manffield
who died Janr 12th
1779 in ye 43d year
of her age

Firm in this hope,
that energies divine
Shall work the laft great
change destroying ill;
And all mankind before
Immanuel's fhrine
wait for the perfect day.

72. WM. MANSFIELD
DIED
July 22, 1839,
Aged 89.

(footstone)
W. M.

73. In memory of
Mis Minerva Butler
Daughtr to Mr Ben
jamin & Mrs Dia
dama Butler who
died April 25th
1784 Phthife in ye
her Age

(footstone)
Mis
Minerva
Butler

74. In memory of
Mifs Lydia Daugh,t
to Mr Elifha Hyde
& Mrs Lydia his
wife who died
April 3d 1780
in ye 39th year
of her Age.

(footstone)
Mifs
Lydia
Hyde

75. In memory of
Mrs Diadama ye
wife of Mr BenJamin
Butler dautr to Mr
Jedidiah & Mrs Jerufha
Hide who died Sept
ye 18th 1771 in ye
31ft year of her age

(footstone)
Mrs
Diadama
Butler

76. In Memory of Mifs
Rofamund Butler,
Daughter to Mr
Benjamin and Mrs
Diadama Butler
Died of a Confum
fion may 5th AD
1783, in ye 17th
year of her Age

(footstone)
Mifs
Rofamund
Butler

77. (footstone)
Mrs
Jerufha
Stark

78.
Alas, poor human nature!
In Memory of Mr
BENJAMIN BUTLER
who died of a Phthiſis
pulmonaris June 17th AD
1787 in the 48th year
of his age

Who without pains advice would e'er be good;
Who without Death but would be good in vain
Heaven gives us friends to bless the perfect ſcene
Reſumes them to prepare us for the next.

(footstone)
Mr
Benjamin
Butler

79. Monumental
of
George Frederick
Turner
died 9th Feby 1813,
aged 21 years.

The youth of great promise
yields resigned & submissive
to the unrelenting stroke of death.

(footstone)
G. F. T.

80. Monumental
of
Charles William
Turner
Born 30th March 1793
Died 13th Feby 1794

God unerring
Gives & takes the Vital Spark

(footstone)
Charles
William
Turner

81.
(Brick Tomb.)
In Memory
of
Eliſha Tracy MD
Who died in ye 71st year of his Age
On ye 1ſt Day of May 1783
A Celebrated Phyſician

Upwards of forty years in Practice
in this and in neighbouring Towns
He died Univerſally Lamented
Eſpecially by all thoſe Gentlemen
of the Faculty within his Acquaintance

In Memory of
Philip Turner Eſq
Capt of ye Troop of Horse
Who died 13th January
1755, in the 39th
year of his age

In Memory of
Mrs Ann Abell
former Conſort
of Philip Turner Esq.
who died June 1759
in ye 39th year
of her age

82. IN MEMORY
LUCY
of the Pious & beloved
wife of Elisha Tracy
Daughter of Deacⁿ
Eben^r & Mrs Sarah
Huntington who died
Octob^r 12th 1751
AEtatis suae 30.

O Death where is thy sting
O Grave where is thy victory

(footstone)
Lucy
Tracy

83. Broken granite stone—sunken.

84. In Memory of M^{rs}
Elisabeth the pious
and beloved wife
of Doct^r Elisha
Tracy who died
the 23^d of march
1781 AEtatis Suae
51 mo

O Death where is thy sting
O Grave where is thy Victory.

(footstone)
Elisabeth
Tracy

85. Here lies the
Body of Mary
wife of Capt
Joseph Tracy
who died Jan^{ry}
16th 1751 in y^e
71st year of
her age

(footstone)
M^{rs}
Mary Tracy

86. IN MEMORY OF
Capt Joseph Tracy
who died April the
10 1765 in the
83 year of his
age

87. In Memory of
Mr Elisha Hyde
who died June
4th AD 1769 in
ye 45th Year of
his age
Mors Omnia Vincit.

88. Here Lies ye Body of
Mr Jedidiah Hide who
Departed this Life
sep^t 1761 in ye 49th year
of his Age.

The sweet rememberance
of the Just shall Flourish
when they sleep in dust

89. In Memory of
Mrs Sarah Hallam
wife of Mr Amos
Hallam late of
New London who
Departed this life
June 19 1785 in
ye 57 year of
her Age

(footstone)
M^{rs}
Sarah
Hallum

90. (footstone)
D   R

91. (footstone)
M^{rs}
Anne Turner
1765

92. (footstone)
Mrs Elisha
Hide

93.
In memory of
Mr JOS. TRACY
who died
April 19, 1777
aged 80 years

Also of
Mrs ANNA TRACY
his wife who died
Jan. 8, 1801
aged 84 years

(footstone)
J   T

94.
SACRED
TO
the Memory of
ELIZABETH
Relict of
Joseph Peck
who died
Dec. 26, 1817
Aged 93

(footstone)
E.   P.

95.
Here Lies Inter'd
ye Remains of
Joseph Peck who
Departed this Life
fept 9th 1776 in ye
70th year of his Age

96.
Here lies the Body of Elisha
Maples who died Feb 24th 1800
in the 4th year of his age

Here do I lie cut down tho'
young
Nor will the readers days
be long

(footstone)
Elifha
Maples

97.
(footstone)
D   L

98.
In Memory of
Eunice Daughtr
to Capt Nehemiah
Waterman & Mrs
Sufannah his Wife
fhe Died Octr 5th
1775 in ye 2d
year of her Age

99.
In memory of Mrs.
Sarah wife of Mr
Nehemiah Waterman
who died Jan, 21ft
1795, in ye 83d
Year of her age

The fweet remem
brance of the Juft
fhall flourifh when
they fleep in duft.

(footstone)
Mrs
Sarah
Waterman

100.
In memory of
Nehemiah Waterman
of Bozrah who de
parted this life
Octr 27th 1796
in ye 88th Year
of his age

O mind you, O mind
you
if you your felves love,
O mind you O mind you
your maker above

(footstone)
Mr
Nehemiah
Waterman

101. Nehemiah Waterman
Eſq
of Bozrah
Born Octr 24th AD
1736
Died Octr 18th AD 1802
aged 66

Amiable in private and
uſeful in public life
The friend of order and
Religion were his friend

(footstone)
Nehemiah
Waterman
Eſq

102. Mrs
SUSANNA WATERMAN
wife of the late
NEHEMIAH WATERMAN
died March 9, 1825
AE 87

(footstone)
S.   W.

(footstone)
103. Mrs   Mr
Margaret   William
Waterman   Waterman

104. Small granite stone, no inscription.

105. Small granite stone, no inscription.

106. HERE LYES INTERRD Ye REMAs
OF MRs ABIGAIL LOTHROP Ye
RELICT OF MR SAMUEL LO
THROP OF NORWICH BORN
AT PLYMOUTH 1631 &
LIVED IN NORWICH 43
YEARS & DIED JANUARY
23   ANOD   17345
IN   Ye   104TH
OF   HER   AGE

(footstone)
MRs ABIGAIL LOTHROP
DIED JANRY 23 ANO 1734/5

107. IN MEMORY OF
Ruth y
Nathan
& Daug
John & Mrs Lidya Ra
ynolds, Who Died Dese
mber ye 11 AD. 1756
in ye 28th year of her Age

(footstone)
Mrs
Ruth Shipman

(footstone)
108. Mrs
Experience
Poſt

109. ELIZA
WATERMAN
WIFE OF JOHN
WATERMAN
DECECED OCT
1708   AGED 29

(footstone)
E   W

110. SERT
THOMAS
WATERMAN
Decd IVNE
1708 AGED 64

(footstone)
T   W

111. HERE LYES Ye BODY
OF MRS SARAH RENELS
LATE WIFE OF MR
JOSEPH RENELS
WHO DIED AVGVST
Ye 14th 1714 AGED
48 YEARS

(footstone)
SARAH RENELS

112. Here lies yᵉ body of Mʳ Joseph
Renalls Who had been the
Huſband of Mʳˢ Sarah Renalls
Who died February yᵉ first
1728/9 Ageed 69 years

Farewel my louing Children all
My Neighbours & my friends
Sarue God in Truth whil in youʳ youth
& till your Lifˢᵉ doth end

(footstone)
Mʳ Joseph
Renalls
who died
1728/9

113. In memory of Mʳˢ
Lydia, relict to the
late John Reynolds
deceaſᵈ & Daughᵗ to
Richard Lord Eſqʳ
of Lyme, who died
July 16ᵗʰ 1786
aged 92 years
Here lies the lover
of truth

(footstone)
Mʳˢ
Lydia
Reynolds

114. Here Lies yᵉ Body
of Nathaniel Son
to Mʳ Nathaniel &
Mrs Ruth ſhipman
Who died July
yᵉ 7 A D 1749
aged 9 Months
& 27 Days

(footstone)
Nathaniel
Shipman

115. Here Lies the Body of
Mr John Renold Born in
Norwich Feb 21 1691
died Augᶠᵗ 16 1742 &
aged 51 years

The power and wiſdom
The mercy and truth of
God encircle the Grave
of a ſaint

(footstone)
Mʳ
John
Renold

116. Here Lyes yᵉ Body of
Mʳˢ Anne Wife to Capᵗ
Thomas Fanning; ſhe
Dyed Dec yᵉ 22 1771 in
yᵉ 49 year of her Age

My Lover Friend Familiar
all, Remov'd from Sight &
out of call, to dark Oblivion
is Retired dead, or at Leaſt
to me Expired.

(footstone)
Mʳˢ
Anne
Fanning

117. This monument is erected
to perpetuate the memory
of
Eliſha Lee Reynolds
who was loſt at sea
in a tempest
on the 18ᵗʰ of Jan 1799
aged 29 years

(footstone)
118. STEPHEN RENELLS
SON OF MR JO
SEPH & MRS SARAH
RENELLS   DIED
NOUEMBER yᵉ 27
1731   in   yᵉ
33   YEAR   OF
HIS   AGE

119. In Memory of Miſs Anne
daugh, to M Joſeph &
Mrſ Phebe Reynolds who
died July 22ᵈ 1786 in
yᵉ 16 Year of her age

This happy youth resign'd her breath
Prepared to live & ripe for Death,
Ye blooming Youth who ſee this stone
Learn early Death to be your own

(footstone)
Miſs Anne
Reynolds

120. HERE LIES
THE BODY OF
SARY CALKINS
WHO DIED
AGED 77 YEARS

121. In Memory of
Absalom King
Arnold yᵉ Son
of Benedict &
Hannah Arnold
died Octo yᵉ
22ᵈ 1750
Aged 3 years

(footstone)
A. K. A.
1750

122. Mary Daughter
of Benedict &
Hannah Arnold
died Septem yᵉ
10 1753 Aged
8 Years 3 Mᵒ
& 4 Days.

(footstone)
M A
1753

123. Elizabeth yᵉ
Daughter of
Benedict &
Hannah Arnold
died Sept 29
1753 aged 3
Years 10 Mᵒ
& 11 Days.

(footstone)
E A
1753

124. IN MEMORY oF
Hannah yᵉ well beloved
Wife of Capᵗ Benedict
Arnold & Daughter of
Mʳ John & Elizabeth
Waterman, (She was a
Pattern of Piety Patience
and Virtue) who died
Augᶠᵗ 15ᵗʰ 1759
AEtatis Suae 52

(footstone)
Hannah Arnold
1759

125. SACRED
TO
the memory of
PHEBE REYNOLDS,
WHO DIED
April 6, 1832,
Aged 72.

(footstone)
P.   R.

126. Sacred to the memory of
Mrs. Phebe relict of
Mr. Joseph Reynolds
who departed this life
Aug 21ᶠᵗ 1818
in the 83ᵈ year of her age

She was lovely in life & peaceful
in death.
She died in faith, the heavenly
land in sight
To Jesus arms her spirit
winged its flight

(footstone)
Mrs
P. Reynolds

127. In memory of Mr Joseph Reynolds the loving and beloved Confort of Mrs Phebe Reynolds who departed this life Decm 10th 1792 in ye 61st Year of his age

Softly his fainting head he lay
Upon his Makers breaſt
His Maker kiſſed his ſoul away
And laid his fleſh to reſt

(footstone)
MR
Joseph
Reynolds

128. The design of this monument iſ to preserve the me: mory of Capt Thomas Fanning who died the 7th day of ſept 1790 in ye 67th Year of his age.

After enduring for many Years The ſtorms of Adversity he Rejoiced in proſpect in finding a peacefull harbour in the Grave where the wicked cease from troubling & the weary are at reſt, full believing that when Chriſt ſhall appear he should appear with him in Glory.

(footstone)
Capt
Thomas
Fanning

129. Here Lies the Body Of Enſign Thomas Waterman who Departed this life In hope of an happy Immortality Decemr 13th 1755 In the 86th year of his age.

(footstone)
Enſign
Thomas
Waterman

130. Here Lies the body of Mrs Eliſabeth Waterman Wife of Enſign Thomas Waterman who died March 15th 1755 in The 86th year of Her age.

(footstone)
Mrs
Eliſabeth
Waterman

131. North-west of the footstone of No. 124 and east of those of Nos. 114 and 115, is a small, granite footstone bearing crudely lettered initials   A   M

132. North of the footstone of No. 124 is that of 125, and back to back with the latter is a small, granite footstone with crude initials   J   M

133.
HERE LYSE Ye BODY OF Mr SAMUEL
POST SEN Ye HUSBAND OF MRS.
RUTH POST WHO DYED APRIL
Ye 23 ANOd 1735 IN THE
68 YEAR OF HIS AGE
RESERUED FOR A GLORIOUS
RESURRECTION   TO   LIFE
ETERNAL.

134. HERE LYES Ye BODY OF Mr STEPHEN POST Ye SON OF Ye AGEED MR SAMUEL & MRS RUTH POST OF NORWICH WHO DYED APRIL Ye 14 1735 AGEED 26 YEARS

HERE LYES Ye BODY OF SAMUEL Ye SON OF Mr SAMUEL & MRs SARAH POST WHO DYED APRL Ye 15 1735 AGEED 1 YEAR

(footstone)
Mr STEPHEN
POST DYED APr
Ye 14 1735

SAMUEL POST
DYED APRIL Ye
15 ANO 1735

135.　　　　HEARE
　　　　LYES THE BO
　　　　DY OF MR JO
　　　　HN POST WHO
　　　　DYED NOUMR
　　　　27　1710　AGED
　　　　84 YEARS

　　　　　　(footstone)
　　　　　　　J　　P

136.　　footstone—no inscription

137.　　　　IN MEMORY
　　　　of Sarah Poſt Dau
　　　　ghter of M Samuell
　　　　Post & Sarah his
　　　　wife Deſt December
　　　　y 4th A D 1746
　　　　Entred in her
　　　　Ninth year

　　　　　　(footstone)
　　　　　　　Sarah
　　　　　　　Poſt

138.　　　　In Memory of
　　　　　Anna Manning
　　　　　　consort of
　　　　　　Diah Manning
　　　　who departed this life
　　　　　Sept. 30, 1851,
　　　　　Aged 89 years

　　　　　　(footstone)
　　　　　Anna Manning

139.　　　　In memory of
　　　　　Mr. Diah Manning
　　　　　　who died
　　　　　Augt 25th 1815,
　　　　　aged 55 years.

　Man that is born of a woman
　is of few days, & full of trouble,
　he cometh forth as a flower & is
　cut down, he fleeith as a shadow
　& continueth not.

　　　　　　(footstone)
　　　　　　D. Manning

140.　Two very small stones. No visible in-
　　　scriptions.

141.　　　　In Memory of Mr
　　　　　Samuel Manning
　　　　　who departed this
　　　　　life Novr 9th AD
　　　　　1783 in ye 59th
　　　　　Year of his Age

　　　　With confidence I
　　　　truſt my dying Lord
　　　　This duſt shall riſe
　　　　according to his word.

　　　　　　(footstone)
　　　　　　　Mr
　　　　　　　Samuel
　　　　　　　Manning

142.　　　　In Memory of Mrs
　　　　　Eunice Waterman
　　　　　wife to Mr John
　　　　　Waterman ſhe Depart
　　　　　ed this Life Octbr
　　　　　15th 1781 in ye 26th
　　　　　year of her Age

　　　　Behold my friend as you
　　　　　　　　　　　Paſs by
　　　　as you are now ſo once
　　　　　　　　　　　was I
　　　　as I am now ſo you
　　　　　　　　　　　muſt be
　　　　Prepare for Death and
　　　　　　　　　　Follow me

　　　　　　(footstone)
　　　　　　　Mrs
　　　　　　　Eunice
　　　　　　　Waterman

143.　　Small granite footstone
　　　　　　　L　　M

144. In Memory of yᵉ three
children of Mʳ Samuel
Manning & Mʳˢ Anne
his Wife. Nemely
Eunis who Died Junᵉ
9, 1750: Agedᵈ 4 year
& Anne Died Septᵗ yᵉ
24 1753: Age 2 year
& Anne yᵉ 2ᵈ Died Septᵗ
3ᵈ 1759 in yᵉ 6ᵗʰ year
of her Age

Death is a Debt to Nature
due
Which we have paid & so
must you.

(footstone)
Eunice   Anne
Anne   Manning

145. HERE LIES yᵉ BODY OF Mʳ
JABEZ POST yᵉ SON OF
Mʳ SAMUEL & Mʳˢ RUTH
POAST yᵉ AGEED WHO DY
MARCH yᵉ 6ᵗʰ 1725 IN
yᵉ 22 YEAR OF HIS
AGE REMEMBER NOʷ
THY CREATOR IN yᵉ DAYS
OF THY YOUTH

(footstone)
JABEZ POST DYED
MARCH 6 1725

146. HER LYES yᵉ BODY OF JOHN
yᵉ SON OF Mʳ SAMUEL &
Mʳˢ RUTH POST WHO
DYED AGEED 18 YEARS
AGUST 26 1718
SEEK FIRST yᵉ KING
DUM OF HEAUEN

(footstone)
JOHN POST DYED
AGUST 1718

147. Granite stone sunken to level of the earth.

148. In Memory of Mʳˢ
Experience wife to
Mʳ Nathaniel Post,
who died June 13ᵗʰ
1792 in yᵉ 89ᵗʰ
Year of her age

It ſhall be known
when we are dead
and left on long record
that ages yet unborn may
read and truſt and praise
the Lord

(footstone)

149. In Memory
of the Well-Beloved
Mʳ Samuell Post
Junⁿ Son to Mʳ Sam
uell Post and Ruth
his wife, Detᵗ Decᵇ
the 7ᵗʰ AD 1746
aged 48 years
B. Collins, Lebanon, fecit

(footstone)
Mʳ
Samuel
Post Junʳ

150 Here lies yᵉ Body
of Mʳˢ Suſannah
Poſt wife of Mʳ
Samuel Poſt ſhe
was a woman of
Piety & virtue
Departed this
Life in hope of
a Better Novᵇ
5ᵗʰ 1762 in yᵉ 28ᵗʰ
year of her age

(footstone)
Mʳˢ
Suſannah
Post

151. Here Lyes intered
the body of mr
Simon Backus who
departed this life
febr the 16th 1764
in the 36th year of
his age

(footstone)
Mr
Simon Backus

152. In memory of
Dea John Backus
who was born Oct 16th 1740
and died April 27th 1814 in
the 74th year of his age

The memory of the Juſt is
Bleſſed

(footstone)
Dea
John Backus

153. In memory of
Mrs. Mary Carew,
who died June 10th
1793 in ye 82d
Year of her age

The memory of ye
Just is bleſſed

(footstone)
MRS
Mary
Carew

154. In memory of
Mrs Margaret Backus
relict of
Elijah Backus Eſq,
& formerly the conſort of
Jared Tracy Eſq.
She died Nov. 13th 1813
aged 73 years

(footstone)
Mrs.
Margaret
Backus

155. In memory of
Nancy, daughter of
James & Dorothy C.
Backus who died
Sept 1ſt 1802 aged
10 MONTHS

(footstone)
N.   B.

156. Sacred
to the memory of
Elijah Backus Eſq
who died Sept 4th 1798,
in the 73d year of
his age

(footstone)
Elijah
Backus Eſq

157. In memory of Mrs Lucy
the amiable conſort of
Elijah Backus Eſqr & daughter
of John Griſwold Eſqr late of
Lyme who departed this life
on the 16th of Decr 1795
in the 70th year of her age

(footstone)
Mrs Lucy
Backus

158. IN MEMORY OF LUEt SA
MVEL BACKUS WHO
DIED NOV 24th A D O
1740 AETATIS SUAE 48

If being pious generous Iust or br
aue
Could rescue human nature from the
Graue
Here lies the man whose much lovd
earthy frame
Had then immortal ben as is his fame

(footstone)
LEUt SAMUEL
BACKUS

159.
IN
MEMORY OF
MRS REBECCA SAVAGE
WHO DIED
Aug. 2, 1846,
AE 91

The sweet remembrance of the just
Shall fourish when they sleep in dust

(footstone)
R.   S.

160.
In memory of
Elizabeth
daughter of
Maj. Thomas & Mrs.
Elizabeth Tracy,
who died Nov. 21ſt
1807, aged 2 years
& 5 months

(footstone)
E.   T.

161.
Sacred
to the memory of
Maj. Thomas Tracy
ſon of Samuel Tracy Eſq
& Mrs Sybel Tracy his wife
who died Dec. 29 1806
aged 39 years

(footstone)
Maj
Thomas Tracy

162.
In memory of
Mrs. Elizabeth Tracy
relict of the late
Maj. Thomas Tracy
& daughter of
Samuel Avery
who died April 22ᵈ
1822 in the 41ſt year
of her age.

(footstone)
E.   T.

163.
Sacred
to the memory of
Samuel Tracy Eſq
who died of the small pox
June 5th 1798 in the 75th
year of his age.

(footstone)
Samuel
Tracy Eſq

164. Granite stone—no visible inscription.

165.
Sacred
to the memory of
Mrs. Sybel Tracy, relict
of Samuel Tracy Eſq
who died Aug. 17 1802
in the 77th year of her
age

(footstone)
Mrs Sybel
Tracy

166.
In Memory
of Mr Daniel Tracy
(Son of Mr Daniel Tracy
loving Husband of
Mrs Abigail Tracy)
who was born 1688
decr 7th died Janr 29th
1771 in the 83ᵈ year of
his Age
Mors Omnia vincit

(footstone)
Mr
Daniel Tracy

167.
Here Lyes ye Body
of Mrs Abigail Tracy
relict of Mr Daniel Tra
cy & Daughtr of Mr
Thomas Leffingwell
& Mary his Wife
born Sepbr 1691, Died
march 10th 1777 AEtat 86

(footstone)
Mrs
Abigail
Tracy

168. In Memory of
Daniel Tracy Eſq
Son of Samˡ Tracy Eſq & Mʳˢ
Sybel his wife, loving Conſort
of Mʳˢ Lucretia Tracy Born
March 27ᵗʰ 1758 Died Dec 6ᵗʰ
1782 AE 24

The only Death thy opning
    years Invade
With wit and Fame & love
    & Beauty bleſt
Tho Earth's cold Mantle
    ſhroud thy head
And peaceful virtue ſink
    beneath yᵉ duſt
Yet o'er thy Grave unfading
    wreaths ſhall riſe
Triumphant Faith ſhall
    burſt yᵉ fable Tomb
A Saviours Hand ſhall crown
    thee for yᵉ ſkies
And love & virtue flouriſh
    in immortal bloom

(footstone)
Daniel
Tracy Eſq

169. In memory of
Hannah daughter
of Elijah & Hannah
Pitcher who died
Feb 12 1796 in the
5ᵗʰ year of her age.

Sleep on ſweet babe
And take unto your reſt
God call'd thee home
He ſaw it beſt

170. GEORGE E. FANNING
died
June 5, 1877
aged 75 yrs.

(footstone)
G. E. F.

171. In Memory of
JANE ABBY
died March 1ˢᵗ 1852
aged 53 years
also
Thomas T.
died in Cincinnati, Ohio,
Dec. 26, 1850,
aged 49 years
children of John & Abigail
Fanning

(footstone)
J. A. F.
T. T. F.

172. Mrs.
Abigail Fanning
Widow of
Capt
John Fanning
died Jan. 3, 1850,
aged 85 years

(footstone)
A. F.

173. Capt
John Fanning
died Suddenly
Aug. 22, 1830
aged 72 years.

(footstone)
J. F.

174. Sacred
to the memory of
THOMAS FANNING Eˢᑫ
who departed this life
May 24ᵗʰ 1812
AEt 62 years
The memory of the juſt is
blessed

(footstone)
THOMAS
FANNING
ESQʳ

175. Beneath this folemn Monument
is Interred
the lifelefs clay of the once
Amiable & virtuous
Mrs Lydia Fanning
the loving & beloved confort
of Mr Thomas Fanning
of Norwich
the daught of
Samuel Tracy Efqr
& Mrs Sybel his wife
the mother of
Lydia, Lucretia & Nancy Fanning
She died Decbr 19th 1787 AE 32 years
The tender friend once fmiling as the morn

(footstone)
Mrs
LYDIA
FANNING

176. INFANT
Son of
John H. &
E. Fanning
DIED
April 14, 1839

177. ISWOLD
IED NOU 1737
N THE YEAR
OF HIS AG

FRANCIS
GRISWOLD
DIED NOV. 1737
IN THE 14th YEAR
OF HIS AGE
Miss Caulkins' list p 38

178. LUCY
Relict of
John Trumbull
Born at New-London
Oct 10, 1758
Died at Norwich Ct.
Aug. 23, 1813.

(footstone)
L. T.

179. MR. JOHN TRUMBULL,
Departed this life, August 14th 1802,
aged 50 Years. He was born in
Cambridge, (Mass) from whence he
early remov'd to this Town in which
he was the first publisher of a
News-Paper; he was a Member of
Somerset Lodge and was the
first interr'd with Masonic
honors in this yard.

My friends forbear why weep for me
Since all should die, was God's decree
Consider me as free from care,
And far more happy than you are.

(footstone)
Mr. John
Trumbull.

180. Sacred to the memory of two
Sons of Mr John Trumbull,
who departed this life after 4
Days illnefs, Dec. 17th 1794. John
in his 15th & Timothy in ye 11th
Year of his age

Beneath this humble fod interrd
Two blooming Youths at once were laid:
Whofe flumbering duft muft one day rife,
And hail their Saviour in the fkies!
Cut by John Walden, Windham

(footstone)
John & Timothy
Trumbull

181. Sunken granite stone—no visible inscription.

182. Sacred to the Memo
ry of Mrs Amy
Robertfon the amia
ble Confort of Mr
James Robertfon
Formerly of Nor-
wich, Printer:
She departed
this Life June 15th
AD 1776 in ye
31ft year of her
Age

(footstone)
Mrs
Amy
Roberton

183. In Memory of Mrs Han
nah Culver confort to Mr
Jonathan Culver who
Departed this life Decbr
31ft 1784 in ye 36th
year of her Age

Behold my friend as you
paſs by
as you are now so once
was I,
as I am now ſo you
muſt be
Prepare for Death &
follow me

(footstone)
Mrs
Hannah
Culver

184. In memory of
Capt Jonathan Culver
who departed this life
May 4th 1807 in the
62d year of his age

(footstone)
Capt Jonathan
Culver

185. In memory of Mrs
Nancy wife to Mr
Richard Carew who
died Novr 11th 1797
in ye 24th Year of
her age

Death is uncertain
yet moſt ſure
ſin is the wound
Chriſt is the cure

(footstone)
Mrs
Nancy
Carew

186. In memory of
Mrs Mary Culver
relict of
Capt Jonathan Culver
who died Aug 7th 1813
aged 62 years

(footstone)
Mrs
M   C

187. DIED MAR
CH 7 1736/7 AG
ED SIX YEARS

188. In memory of Eliſa
beth Daught of Mr John
& Mrs Tuzah Allen ſhe
died Augſt 30th 1786 aged
6 months & 12 days

Sleep ſweet babe
& take your reſt
God call'd the home
He ſaw it beſt

(footstone)
Eliſabeth
Allen

189. In Memory of Mrs Eu
nice Daught of Mr Pe-
ter & Mrs Elisabeth Mor-
gan who died Augſt
30th 1786 in ye 28th
year of her Age

190. In Memory of Mr
Samuel White of
Long Iſland he Depart
ed this Life May 21ſt
1778, in ye 32:
year of his Age

191. (footstone)
Mr
Joſhua
Woodward

192. In Memory of
Samuel fon to Mr
Samuel & Mrs Marcy
Clevelnad who died
novr 1ft AD 1785
Aged 13 Months

193. Sally Daughter of Mr.
Solomon Williams died
Feb. 18th AD 1795, in the 9th
Year of her age.

The blooming flower how foon decayd
And I am numbered with the dead;
From Death's arreft no age is free,
Prepare for death and follow me.

(footstone)
Sally Williams

194. In
Memory of
Hannah
wife of
Solomon Williams
who died Feb. 2, 1822,
in her 61 year

Blessed are the dead which die in the Lord from henceforth they may rest from their labours; and their works do follow them.

(footstone)
H. W.

195. In memory of
SALLY
wife of
Solomon Williams
& daughter of
Z. Lathrop who died
Sept 10, 1825
aged 50 years

Sleep on dear fiend & take thy rest
God called the home he saw it best.

(footstone)
S. W.

196. In
Memory of
Solomon Williams
who died
Aug 30, 1837,
Aged 81 yrs

(footstone)
S. W.

197. (footstone)
Mrs
Hannah
Tracy

198. In
Memory of
SARAH E.
wife of
Nathan Pratt
died
Sept 1, 1848
aged 31.

(footstone)
S. E. P.

199. Here Lies Interred ye
Remains of Capt Sam
uel Griswold the firft
Captain of the 2nd
Company or Train band
in Norwich he was
born in Norwich
Septr 1665 & died
on ye 2d Day of
Decemr 1740 in
the 76th year
of his Age

200. IN MEMORY OF
Mrs Abigail Grifwould
wife to Mr Francis
Griswould who died
Febry the 18th 1754 in
the 57th year of her age

Beneath this Stone Deaths Iron Slum
                          bers bind
A wife obedient & a Mother kind

(footstone)
Mrs
Abigail
Griswould
B. Collins Sculp Lebanon

201. Here is interred the
Body of mr Francis
Griswould who died
April the 10th 1760
in the 69th year of
his age

(footstone)
Mr
Francis Grifwould

202. Here Lyes intered
the body of mrs
patience wife of mr
Francis Grifwould
who died aprill ye 19th
1761 in the 59th
year of her age.

(footstone)
Mrs
Patience Griswould

203. In Memory of
Dyar fon to Mr
Afa & Mrs Elifa
beth Woodworth
he died June
2d 1783 in
ye 15th year
of his Age

204. In memory of
Mr Afa Woodworth
who departed this
life Feb 22d 1813 in
the 69th year of
his Age

(footstone)
Mr
Afa Woodworth

205. Here is inter'd ye
Body of Mrs Ruth
Late Wife to Mr
Abel Grifwold
Who died Febr 1ft
1772 in ye 37th year
of her Age,
very Juftly La
mented

(footstone)
Mrs
Ruth
Grifwold

206. Sacred
to the memory of
Mr. Abel Grifwold
who died May 8th
1804 in the 74th year
of his age

(footstone)
Mr. Abel
Grifwold

207. In memory of
Mifs Phebe Hunn
who died Feb 27th
1811 aged 62

(footstone)
Mifs Phebe
Hunn

208. In memory of Mrs
Lydia wife to deac
Joſeph Griſwold
who died Janr 3d
1801, in ye 87th year
of her age

Death is uncertain
  yet moſt ſure
ſin is the wound
Christ is the cure

(footstone)
Mrs
Lydia
Griſwold

209. In memory of
Parker H. & Barre
Durkee, ſons of Mr
Eliphalet & Mrs
Sally Durkee
Parker H. died Nov
13th 1797, in the 5th
year of his age
Barre died July 16th
1797 in the 2d year
of his age

(footstone)
Parker H
&
Barre Durkee

210. In Memory of
Mr Parker Hall
who departed
this life Novr
8th 1788 in ye
25th Year of
his age

Death is uncertain
  yet moſt ſure
Sin is the wound
Christ is the cure.

(footstone)
Mr
Parker
Hall

211. Granite stone, deeply sunken, no visible inscription.

212. In memory of Mrs
Molly conſort of An
drew Tracy Eſqr who
died Nov 27th 1794
in ye 45th Year of
her age

The bleſt remem
brance of the Juſt
ſhall flouriſh when
they ſleep in duſt

(footstone)
Mrs
Molly
Tracy

213. In memory of Mr.
Samuel Gifford 3d
ſon to Mr Samuel
& Mrs. Anne Gif
ford who died
Augſt 4th 1792,
in ye 24th Year
of his age

(footstone)
Mr
Samuel
Gifford

214. Granite stone, no inscription.

215. In Memory of
Mr James
Gifford he De
pated this Life
April 2 1783
in ye 54th year
of his Age

216. To
the memory of
JAMES GIFFORD
Son of Samuel Gifford,
One of the Original Settlers of Norwich
who died April 1783
aged 54.
AND HIS CONSORT
SUSAN GIFFORD
who died March 1792,
aged 62.
This Monument is erected by
Their Grandson, James Gifford
of Elgin, Ill. Sept. 1845.

(footstone)
J. G.
S. G.

217. In Memory of M^r
Samuel Gifford He
Died
30 A D 1753

(footstone)
SAMUEL
GIFFORD

218. Unlettered granite stone.

219. In Memory of
POLLY TRACY
daught to Andrew
Tracy Esqr &
Mrs Molly his wife
who died March
28th AD 1788
in ye 17th year

220. In memory of M^{rs}
Lucy wife to M^r
Samuel Crocker who
died Octr 21^{ft} 1789
in ye 23 Year of
her age.

My lover friend familiar all
Remov'd from fight & out of call
To dark oblivion is retir'd
Dead or at leaft to me expir'd

(footstone)
M^{rs}
Lucy
Crocker

221. Broken granite stone, without visible inscription.

222. Beneath this humble
fod lies interred
the body of M^{rs} MA
RY, late confort of M^r
RICHARD COLLIER
Who perfectly refigned
to the will of HIM who
animates the duft,
Calmly died Octo^{br}
11th 1786 aged 49
To whofe memory this
monument is facred

(footstone)
M^{rs}
Mary
Collier

223. Lucy, daughter of Mr.
Benjn Collier, died May
30th 1795, in the 7th Year
of her age.

(decay'd
The blooming flower how foon
And I am numbered with the dead
From death's arreft no age is free
Prepare for death and follow me.

(footstone)
Lucy Collier

224. Well-sunken, unlettered granite stone.

225. SE^R HUGH
CALKINS DYED
SEP Y 15th 1722.
IN THE 63 YEAR
OF HIS AGE

226. HERE
LYES THE BOD
Y OF THOMAS
BINGHAM WHO
DIED THE 43 YEAR
OF HIS AGE APRIL
1st 1710.

(footstone)
T B

227.   IN MEMORY of
       Elizabeth Wife
       of Capt ZABDIEL
       ROGERS & Daughter
       of Mr ISAAC TRACY
       who died March 1ſt AD
       1772, Aged 34 Years

O! Tyrant Death how ſavage is thy Sway
No Age or ſex but falls thy Greedy Prey,
But ſhort's thy triumph
Virtue ſoon ſhall Riſe
And dwell with God in yon Celeſtial
                                Skies

       (footstone)
       ELIZABETH
       ROGERS
       1772

228.   Sophia
       Daughter of
       Capt Zabdiel
       Rogers and
       Elizabeth
       his Wife died
       March 23d 1772
       in the 3d Year
       of her Age

       (footstone)
       SOPHIA
       ROGERS

229.   In Memory of
       Mrs Hannah Griſ
       would of Norwich
       Relict of Capt.
       Samuel Griſwould
       late of Norwich
       who died Feb ye
       25th 1752 in ye 77th
       Year of her Age.

       (footstone)
       Mrs Hannah
       Griswould

230.   In Memory of
       Miſs Hannah
       Hunn Daughter to
       Mr Jonathan Hunn
       & Mrs Betſy his wife
       who departed this life
       March ye 22 AD 1790
       in the 18th year
       of her Age

231.   In Memory of Mr David
       Hunn he Departed
       this Life march 2d
       AD 1781 in ye 20th
       Year of his Age

       (footstone)
       Mr
       David
       Hunn

232.   In Memory of
       Mrs Sarah Conſort
       of Mr Aaron Fargo
       who departed this
       Life Decr 7th 1780
       in ye 74th year of
       her Age

       (footstone)
       Mrs
       Sarah
       Fargo

233.   In Memory of
       Mr Aaron Fargo
       he departed this
       Life Novr 9th 1782
       in ye 82d year of
       his Age

       (footstone)
       Mr
       Aaron
       Fargo

234. Here Lies the
Body of Mrs Expe
rience Johnſon wife
of Mr Iſaac Johnſon
Daughter of Mr
Samuel and Mrs
Experience Gifford
Who died May
ye 5th 1755 in ye
22d Year of her
Age

(footstone)
Mrs
Experience
Johnſon

235. Here lies ye Body
of Mr Jabez Back
us who lived a So-
ber virtuous life
and died July ye
15 1761 in ye 49
Year of his Age

(footstone)
Mr
Jabez
Backus

236. (footstone)
Mrs
Eunice
Backus

237. M CA EL
DIED AU UST
ye 7 1731 &
JN ye 85 YEAR
OF HIS AGE

(footstone)
MR
CALEB
ABELL

238. HERE LIES Ye
BODY OF THEO
PHELVS ABELL
WHO DIED AUGUST
ye 31 1724 AGED
44 YEARS

(footstone)
THEOPHILUS
ABELL

239. MR JOHN HIDE
DIED JULY Ye
26 1727 &
IN YE 60ETH
YEAR OF
HIS AGE

(footstone)
MR
JOHN
HIDE

240. Here lies ye Body
of Mrs Abigail ye
Wif of Mr Chriſtopher
Huntington Junr
of Norwich who
Aftar Shee had
Liueed A pios lif fell
Aſlep in Jeſus 1730
Ageed 46 years

241. HERE LYES ye BODY oF MRs
ELIZABETH HUNTINGTON
WIFE OF Mr CHRISTOPHER
HUNTINGTON LUNr SHE
WAS A DISCREET WORTHY
VIRTUOUS WOMAN WHO
LEFT ye EARTH FOR HEAVEN
MARCH 2: 1735 IN ye FORTY 2
YEAR OF HAR AGE

(footstone)
MRS E H

242. In memory of Miſs
Lois daughter of Mr
Gideon & Mrs Eunice
Birchard who died
July 15th 1789 in ye
19th year of her age

Death is uncertain
yet moſt ſure
ſin is the wound
Chriſt is the cure

(footstone)
Miſs Lois
Birchard

Mr. John Post, 1710
(Founder)
See Page 20

Sergt. Thomas Waterman, 1708
(Founder)
See Page 16

Deacon Simon Huntington, 1706
(Founder)
See Page 95

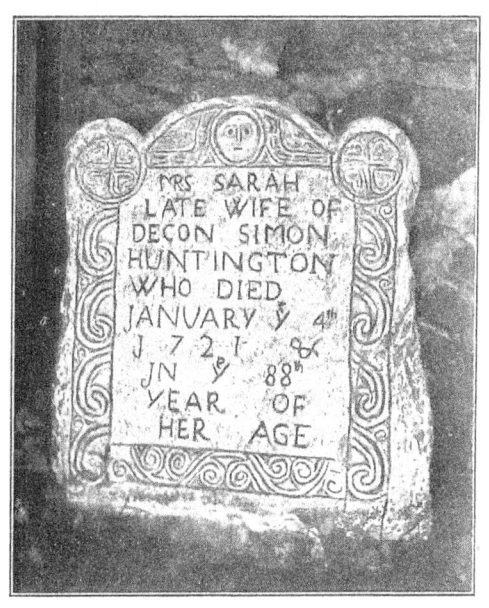

Mrs. Sarah Huntington, 1721
See Page 94

243. (footstone)
      Mrs
      Mary
      Huntington

244. In memory of
      Eunice wife of
      Thomas L. Thomas
      and daughter of
      Gideon Birchard
      who died Novr 3d
      1796 in the 37th
      year of her age

      (footstone)
      Eunice
      Thomas

245. Here   ye Body
      of Mrs Mary Hunting
      late Virtuous &
      Loving Confort of Mr
      Chriftopher Huntington
      She   lived   beloved
      &   died   lamented

                        ia
246. Here lies ye Body of lyd
      Abel ye Daughter of
      Samuel & Mrs Lydia
      Abel who died April
      ye 1 1739 & About
      14 years of Age

      (footstone)
      Lydia Abell
      The Daughter of
      Mr Samuel Abel

247. In Memory of Mr
      Samuel Abell Died
      Nouemb ye 26th
      AD   1761
      Aged 89 years

      Blessed Are ye Dead
      That Die in ye Lord

248. In memory of
      William H fon
      of Elisha and
      Thankful
      Burchard who
      died Septr 10th
      1797 age 9
      months

      (footstone)
      William Burchard
      Burchard

249. (footstone)
      MRS
      ELISABETH
      ABELL

250. (footstone)
      MRS
      JERUSHA
      ABELL

251. Unlettered granite stone.

252. IN MEMORY
      OF Mrs JERUSHA WIFE
      to Mr Joshua Abell
      Who Died March the 1
      A d 1741/2 in the 38th
      Year of her Age
      (footstone No. 250)

253. In Memory of Ri
      chard fon to John &
      Abigail Huntington
      he died Febr 11th
      1784 in ye 6th
      year of his Age

           the
                  o d
      He clos'd his Eyes
      and faw his God

254. Unlettered granite stone.

255. In memory of Capt
Afa Waterman
who departed this
life Feb^r 26th AD
1789 in ye 50th
Year of his age

Death is uncertain
yet moſt ſure
ſin is the wound
Chriſt is the cure

(footstone)
Capt
Afa
Waterman

256. In Memory of M^rs
Lucy wife to M^r
Afa Waterman who
departed this life
Novr 16th A D 1790
in ye 77th year
of her age

(footstone)
M^rs
Lucy
Waterman

257. In Memory of
Mr Afa Waterman
who Departed
this life nov^r 14th
1783 in ye 76th
year of his Age.

(footstone)
M^r
Afa
Waterman

258. In Memory of M^rs
Marey Hyde wife
to Capt Jedediah
Hyde. ſhe died
ſep^t 2^d 1780 in y^e
42^d year of her age
ſhe was an agreeable
Companion & the
moſt tender mother

(footstone)
Marey
Hyde

259. Here Lyes ye Body
of Mr Thomas Wa-
terman, Son to M^r
Afa & Lucy Waterman
he was Drowned
May 22^d: AD 1773 in
ye 39th year of his
Age.

(footstone)
Mr Thomas
Waterman

260. In memory of
Mrs Eunice Waterman
relict of
Mr. Thomas Waterman
who died
March 28th 1808
aged 68 years

(footstone)
M^rs
Eunice
Waterman

261. Here Lies ye Bo
dy of Mrs Zepo
rah wife to M^r
Jabez Tracy
ſhe Died Feb^r
26 1769 in y^e
28th year of
her Age

(footstone)
M^rs
Zeporah
Tracy

262. In memory of
Mr Jabez Tracy
who died June
15, 1828,
Aged 88 years

They die in Jesus, and are blest
How kind their slumbers are!

(footstone)
J.   T.

263. In Memory of
Clarina Daught
to Mr Mun-
dator Tracy
& Mrs Carolina
his wife who
died Decbr 2d
1781 in ye 6th
year of her Age

264. In Memory of ye pious
Beloved & very Aged
Mr Simon Tracy who
Died fept 14th 1775
in ye 96th year
of his Age

(footstone)
Mr
Simon Tracy

265. Here Lies Inter'd
ye Body of Mrs Abigail
Tracy the virtuous
Confort of Deacon
Simon Tracy who
died July 6th 1774
in ye 56th year
of her age

(footstone)
Mrs
Abigail
Tracy

266. IN MEMORY
of Mrs Hannah Morgan
the Prudent Virtuous
and Well beloved wife
of Decon William
Morgan who by the
Will of God fell
afleep in the Cradle
of Death on the 26
Day of June A D
1747 aged about
48 years

(footstone)
Mrs
Hannah
Morgan

267. IN MEMORY
of Mrs Margret Mor
gan Decd September
the 12 A D 1745
Daughter to Deacon
William Morgan
and Mrs Hannah his
wife

(footstone)
Mrs
Margaret
Morgan

268. IN MEMORY
of Mrs Abigail Morgan
Daughter to Deacon
William Morgan &
Mrs Hannah his wife
Decd June the 5th
A D 1746 aged
18 years and 10
months

(footstone)
Mrs
Abigail
Morgan

269. Here lies ye Body of
Mrs Anne Morgan
Daughter to Deacon
William Morgan &
Mrs Hannah his wife
who died Oct ye 2
A D 1750 in the
21 year of her age

(footstone)
Morgan

270. to Mr Jabez
Avery & Lucy
his wife fhe
died Oct 30th
1775 Aged 8
months

(footstone)
Lydia
Avery
(daughter of above)

271. In Memory of Mrs Carolina Tracy loving Confort of Mr Mundator Tracy who died on ye 25th day of Jan^r 1785 in ye 38th year of her age

Hark ye fmall voice
that whifpers from ye tomb
Here ends this life:
another life to come
In this life then let
virt'ue guide your ways
And death fhall waft
you to immortal day

272. In memory of Dea^n Simon Tracy who departed this life on the 9th of Auguft 1793 in the 83^d year of his age Bleffed are the dead who die in the Lord

(footstone)
unlettered

273. In memory of Mr Mundator Tracy who died June 26th 1816 aged 66 years

(footstone)
Mr
M. T.

274. In memory of Mrs Nabby Tracy relict of Mr Mundator Tracy and daughter of Mr. Eleaser Lord She died March 8th 1821, aged 68 years

(footstone)
Mrs
N. T.

275. In memory of Jabin Tracy fon of Dorastus & Lovifa Tracy who died May 3^d 18^04, aged 14 months

(footstone)
J. T.

276. In memory of Mr Daniel Douglafs who depart'ed this life Feb 13th 1794 in the 81ft year of his age

In memory of Mrs Lois Douglafs Confort of Mr Daniel Douglafs who died May 25th 1803 AEt 78

(footstone)
Mr
Daniel
Douglafs

Mrs
Lois
Douglafs

277. In Memory of Mr Jabez Avery who died of the fmall pox Jan^r 30th 1779, in ye 45th Year of his age

In Memory of Mrs Lucy wife to Mr Jabez Avery who died Aug^ft 19th 1788 in ye 56th Year of her age

278. In memory of Mifs Lucretia daugh^t to Richard Hyde Efq^r & Mrs Anne his wife. fhe died dec^r 18th AD 1786, in ye 45th Year of her age.

(footstone)
Mifs
Lucretia
Hyde

279. In
Memory of
Mr. Zebadiah Hyde
who died
March 5, 1821;
aged 71 years

(footstone)
Z.   H.

280. Here lies yᵉ Body
of Mrs Mehitable
Wife to Mr Nathan
Hibbard ſhe Died
June 12th 1773 in yᵉ
35 year of her Age

(footstone)
M
Mehitable
Hibbard

281. In Memory of
Mr Hezekiah
Douglaſs he Depart
ed this life Augſt
10th   1781   in
yᵉ   33d   year
of his Age

(footstone)
Mr
Hezekiah
Douglaſs

282. In memory of Mrs.
Sarah relict of Mr
Theodore Hyde who
died July 30th 1793
in yᵉ 54th Year of
her age

Death is a debt
to nature due
Which I have paid
& ſo muſt you

(footstone)
Mrs
Sarah
Hyde

283. In Memory of Mr
Theodore Hyde
who died Decbr 29th
1787 in yᵉ 55th
year of his age

The ſweet remem
brance of the Juſt
ſhall flouriſh when
they ſleep in duſt

(footstone)
Mr
Theodore
Hyde

284. In Memory of Mrs.
Sarah Birchard
wife of Mr. John
Birchard, and late
widow of Mr.
Eleazer Hyde, who
died Janr the 1ſt
1777 in the 69th
Year of her Age.

(footstone)
Mrs
Sarah
Birchard

285. Here lies yᵉ Body
of Mr Eleazer Hyde
Who departed this
Life May 11th 1772:
in yᵉ 68th year
of his Age

(footstone)
Mr
Eleazer
Hyde

286. Here Lyes yᵉ
Body of Mr Iſsa
char Hyde Son
to Mr Elezr &
Sarah Hyde he
Died Octr 16th 1772
in yᵉ 25th year of
his Age.

(footstone)
Mr
Issachar
Hyde

287.
   ory of
   Daniel
   kins who
  eparted this
  life ſept 10th
   AD 1786 in
   ye 85th year
   of his Age

   (footstone)
    Mr
    Daniel
    Calkins

288. Sunken granite stone.

289. In Memory of Capt
   Oliver Arnold who
   died ſept 15th 1781 in
   ye 60th year of his Age

(289.)
    (2nd stone)
   In Memory of Capt
   Oliver Arnold who
   died ſept 15th 1781 in
   ye 60th year of his Age

  Ye living think as you paſſ by,
  And learn from me you-re
      Born to die,
  And ſince you ſee to what
      I've come
  Think of your impend
      ing doom
  For Cruel Death that ty
      rant' Grim
  Will ſlay when you think
      not of him

290. Here Lies the Body
   of Mrs perients
   Hide parted
   this Li ye 24th
   1765 in the 91ſt
   Year of her Age

   (footstone)
    Mrs
   Experients
    Hide

291. Here lies the Body
   of Mr Eliab Hide
   ſon of Mr Eleazer
   & Sarah Hide
   Who died April
   21 1760 in the
   22 year of
   his age

   (footstone)
    Mr
   Eliab Hide

292. In memory of Mr Na
   than Chapel Jn who
   died may 14th 1792
   in ye 41ſt year of
   his age

  Death is uncertain
   yet moſt ſure
   ſin is the wound
   Chriſt is the cure

   (footstone)
    Mr
   Nathan
   Chappel

293. In memory of Mrs
   Suſannah wife to Mr
   Nathan Chappel who
   died decbr 16th 1791
   aged 35 Years

  Alſo in memory of their
   Infant who died
   Octr 21ſt 1787

   (footstone)
    Mrs
   Suſannah
   Chappel

294. In Memory of
Mrs Sally wife
to Mr Thomas
Marſhall and
Daught to Capt
Benjamin
Edgerton & Mrs
Suſanna his wife
ſhe died April
21ſt 1785

    (footstone)
    Mrs
    Sally
    Marshall

295. John Harknes Son
Mr Jared Wentworth
& Abigail his Wife
in ye 2d year of his
Age

    (footstone)
    J. H. W.

296. In memory of Capt
Jacob Hazen who de-
parted this life Novr
14th 1790 in ye 61ſt
Year of his age

Death is a debt
To nature due
which I have paid
and ſo muſt you

    (footstone)
    Capt
    Jacob
    Hazen

297. In memory of Abigail, Clariſa
& Sophia children of Mr
Frederick & Mrs Sarah Hazen
Abigail died May 22d in the 8th
year of her age. Clariſa May
16th 3d year of her age.
Sophia June 1ſt aged 5 weeks
    AD 1776

    (footstone)
    Abigail
    Clariſa &
    Sophia Hazen

298. IN MEMORY OF
Mr. Silas Hide who
Departed this Life
October the 18th
A. D. 1776 in the
50th year of his
    Age

Stop, as you paſs by,
As you are now, So once was I,
As I am now, So you muſt be,
Prepare for Death & follow me.

    (footstone)
    Mr
    Silas
    Hide

299. The remains of
Capt ISAAC ABEL
Lie here inter'd
He died
June ye 3d AD 1783
In the 40th year of his
    Age

    (footstone)
300.   Sidney
    Tracy

301. In memory of Mr
Palmer Carew, who
Died Augſt 22d 1792
in ye 53d Year of
    his Age

How ſoon! How ſudden
death may cloſe our
mortal eyes in long repoſe
hear then the voice
    of wisdom cry
he dies to live
who lives to die

    (footstone)
    Mr
    Palmer
    Carew

302. In memory of
Mrs Susannah consort of
Mr Peleg Hyde who die
April 28th 1788 in the
45th year of her age
Memento mori fugit hora

(footstone)
Mrs
Susannah
Hyde

303. Broken granite stone.

304. In Memory of
James Jarvis Hyde
son to Mr Peleg &
Mrs Susanna Hyde
died June 7th AD
in the 8th
year of his age

305. Piece of 306 bearing last line of the inscription.

306. Here Lyes ye Body
of James Jarvis
Hyde son to Mr
Peleg & susanna
Hyde who Died
May 25, 1776
in his 3 year.

(footstone)
James Jarvis
Hyde

307. In Memory of
Mr Simeon
Backus he Depart
ed this Life Janr
7th 1782 in
ye 30th year
of his Age

(footstone)
Mr
Simeon
Backus

308. In Memory of
Mrs Abigail wed
ge Daughter to
Joshua & Rebecca
wedge who died
May ye 31st 1773
in the 66th year
of her Age

(footstone)
M   A gail

309. IN MEMORY OF
mrs Rebecca Wedge
Dad of mr Joshua &
Mrs Rebecca Wedge
Who departed this
life July ye 11th 1764
in ye 64th year of her
Age

(footstone)
Mrs
Rebecca Wedge

310. Here Lies the Body
of Mrs. Elizabeth Avery
wife to Mr. Jonathan
Avery who died
January ye 5th A D
1752 in ye 49th
Year of her age

311. Granite stone   H   A

312. In memory of Ozias
Backus son of Josiah
Backus and Love
His Wife & Husband
to Lydia Backus
Daughter to Elisha
& Sarah Waterman
who died Jan 25
1764 in the 25
year of his age

(footstone)
Mr
Ozias
Backus

313. He lies the Body of
Abſalom ſon to Joſiah
and Love Backus who
Died March yᵉ 17 1760
in the 13 year of his
Age his Siſter Ann
Lying at his right hand
Mors vincit omnia

    (footstone)
    Abſalom
    Backus

314. In Memory of
Mʳ Joſiah Backus
who departed
this life June
18ᵗʰ 1779 in yᵉ
70ᵗʰ year of
his age

    (footstone)
    Mʳ Joſiah
    Backus

315. In memory of Mʳˢ
Love Backus, who died
the 29ᵗʰ of Decemʳ
1778 in the 68ᵗʰ
Year of her Age

    (footstone)
    Mʳˢ Love
    Backus

316. To the memory
of Mrs Betſey
Tracy conſort of
Mʳ Peleg Tracy, &
daughᵗ of Mr Jeſſe
Brown, who died
March 19ᵗʰ 1792,
aged 19 years &
8 months

Bleſſed are the dead
that die in the Lord.

    (footstone)
    Mrs
    Betſey
    Tracy

317. In memory of Mr.
Ruſſel Brown ſon
of Mr. Jeſſe Brown
& Mrs Anne his wife
who died ſeptᵗ 24ᵗʰ
1795 in yᵉ 22ᵈ
Year of his age

    (footstone)
    Mr
    Ruſſel
    Brown

318. In Memory of
Miſs Phylena
daughᵗ to Mʳ
Jeſſe Brown &
Mʳˢ Anne his
wife ſhe died
March 3, 1785.

    (footstone)
    Miſs
    Phylena
    Brown

319. IN MEMORY
of Mary yᵉ Wife of
Jacob Perkins Junʳ
& Daughter of James
& Ann Brown who
died July 25ᵗʰ 1759
in yᵉ 23ᵈ Year
of her Age

    (footstone)
    Mary
    Perkins
    1759

320. LUCRETIA CAREW
died Aug. 12, 1778,
aged 1 year & 10 Mos.
MARY died March
22, 1775, aged 1 day.
Children of Daniel
and Lucy Carew

    (footstone)
    L. C.
    M. C.

321. Small granite stone, no visible inscription.

322.   In Memory of
       Mrs Mary Wife
       to Mr William
       Morgan fhe De
       parted this Life
       Auguft 15th 1770
       in ye 53d year
       of her Age

323.   In memory of Mrs. Mary
       wife to Mr. Abiel Hyde,
         who died Novr 3d 1791,
       in ye 31ft Year of her age
       alfo died Abial their fon
       Augft 26th 1791, aged 8 months

       Heav'n gives the needful but
                     neglected call
       What day what hour, but knocks
                     at human hearts
       To wake the foul to fenfe of
                     future fcenes
       And kindly point us to our
                     Journey's end

                (footstone)
                   Mrs
                   Mary
                   Hide

324.   Sacred
          to the memory of
          Mr. Abiel Hyde
          who died March 2d
          AD 1808 aged 50 years.

                (footstone)
                   Mr
                Abiel Hyde

325.   Sacred to the memory
       of Mrs. Anne Miner
       wife of Capt Seth
       Miner, who died Novr
       3d 1804 in the 60th year
       of her age
       Alfo of their 2 Children
       Sarah died Decr 7th
       1775 aged 3 years &
          7 days. Charlott di
       ed Novr 1ft 1774 aged
       6 weeks & 2 days.

                (footstone)
                   Mrs
                   Anne
                   Miner

326.   In memory of two children
       of David & Eunice Beebe,
       David Beebe   Cushing Beebe
       died Augt 15th   died Novr 29th
       1793, aged 2   1811, aged a
       years & 4   years & 8
       months.   months.

       Sleep on sweet babes & take your reft
       God called you home he saw it beft.

                (footstone)
          D. B. Jr   C. B.

327.   Cary ye Son
       of Cary &
       Ann Dunn
       died Septemr
       ye 25 th 1756
       aged 1 year

                (footstone)
                   C. D.

328.   Here lies the Body of
       Mrs Ann Brown
       wife to Mr James
       Brown Jur who
       Died Octor 22 1754
       In the 52 Year
       of her age

                (footstone)
                   Mrs
                Ann Brown

329. Here Lies the Body of
Mr James Noyce
Brown who died
Novemb the 8 day
1756 in the 27
Year of his age
Mors vincit omnia

    (footstone)
    Mr
    James Noyce
    Brown

330. In Memory of Daniel
son to Mr Eliphalet
Carew and Mary his
Wife he Died June
8th 1777 in ye 12th
year of his Age

    (footstone)
    Daniel
    Carew

331. In memory of
Mr Blancher
Darby who died
Novr 25th 1791
in ye 56th Year
of his age

The sweet remem
brance of the Just
shall flourish when
they sleep in dust.

    (footstone)
    Mr
    Blancher
    Darby

332. In memory of Willi
am son to Capt Silas
Goodell & Mrs. Sarah
his wife he was drown
ed June 28th 1790
in his 4 Year

Death is uncertain
    yet most sure
sin is the wound
Christ is the cure

    (footstone)
    William
    Goodell

333. In memory of
George son to Mr John
Richards & Martha his
wife he Died of the Rat
tles Octr 9th 1781 Aged
2 years & 9 days.

My date on earth was very
short my voige of life soon
ore Being Clothed in
robes which Jesus wrought
My soul shall rest secure

    (footstone)
    George
    Richards

334. Here Lies ye Body of Mr
Charles Avery who
Departed this Life
April 3d; AD 1774
in ye 45th year of
his Age

    (footstone)
    Mr
    Charles
    Avery

335. Here Lies ye Body of Mrs
Chloe Late Wife to Mr
Hugh Ledlie & Daught
to Mr Dan & Mrs Joanna
Stoughton she died
April 6th 1769 in ye 38th
year of her Age

Now you Behold this
monument Consider
how your time is Spent

    (footstone)
    Mrs Chloe
    Ledlie

336. In memory of Henry & Eu
nice Children of Mr Samuel
and Mrs Candace Avery. Henry
died June 22d 1783 AEtat 2
months & 15 days. Eunice
died Octr 17th 1792, AEtat
3 Years & 5 months.

Sleep sweet babes &
take your rest, God call'd
you home He saw it best.

    (footstone)
    Eunice &
    Henry Avery

337. In memory of M^rs
Eliſabeth wife to
Mr David Rogers who
died dec^r 4th 1786 in
ye 54th Year of her age.

This the laſt token of
eſteem receive
Tis all a husband
all a friend can give

338. Here Lies the Body
of Lidia ye Wife of
M^r Joſeph Emes &
Dau^tr to Mr Robert
Roath Who died
May ye 26th 1768
in ye 24th year
of her age

339. Here Lies the
Body of M^rs
Anna ye wife of
M^r peter Roath
who died March
26th 1769 in
ye 80th year of
her age

(footstone)
M^rs
Anna Roath

340. (footstone)
M^r
James
Gifford

341. In memory of Mrs
Mary wife to Mr,
Joſeph Shapley,
who died ſept 8th
1793, in ye 58th
Year of her age

342. IN MEMORY OF
Abigail ye Wife of
Mr William Bradford
Whiting who died
May ye 20th 1756
in ye 28th Year
of her Age

(footstone)
Abigail
Whiting
1756

343. In Memory of M^r   In Memory of M^rs
Thomas Carew,   Abigail Carew
he Departed this   Wife to Mr Tho-
Life Jan^r 13th   mas Carew, ſhe
1761 in ye 60th   Departed this
year of his   Life June 14th
Age   1777 in ye 70th
                        year of her Age

(footstone)
M^r   Abigail
Thomas   Carew
Carew

344. IN MEMORY of
Abigail ye Wife of
Mr Simeon Perkins
& Eldeſt Daughter
of Ebenezer
Backus Esq
who died Dec 22
AD 1760 in y^e
59 Year of
her Age

(footstone)
Abigail Perkins
1760

345. In memory of Mrs
Eunice the beloved
wife of Mr Jabez Avery
who died June 16th
1790 in ye 24d Year
of her age
Also Elisbeth their
daught who died July
12th 1790 aged 10
months & 4 days

(footstone)
Mrs
Eunice
Avery

346. In Memory of Miſs
Anne, daught to
Mr Thomas & Mrs
Anne Marſhall,
who died march
27th 1786 in
ye 25th year
of her Age

(footstone)
Miſs
Anne
Marſhall

347. In memory of the
widow Anne Marſhall
who died Janr 26th
1799 aged 74 years

The ſweet remem
brance of the Juſt
ſhall flourish when
they ſleep in duſt

(footstone)
Mrs
Anne
Marſhall

348. In memory of Mrs
Lucretia Daught to
Mr Thomas Marſhall
& Anne his Wife
ſhe Died Janr ye 3d
1774 in ye 20th year
of her Age

(footstone)
Mrs
Lucretia
Marſhall

349. Here lies the
Body of Mrs
Lydia Roath
wife of Mr Ro
bert Roath
who died A
priel 11th 1760
in the 45th
Year of her
Age

(footstone)
Mrs
Lydia
Roath

350. Here Lyes ye
Body   Hannah

John   Zip
orah Hughes who
died July ye 10th
1754 aged 2 year
2 months & 18 days

(footstone)
Hannah
Hughes

351. Sunken, unlettered stone.

352.   In M   of
       Cap   les
       wh   he 12th
       1771   year
       of

   The ſweet Remembr   of ye Juſt
   ſhall flouriſh when   he ſleep in
                         durſt

           (footstone)
             Capt
           John Bolles

353.   In memory of two
       children of Mr
       Sylvanus Jones & Mrs
       Keziah his wife
       viz Tryphena who
       died Auguſt 31 1751
       aged 2 years & 3
       months & Eliſabeth
       who died ſept. 1, 1751
       aged 4 years & 10
       months

           (footstone)
             Tryphena
                &
             Eliſabeth
               Jones

354.   In Memory of Mrs
       Chloe Hyde, loving
       conſort to Mr Ebenezer
       Hyde & eldeſt daught
       of Daniel Elſworth Eſqr
       & Mrs Mary his wife of
       Ellington who died
       June 30th AD 1787 in
       ye 35th year of her age

       Death is uncertain
         yet moſt ſure
         ſin is the wound
         Chriſt is the cure

           (footstone)
             Chloe
             Hyde

355.   In memory of Mrs Eliza
       beth Huntington wife to
       Mr James Huntington
       who died June 12 1790
       in ye 72d Year of
       her age

   Behold my friend as you paſs by,
   As you are now ſo once was I
   As I am now ſo you muſt be,
   Prepare for death & follow me

356.   In Memory of Mr
       James Huntington,
       who departed this
       life May 12th 1785:
       in ye 79th year
       of his age

   My lover friend Familliar all
   Removed from ſight & out of call
   To dark oblivion is retired
   Dead or at leaſt to me expir'd

           (footstone)
              Mr
             James
           Huntington

357.   In memory two Sons & two
       daughters of Capt James Hyde &
       Mrs. Martha his Wife. Sarah di
       ed Novr 1777 in her 2d Year,
       James died Octr 1778 aged 8 Mo
       James 2d died July 3d 1781 aged 7 Mo
       Betſey died June 16th 1792 aged 9 Mo

   Sleep ſweet babes & take your reſt
   God called you home He ſaw it beſt

           (footstone)
           Sarah, James, James
             Betſey Hyde

358.   In memory of
       Charles ſon to Capt
       James Hyde & Mrs
       Martha his wife
       who died febr
       10th 1795 in his
       2d year

359. Here lies yᵉ Body
of Mʳˢ Sarah
Wife to Mʳ James
Hide ſhe De-
parted this Life
Nov, 3ᵈ 1773 in yᵉ
54: year of her
Age

360. In memory of
Mr James Hide who
died April 24ᵗʰ 1793 in
yᵉ 87ᵗʰ year of his age

What once he was forbear to ſay
Twil beſt be known in that great day
   when you & I & everyone
Muſt give account of what
      we have done
To ſay no more he lived approved
And died lamented & beloved

361. In memory of
Mʳˢ Abiah Randal
relict of
Mʳ Amos Randal
who died April 6ᵗʰ 1812
aged 82

(footstone)
Mrs Abiah
Randall

362. In
memory of
Ebenezer Hyde
who died
Dec. 28ᵗʰ 1816
Æ 67

(footstone)
E. H.

363. Granite stone—no visible inscription.

364. In memory of Colᵒ John Durkee
who departed this life May
29ᵗʰ 1782 in the 54ᵗʰ
Year of his age

In memory of Mrs Martha
wife to Colᵒ John Durkee
who died May 27ᵗʰ 1787
in yᵉ 60ᵗʰ Year of her age

In memory of Doctʳ Dominic
Touzin who was loſt in a
at ſea
hurricane March 1782 in
yᵉ 31ſt Year of his Age

(footstone)
Colᵒ John Durkee
Mrs Martha Durkee

365. Sunken granite stone—no visible inscription.

366. Oct. 25ᵗʰ 1773 De-
parted this Life
Lucy Daughᵗʳ to
Mʳ Joſhua Prior Jⁿʳ
& Sarah his Wife
Age 4 year & 4 Month

Sleep My Babe
& take thy reſt
God call'd yᵉ home
He saw it Best

(footstone)
Lucy
Prior

367. Here lies yᵉ Body
of Abigail dauᵗʳ to
Mʳ Joſhua Prier ᴶⁿʳ
& Sarah his
wife who   ied
octᵗ yᵉ   6
aged 3 y   &
6 months

(footstone)
Abigail prier

368. Beneath lie the Remains of
four infant children of Caleb
& Anne Huntington, a daught
who died Sept 7th 1796. A fon
& daughter June 17th 1797. And a
daughter May 16th 1798.

369. In memory of
Mrs Mary the vir
tuous wife of Mr
John Huntington
who died march
7th 1786 in ye
72d year of
her age

370. Granite stone—much sunken.

371. In Memory of
Mr Ozias Huntington
who died July 20
1810 in ye 36 Year
of his age

(footstone)
Mr Ozias Huntington

372. In memory of
Mrs Mahetibel relict
of Mr Simeon Case
who died Novr 4th
1788 in the 56th
year of her age.
Alfo of Mr John Cafe
who died Febry 19th
1788 in the 24th
year of his age

(footstone)
Mrs
Mahetible
&   Mr
John Cafe

373. This stone is erected
as a monument of
repect to the
memory of
Mrs Katharine Cobb
Confort of Mr
Nathan Cobb
who died April 15th
1795 aged 64 years

(footstone)
Mrs
Katharine
Cobb

374. A monument of refpect
to the memory of
Mr Nathan Cobb
who died Dec 1ft
1805 aged 71 years

(footstone)
Mr Nathan
Cobb

375. Mary Cobb

(footstone)
Mary Cobb

376.
(footstone)

377. Here Lies ye Body of the
Wel-beloved Mrs Sarah Dan
forth wife to Mr Thomas
Danforth & Daughter of Capt
Jeams Leonard ye 2d (of Tanton)
& Mrs Hannah his wife (fhe
was a Pattern of Piety
Patience & Virtue) who
died May the 22d A D
1742 AEtatis Sua
About 34
& Six Children of Sd Dan
forth Near the Same Place

(footstone)
Mrs
Sarah
Danforth

378.　In memory of Doctr
John Danforth, ſon to
Mr John & Mrs Eliza-
beth Danforth who
died Octr 31ſt 1791,
aged 23 Years

This happy youth reſign'd his
　　　breath
Prepar'd to live and ripe for death
Ye blooming Youth who read this stone
Learn early death to be your own

(footstone)
Doct
John
Danforth

379.　In memory of Mr.
John Danforth who
died Janr 31ſt 1799
in ye 58th year
of his age

Behold my friend as
　　　you paſs by
As you are now ſo
　　　once was I
As I am now ſo you
　　　muſt be
Prepare for death &
　　　follow me

(footstone)
Mr
John
Danforth

380.　Sacred
to the memory of
Mrs. Deborah Thomas
relict of
Mr Ebnezer Thomas
who died Oct 5th 1803,
aged 89 years

(footstone)
Mrs
Deborah
Thomas

381.　Here Lies ye Body
of Mr Ebenezer Tho
mas he Departed
this Life Oct 16th
1774, in ye 72d year
of his Age

(footstone)
Mr
Ebenezer Thomas

382.　Sacred
to the memory of Miſs
Lucretia Thomas
who died Dec 10th
1812, aged 74 years

(footstone)
Miſs Lucretia
Thomas

383.　Here Lies ye Body
of Mrs Elizabeth
Daught to Mr
Ebenezer Thomas
& Mrs Hannah his
Wife, ſhe Died Janr
4th 1777 in ye
29th year of
her Age

(footstone)
Mrs
Elizabeth
Thomas

384.　Two small, much sunken, unlettered granite stones.

385.　Two similar stones.

386. (Tablestone)
In memory of Mrs Sarah
Huntington the amiable
conſort of Capt Frederick Hunt
ington & only daugh^r of M^r
John Bliſs & Sarah his wife
ſhe died Aug^ſt 6th 1786 aged 29 Years
& in Memory of their two ſons
John, who died July 19th 1786
in his 2^d year & Frederick who
died Aug^ſt 1ſt 1786 aged 4 Months

Stop here kind friend & drop a tear,
Upon the duſt that ſlumbers here.
And while you read the fate of me
Think on the glaſs that runs for thee

Sleep my friend and take thy reſt
The babes & you I truſt are bleſt.

(footstone)

387. In Memory of M^rs
Ruth the wife of
Mr Peter Huntin
gton who died
ſep 18th 1761 in
ye 46th year
of her age

(footstone)
Mrs
Ruth
Huntington

388. In memory of
Mrs Phebe, wife to Mr.
Ebenezer Hyde who died
July 5th 1799, in ye 52^d
year of her age

The ſweet remembrance
of the Juſt
ſhall flouriſh when they
ſleep in duſt

(footstone)
Mrs
Phebe
Hyde

389. IN MEMORY
of Mrs Elizabeth the
wife of Mr Simon
Tracy Daughter of
Capt Jabez Hyde Eſq
and Mrs Elizabeth
his wife who died
Auguſt the 23 Anno
Domini 1741 Aged
30

          lie
Let not ye dead forgotten
Leaſt men forget that they
          (muſt die

(footstone)
probably No. 448.

390. In memory of
Mrs. Abigail relict of
Mr. Azariah Lathrop
who died
March 9th 1820,
aged 80 years

(footstone)
A. L.

391. In memory of
Mr Azariah Lathrop
who died
Feby 25th AD 1810
aged 82 years

(footstone)
Mr
Azariah
Lathrop

392. In Memory of M^rs
Anna late Conſort
of Mr Nath^ll Lathrop
ſhe Died aug^ſt 24th
AD 1761 in y^e
66th year of her Age

(footstone)
M^rs
Anna
Lathrop

393.   In Memory of Mr
Nathll Lathrop he
Departed this
Life march 20th
AD 1774 in ye
81ft year of
his Age

394.   Sacred
To the memory of
Mrs. Nabby Whiting,
wife of
W. B. Whiting, of Albany,
And Daugr of Azariah Lathrop Efqr.
who died
Augt 25th. 1805;
Aged 33 years.

(footstone)
Mrs
Nabby Whiting

395.   In
memory of
Mr Charles T. Wood
who died
March 20, 1807,
aged 28
Also of
Betsey
wife of Charles T. Wood,
who died April 8, 1826,
aged 46.
And of Mary B. who died
Dec. 7, 1801 aged 1 year

(footstone)
C. T. W.

396. Sunken granite stone—no visible inscription.

397.   In memory of
Mr John Leach,
who died Dec. 22d
1803 in the 26th
year of his age

(footstone)
Mr. John
Leach

398. Sunken granite stone—no visible inscription.

399.   In
Memory of
MRS. WELTHEA FOSTER,
widow of
Capt. Daniel Foster,
who died
Feb. 11, 1851,
aged 88.

"Blessed are the dead who die in the Lord"

(footstone)
W. F.

400. Two unlettered, granite stones which may indicate one grave.

401.   IN MEMORY OF
ASAHEL CASE
died
Nov 11, 1828,
AE. 58
ALSO
ROSANAH,
wife of
ASAHEL CASE
died March 27, 1849,
AE 84.
ALSO
LOUISA,
their daughter died Jan 10, 1806
AE 4 Yr's
AND ALSO
JAMES V
Son of Varney & Eleanor S. Parkerson
died Sept. 5, 1829, aged 9 years.

(footstone)
A. C.

402. Small granite stone.

403.   In memory of Doctr
Jonathan Marsh who
died April 18th 1798 in
the 44th year of his age

God my redeemer lives
And often from the fkies
Looks down and watches
all my duft
Till he fhall bid it rife.

(footstone)
Doctr
Jonathan
Marsh

404. EBENEZER LATHROP
died
April 7, 1870.
Aged 89 years.

(footstone)
E. L.

405. In memory of Mrs
Elizabeth Manwaring
relict of
Robert Manwaring
who died Feb 13th 1802,
in the 39th year
of her age

(footstone)
Mrs Elizabeth
Manwaring

406. In memory of
Dea. Robert Manwaring
who died
March 29th AD. 1807,
in the 62d year
of his age

(footstone)
Dea. Robert
Manwaring

407. In memory of Mrs
Sufan Manwaring
relict of Dea
Robert Manwaring
who died April 9th
1814 in the 47th year
of her age

(footstone)
Mrs
S. M.

408. In memory of Civil
Confort of Jedidiah Lathrop
who died June 19th 1797
in the 46th year of her age

We fee our friends around us falling,
We fee them bury'd in the duft,
In folemn filence ftill they're calling,
Prepare for death for die you muft.

(footstone)
Civil Lathrop.

409. In memory of
Mr. Jedidiah Lathrop
who died June 19th 1817
age 69

Heav'n gives us friends to
blefs the perfect fcene
Returnes them to prepare
us for the next

(footstone)
J. L.

410. In memory of
Mrs. Eunice Bailey
wife of
Mr. Samuel Bailey
who died July 26th
1819 in the 53d year
of her age

(footstone)
Mrs
E. B.

411. Sacred
to the memory of
Mrs Cynthia Bailey
wife of
Mr Samuel Bailey,
who died Feb 9th 1808
in the 44th year of
her age

(footstone)
Mrs Cinthia
Bailey

412. In
MEMORY OF
SAMUEL BAILEY
WHO DIED
March 7, 1848
aged 83

(footstone)
S. B.

413. In memory of
Mrs Catharine
confort of
Mr Samuel Bailey
who died Oct 8th
1820 in the 35th
year of her age

(footstone)
Mrs
C. B.

414. In memory of Mrs
Eunice, confort of
Mr. Joseph Carpender
who died June 18th
1797, in ye 42d
year of her age

The sweet remem-
brance of the Juft
shall flourish when
they sleep in dust

(footstone)
Mrs
Eunice
Carpender

415. In memory of
Charles fon to
Mr Ezra & Mrs
Elifabeth Hunt
ington, who died
July 25th 1775
in ye 8th year
of his Age

(footstone)
Charles
Huntington

416. In memory of
Silas
Huntington
who died Feb. 21ft
1799 in the 25th
year of his age

(footstone)
Silas
Huntington

417. In memory of
Mary Huntington
2d wife of
Ezra Huntington
who died Nov 12th
1804 in the 53d year
of her age

(footstone)
Mary
Huntington

418. In memory of
Elifabeth wife of
Ezra Huntington
who died octr 19th
1796 in the 48th
year of her age

(footstone)
Elifabeth
Huntington

419. IN MEMORY OF
Mrs Sarah late
virtuous confort
of Deacn Ebenezer
Huntington & daur
of Deacn Thomas
Leffingwell who
died April 1ft 1770
in ye 72 year of her age

(footstone)
Mrs
Sarah
Huntington

420. IN MEMORY OF DEACON
Ebenezer Huntington of
Norwich fon of Deacon Simon
Huntington Born May 10th
1692 Chosen Deacon of
the firft Church Janry 18th 1737
lived an Exemplary life &
being well Reconciled to death
died fuddenly feptr 12th 1768
in the 77th year of his
age

(footstone)
Deacon
Ebenezer
Huntington

421.   In Memory of
M. Roger Hunting
ton ſon to Deacn
Simon Huntington
& Mrs Zipporah
his wife who liv'd
beloved & died la-
mented Sept 7th
1780 in ye 21ſt
year of his age

(footstone)
Mr
Roger
Huntington

422.   Here is Buried Mr Simeon
Wartermans wife & Child
Who Died May 30th 1764 in
ye 21d year of her age,

Altho Death Diſolved ye uni
on Between them, nipt him in
the Topmuſt Bow, in the height
of his Feliſity, yet Comfort Re
mains in ye foloing Epitaph

Silent She lies Here in this Place
And so to Rest Till Christ Shall
Come to Raise her Duſt & Crown
that Grace Which in her
Life so Nobly Shone

(footstone)
Mrs Hannah
Warterman

(Cut and signed by J. Manning)

423.   IN
memory of
EZEKIEL BARRETT
who died
Feb 10, 1838,
aged 95 yr's

(footstone)
E. B.

424.   IN
Memory of
SARAH BARRETT
Relict of
EZEKIEL BARRETT
DIED
April 3, 1842,
Aged 74

(footstone)
S. B.

425.   In Memory of
Mr William Lathrop
Who Departed
this life Sept
27th 1778 in
ye 90th year
of his Age

The ſweet remem
brance of the Juſt
ſhall flouriſh when
they ſleep in duſt

426.   In Memory of
Mrs Mary the
amiable Conſort
of Mr Benjamin
Huntington Junr
ſhe died April 24th
AD 1777 aged 42

(footstone)
Mrs
Mary
Huntington

427.   In memory of
Benjamin Huntington
Eſq
who departed this life
Sept 3d 1801 in the
65 year of his age

(footstone)
Benj
Huntington Eſq

428. Here lies the Body of
Mr William Lothrop Junr
Son to Mr William Lothrop
& Sarah his wife
of Norwich who died
July 15th 1770 aged 55
years & 1 month

(footstone)
Mr
William
Lothrop

429. In memory of
SARAH
Wife of
Ezekiel Barrett
who died
Octr 27th 1811,
in the 63 year
of her age

(footstone)
Sarah
Barrett

430. In Memory of Doct
Eliſha Lord who
departed this life
march 15th AD
1768 in ye 40th
year of his Age.

With confidence I
truſt my dying Lord
Thiſ duſt ſhall riſe
according to his word

(footstone)
Doctr
Eliſha
Lord

431. In
MEMORY OF
SAMUEL CASE
who died
Jan 8, 1791,
aged 27 years.
ALSO
SUSANNA
his wife who died
May 24, 1848,
aged 86 years

(footstone)
S. C.

432. SUSAN CASE
DIED
Apr 29, 1820,
aged 33 years

(footstone)
S. C.

433. In Memory of Mr
Andrew Parish
who departed
this life Sept
9th 1764 in ye
24th year of
his age

(footstone)
Mr
Andrew
Pariſh

434. Two sunken, unlettered stones—may be one grave.

435. Two similar stones to 434.

436. In memory of
Mr. Ebenezer Pariſh
who died Feby 4th
1799 in the 25th year
of his age

(footstone)
Mr. Ebenezer
Pariſh

437. In memory of
Mr Elijah Pariſh
who died March 28th
1800 in the 27th year
of his age

(footstone)
Mr Elijah
Pariſh

438. In memory of
Miſs Mary Stroud
who died Dec. 12th
1801 in the 24th year
of her age

(footstone)

439. ncertainty
(footstone)
Capt. Andrew
Parish

Capt. Andrew Parish 1805
Let this stone in eloquent silence teach
the uncertainty of life

(Pastoral Library, Records of the
First Congregational Church, Norwich, p. 92.)

440. Sacred
to the memory of
Mrs Susanna Parish
wife of Capt Andrew
Parish who departed
this life Dec. 1st AD
1811 Aged 44 years

We sorrow not as those
without hope, because
there remaineth a rest
for the righteous.

(footstone)
Mrs Susanna
Parish

441. In m   ry of
Harri   ughter
of Mr   uel &
Mrs   cy
Danfo   who
died Nov. 3d 1801,
aged 1 year &
10 months

(footstone)
H. D.

442. In memory of Gur
don ſon to Capt
Thomas L. Thomas
& Mrs Eunice his
wife who died Augſt
18th 1793 in his 7th Year

Weep not for me
my parents dear
I am not dead
but ſleeping here

(footstone)
Gurdon
Thomas

443. Sacred
to the memory
of Henry, ſon of
Charles & Fanny
Thomas who
died Oct 5th 1814,
aged 1 year

(footstone)
H. T.

(footstone)
444. Mr
Thomas
Danforth

445. In memory of Mrs.
Chloe wife to Mr.
Ebenezer Thomas
who died June 28th
1789, in ye 42d Year
of her age.
& their daughter Jeruſha Thomas who died
Febr, 9th 1793, aged 8 Years.

The ſweet remem
brance of the Juſt
ſhall flouriſh when
they ſleep in duſt

(footstone)
Mrs
Chloe
Thomas

446. Sacred
to the memory of
Ebenezer Thomas
who died April 9th 1808
aged 63

(footstone)
Ebenezer
Thomas

447. Hannah Thomas
DIED
Sept 18, 1834,
AGED 85

(footstone)
H. T.

Deacon Thomas Adgate, 1707
(Founder)
See Page 75

Mrs. Mary Adgate, 1713
See Page 75

Mr. Stephen Gifford, 1724
(Founder)
See Page 11

Mrs. Hannah Gifford, 1724
See Page 11

448.
IN MEMORY
of Mrs Elizabeth
Tracy OB Augt
the 23d A D
1741 AEtatis
Suae 30

449.
In memory of
Mrs Mary Hubbard
relict of
Mr Ruſſell Hubbard
who died Oct 30th
1806 in the 78th
year of her age

450.
In memory of
William Hubbard
ſon of Thomas &
Mary Hubbard
who died Oct 9th
1802 aged 2 years

(footstone)
W. H.

451.
In memory of Mr
Ruſſell Hubbard
who Departed
this life Aug{ſt} 5th
1785 in ye 54th
year of his age

(footstone)
Mr
Ruſſell
Hubbard

452.
Sacred
to the memory of Mrs
Zepporah Huntington
relict of
Dea Simon Huntington
who died March 30th
1814 in the 81{ſt} year of
her age

(footstone)
Z. H.

453.
Sacred
to the memory of Deacon
Simon Huntington, ſon of
Deacon Ebenezer & Mrs
Sarah Huntington who
was born Sept 12th 1719
& died Dec 27th 1801, in
the 83d year of his age

(footstone)
Deacon
Simon
Huntington

454.
Here lies ye Body
of Mrs Lucy Hunting
ton, the Virtuous con-
ſort of Mr Andrew
Huntington, was born
July 2{D} 1746; & died
may 9th 1776 in ye
twenty ninth year of
her Age

The memory of the Juſt
is Bleſſed

(footstone)
Mrs Lucy
Huntington

455.
In memory of Capt
Ebenr Lathrop Who
was born Jan{r} 7th
1703, & died Jan{r}
28th 1781 in ye
79 year of his Age

My lover friend Familiar all
Remov'd from ſight & out of call
To dark Oblivion is retir'd,
dead or at leaſt to me expir'd

(footstone)
Capt
Ebenezer
Lathrop

456.
    Her   Remains
    of   virtuou^s
    c   of
    Ca   hrop of
    No   of
    T

(footstone)
M^{rs}
Lydia Lothrop

457. In memory of Mrs Eliſabeth Lord re- lict of Mr Cyperon Lord who died Aug^{ſt} 7th 1787, in ye 82^d Year of her age

458. The Remains of Eben^r Backus Eſq^r who died the 4th day of Novem^r A. D. 1768: in ye 57th year of his Age.

Earths highest Station ends, in here he lies: and duſt to duſt Concludes her noblest Song.

(footstone)
Eben^r Backus
Esq
(Signed by initials J. M.—"Josiah Manning.")

459. Sunken, unlettered, granite stone.

460. Similar stone to 459.

461. Sacred to the Memory of Mouſ^r Claudius Dumont who Died Octr 2^d 1782 Aged 38 years

If virtue to the Christian were
                confin'd
And ſuch alone poſses the noble mind
    Elogiums are Juſtly due
But commendations of the
                Chriſtian few
The penſive muſe would
             only drop a tear
And ſay "The Body of Dumont
                lies here"
But ſenecas there are in whom
                we find
Tenacious Virtue filling all
                the mind
d thus great and good
              Yet half unknown
Inspir'd the duſt inter'd
             beneath this ſtone

(footstone)
Mouſ^r
Clauldious
Dumont

462. Rough granite stone—no visible inscrip- tion.

463.
IN
Memory of
M^{RS} REBECCA
WIFE OF MR SIMON
CHAPMAN who
died July 9th 1757
Aged 40 years

464. In memory of Miſs Anne Gookin who departed this life May 23^d 1810 aged 79

(footstone)
Miſs
Anne Gookin

465.
In memory of
Miſs Mary
Thompson who
departed this
life Janʸ 23ᵈ
1787 in yᵉ 64th
Year of her age.

(footstone)
Miſs
Mary
Thompſon

466. Here Lyes intered the Body of
Mʳ JABIS BALDWIN
The Son of Mʳ THOMAS and
Mʳˢ ABIGAL BALDWIN
Who Died Decᵇ 15 1737 in
The 25 year of his age
MEMENTO MORI
MORS VINCET OMNIA

(footstone)
Mʳ Jabis Baldwin
Died Decbʳ 15 1737

467. Here Lies yᵉ Body
of Mʳ Lake Cotton
Son of Deanⁿ Thomas
Cotton of Pomfret
who die Septem
yᵉ   AD   1751
in his   year

(footstone)
Mr
Lake
Cotton

468. Mrs MARGARET
WIFE OF
CAPT. TIMOTHY LESTER,
DIED
Dec. 26, 1839,
Aged 69 Years,
and 6 Mo's

(footstone)
M.   L.

469.
Sacred
to the memory of
Capt. Timothy Leſter,
who departed this life
Aug 23ᵈ 1810
aged 42

(footstone)
Capt Timothy
Leſter

470.
Albert
ſon of Timothy &
Peggy Leſter
was born Feb 9th
AD 1799
and died May 18th
AD 1800

(footstone)
A.   L.

471. MARY LESTER
DIED
1846,
aged 50

(footstone)
M.   L.

472. In memory of
Mʳ Hezekiah Allen
who died Novʳ 6th
1794 in the 63ᵈ
year of his age.

(footstone)
Mʳ
Hezekiah
Allen

473. In memory of
Mrs Mary Allen conſort
of Mr Hezekiah Allen
who departed this life
May 2ⁿᵈ 1813 in the 71ᶠᵗ
year of her age

(footstone)
Mrs Mary
Allen

474. In memory of Mrs.
Amelia Pendleton
wife of Mr
Joſhua Pendleton jun
who died Jan 8th 1801,
in the 23d year
of her age
(footstone)
Mrs Amelia
Pendleton

475. In memory of
DEA
JOSHUA PENDLETON,
WHO DIED
April 9, 1824,
Aged 80

"Blessed are the dead
Which die in the Lord."

RENDERED LOYAL SERVICE
IN THE CAUSE OF AMERICAN
INDEPENDENCE AS CAPT. OF
THE FIRST WESTERLY CO. R. I.
STATE MILITIA FROM MAY
1776 TO THE CLOSE OF THE WAR.

(footstone)
J. P.

476. Mrs. ANNA
Relict of
Dea. Joshua Pendleton
died June 27, 1842
aged 92.
(footstone)
A. P.

477. Sunken, granite stone.

478. In memory of
Mrs RHODA WITTER
wife of
Mr JACOB WITTER
the daughter of
Capt Ebenezer & Mrs Bethiah Baldwin,
ſhe died Octr 10th AD 1793, aged 54 Years,
in the midſt of a uſeful life
of affectionate attention to her husband,
and kindness to her friends & the poor
of uncommon induſtry
ſtrict economy
and ſingular patience and fortitude
under her peculiar trials
in the bright proſpect of a
glorious Immortality

(footstone)
Mrs
Rhoda
Witter

479. In memory of Mr.
Jacob Witter, who
died Janr 29th 1798
in ye 64th year of
his age.

Death is a debt
to nature due
Which I have paid
& ſo muſt you.

(footstone)
Mr
Jacob
Witter

480. (Western Front)   (Southern Face)   (Northern Side)
HEZEKIAH   JOHN WILLIAMS   HEZEKIAH H.
WILLIAMS   DIED   Son of
died   Aug. 10, 1878,   Hezekiah & Dorothy H.
Nov. 2, 1790,   Aged 28.   WILLIAMS
Aged 28.   died
                                             March 13, 1815,
DOROTHY H.   Aged 25.
WILLIAMS
his Wife   (footstone)
died Sept. 11,   Mr John Williams
1841   Mr Hezekiah Williams
Aged 77.

481. To the Memory of
Mrs Dorothy, Second
Confort of the Honble
Hezh Huntington Efqr
Who died Febr 27th
1774 AEt 67.

(footstone)
Mrs
Dorothy
Huntington

482. To the Memory of ye Honbl
HEZEKIAH HUNTING
TON Efqr who died at New
London in ye Sefsion of ye Court
Febry: 10th: 1773, AEtat: 76, Deacon
of ye first Church in Norwich,
one of ye Councel of ye Colony,
Cheif Judge of ye Inf: Court &
Judge of Probate: his Piety &
Affability, Prayers & Example,
Wisdom & Experience endeared
him to his Friends, to ye Church
& ye State.

"And all Judah & ye Inhabi-
tants of Jerufalem
Did him Honour at his
Death."

(footstone)
The
Honobl
Hezekiah
Huntington

483. In memory of
Rofwell fon to
Mr Jedidiah &
Mrs Civil Lathrop
he died April
15th 1783 in
ye 7th year
of his age

484. Here Lies Buried ye
Body of Gurdon
Huntington A. M. Son
to the Honble Hezekiah
Huntington Efyr who
departed this life
Decmr ye 28th A. D.
1767 in the 28th
Year of his age

Mors omnia vincit.

(footstone)
Gurdon
Huntington, A. M.

485. IN MEMORY OF
Mr John williams lost
at Sea march 1764 & of
Eunice his
here Lyes
of ye
Hez
die
in

(footstone)
Mrs
Eunice Williams

486. In Memory of
Charlotte Daughr
to Mr Azariah
Lathrop & Mrs
Abigail his wife
fhe died Nov
3d 1777 in ye 4th
year of her Age

(footstone)
Charlotte
Lathrop

487. In Memory of
Hannah Daught
to Mr Azariah
Lathrop & Abigail
his Wife fhe
was ftill fept
22d 1767

(footstone)
Hannah
Lathrop

488.   In memory of
       MRS
       MERCY LATHROP
       relict of
       Deacon Joshua Lathrop,
       WHO DIED
       July 7, 1833,
       in the 91st year of
       her age

       (footstone)
       M. Lathrop

489.   In memory of
       Deacon Joſhua Lathrop
       He died Oct 29th AD. 1807,
       in the 85th year of his age.

       A ſoul prepared needs no delays
       The ſummons come, the ſaint obeys.
       Swift was his flight & ſhort the
       road
       He clos'd his eyes & ſaw his God

       (footstone)
       Deacon
       Joſhua Lathrop

490.   IN MEMORY of
       Hannah the loving
       Conſort of Mr Joſhua
       Lathrop & Daughter of
       Mr David Gardiner
       who died July 24th 1760
       in ye 30th Year of her Age

       The Spider's moſt attenuated
       Thread is Cord is Cable to
       Man's tender tie; on earthly
       Bliſs it breaks at every Breeze

       (footstone)
       Hannah
       Lathrop
       1760

491.   In Memory of Mr
       Thomas Lathrop
       he Died May 25th
       1774 Aged 92
       years & 8 months

       Write Bleſſed are
       ye d   d which die
       in ye Lord
       Rev. 14th : 13th

       (footstone)
       Mr
       Thomas
       Lathrop

492.   Here Lies the
       Body of Mrs
       Lydia Lothrop
       wife to Mr Th
       omas Lothrop
       She was Born
       March 1688 and
       Died March
       the 22d 1752.

       (footstone)
       Mrs
       Lydia
       Lathrop

493.   Tablestone—inscription plate missing.

494.   Footstone—no visible inscription.

495.   To the Memory of
       Doct Joſeph Coit he
       departed this Life
       Decr 18th 1779 in ye
       30th year of his Age

       Stop here kind Friend
       and drop a tear
       Upon ye youthfull duſt
       that ſlumbers here.
       And while you read
       the fate of me
       Think on the glass
       That runs for thee

       (footstone)
       Doct
       Joſeph
       Coit

496.   In Memory of
Joſeph Coit Eſqʳ
who died on the
27ᵗʰ day of
April 1787 in
the 90ᵗʰ year
of his age.
The memory of
the Juſt is Bleſſed

(footstone)
Joſeph
Coit
Eſqʳ

497.   In memory of Mrs
Lydia Coit relict of
Joſeph Coit Eſqʳ
who died Janʳ 10ᵗʰ
1794 in yᵉ 76ᵗʰ
year of her age
Memento mori

(footstone)
Mrs
Lydia
Coit

(Table stone)
498.   In memory of Elizabeth wife of
Chriſtopher Leffingwell & daughter
of Joſeph Coit whoſe exit was on the
9ᵗʰ day of Novʳ 1796, aged 53 years

(Table tomb)
499.   The remains of
CHRISTOPHER LEFFINGWELL Esq.
who died
November 27ᵗʰ AD. 1810,
aged 76 years.

(Table stone)
500.   In memory of
of
MRS RUTH LEFFINGWELL,
Relict of the late
Christopher Leffingwell
And daughter of
the late
Palatiah Webster,
WHO DIED
Dec. 18, 1840,
aged 85
years.

501.   Rough, unlettered granite stone.

502.   Here Lies the Body of
Mʳˢ Martha Waterman
The Beloved wife of
Mʳ Eleazer Watermaⁿ
Daughter of Deacon
Thomas Adget & Mʳˢ
Ruth his wife who
Died May 6ᵗʰ 1755 in
Yᵉ 45ᵗʰ year of her age

A virtuous woman Leaves
Her Name   Fame
On yᵉ Refulgent wings of

(footstone)
Mʳˢ
Martha Waterman

503.   HERE LYES Yᵉ BODY
OF CAPᵀ OBADIAH
SMITH WHO DIED
MAY Yᵉ 11ᵗʰ 1727 &
IN Yᵉ 50ᵗʰ YEAR
OF   HIS   AGE

NOW BETWEEN
THESE CARVED STONS
RICH TREASVRE LIES
DEER SMITH HIS BONES

(footstone)
Cap
OBADIAH
SMITH

(footstone)
504.   Mʳˢ
Freelove
Cheſter

505. Here Lies ye Body of
Mi{s Anne Relick of Mr Abiel
Mar{hall & daut^r of M^r
William & Anne Hide both
dec^{e'd} {he died april ye 1{t
1766 in ye 69 year of
her age

in faith {he dy^d in du{t {he lyes
but faith for{ees th^t du{t {hall Ri{e
when Je{us calls while hope a{ume^s
& boa{ts her joy among ye tomb^s

(footstone)
M^{rs}
Anne Mar{hall
1766

506. In memory of
Sarah Daugh^r to
Capt Samuel Wheat
& Sarah his Wife
{he died Aug{t 1{t
1776, Aged 7
months

(footstone)
Sarah
Wheat

507. In Memory of
John De{hon
{on to Samuell
Wheat & Sarah
his wife died
Dec^{br} 6th 1771
aged 20 days

(footstone)
John De{hon
Wheat

508. Here Lyes Interd ye Body
of ye Much re{pected Doct^r
Benjamin Wheate of
Cambridge New-England,
Who after a Laborious Life
Spent to Sarve Mankind
Re{igned his Mortal Life
In ye full hope & Expecta-
tion of a Better in ye Future
World Dyed Jan^r 27th
1758 in ye 49th year
of his Age.

(footstone)
Doct^r
Benjamin
Wheat

509. Elijah ye Son
of Ebenezer &
Bethiah Baldwin
died Jan^{ry} 16th
1750/1   Aged
11 M^o & 8 Days

510. In Memory of 2 Lovely babes
Children of M^r Jo{hua & M^{rs}
Sarah Whipple
Joanna Starr   Sarah died {ept
Whipple died   9th 1787 aged 2
{ept 5th 1787   Years & 9 months
aged 13 months

Sleep my babes till Chri{t
{hall come & take the to his
Eternal home

511.   M e m e n t o   m o r i
In memory of   In memory of
Mi{s Charlotte   Mi{s Bernice
Whiting who   Whiting who
died Octr 15th died May 27th
1794 in ye 24th 1793 aged 20
Year of her age   Years.
Daughters of Maj^r Ebenezer
Whiting & Mrs Anne his wife

Tho{e happy youths re{ign'd their
                                    breath,
Prepared to live & ripe for death,
Ye blooming youth who {ee this {tone,
Learn early death to be your own.

(footstone)
Mi{s Charlotte
& Bernice Whiting

512. How loved how honoured once
         avails thee not,
    To whom related
         or by whom begot,
    A heep of Duſt is all
         remains of thee
    'tis all thou art

    (footstone)
    Capt
    CHARLES
    WHITING

513. In Memory of Mrs
    Philena Whiting Re-
    lick to Col John Whit
    ing Who Died July
    7, 1776, in ye 52nd
    year of her Age

514. In Memory of
    Mrs Abigail Jarvis
    Relick of Capt James
    Jarvis of Roxbury
    ſhe died Sept 17th
    1776 Aged 71
    years

    (footstone)
    Mrs
    Abigail
    Jarvis

515. February 23d 1772
    Departed this
    Life Anne, Daughtr
    to Capt Ebenzr
    Whiting & Anne
    his Wife, Age'd
    1, Month.

    (footstone)
    Anne
    Whiting

516. Joſhua Lathrop
    Son to Mr Joſhua
    Lathrop & Mercy
    Lathrop died Augſt
    20, 1773 Aged 30
    days

517. Here Lyes ye Body
    of Mr Burrel Lathrop,
    Son to Mr Nathll Lath-
    rop Jnr & Margret his
    Wife, Who Departed
    this Life Augſt 4th:
    A.D. 1773: in ye 25th
    year of his Age.
    Memento Mori fugit
    Hora.

    (footstone)
    Mr
    Burrel
    Lathrop

518. Daniel Lathrop
    Son to Mr
    Joſhua & Mercy
    Lathrop who
    died June ye
    29th 1766
    aged 3 months
    (footstone)

519. In memory of
    William ſon to Mr
    Aſa & Mrs Eliſa
    beth Lathrop he
    died ſep. 13th
    1793 aged 12
    days

    Weep not for me
    my parents dear
    I am not dead
    but ſleeping here

    (footstone)
    William
    Lathrop

520. In memory of
    Mary Lathrop
    daughter of Thomas
    & Hannah Lathrop
    who departed this life
    at the Boarding-School
    in Bethlehem Penn-
    ſyvania July 31ſt
    1809 in the 14th year
    of her age

521. Here Lies yᵉ Bodys of
Daniel James & Joſeph
the Sons of Mʳ Daniel &
Mʳˢ Jeruſha Lothrop Joſeph
died June 22 1751 aged
17 Months 26 days. Daniel
died July 16 aged 5
year 5 Months & 15 Days
James died July 26
aged 3 years & 3 months

    (footstone)
Daniel ⎫
James ⎬ Lothrop
Joſeph ⎭

522. In Memory of Docʳ
Daniel Lathrop who
Departed this Life
on yᵉ 9ᵗʰ of Janʳʸ
1782 in yᵉ 70ᵗʰ year
of his Age
What though we wade
in wealth or Soar in fame
Earthˢ higheſt Station
ends in: here he Lies
And Duſt to Duſt
Concludes her nobleſt ſong

    (footstone)
Docʳ
Daniel
Lathrop

523. In memory of
Mrs. Jeruſha Lathrop
daughter of
Governor Talcott,
relict of the late
Doct. Daniel Lathrop ſhe
died Sept. 14ᵗʰ 1805, in the
89ᵗʰ year of her age,
poſſeſſed of that good
name which is better
than precious ointment

    (footstone)
Mrs. Jeruſha
Lathrop

524. In Memory of
Mʳˢ Abigail
Wadſworth daughʳ
to the Revᵈ Mʳ
Daniel Wadsworth
of Hartford who
died April 20ᵗʰ
1783 in yᵉ 49ᵗʰ
year of her Age

    (footstone)
Mʳˢ
Abigail
Wadſworth

525.
(Tablestone)
In memory
of
FRANCES M. WHITING
Wife of Samuel Whiting of the
City of Albany
and Daughter of
Chriſtopher Leffingwell Eſq.
who died the 8th of Dec. 1804
in the 22d year of her age

Death! 'tis an awful theme to guilty man!
But to the Saint whose faith can pierce the Vail
And wear the Crown of life which JESES holds
The welcome herald of immortal joys
Thus welcomes SAINTED SHADES as death to thee
For Sovereign Grace had seal'd thy title sure.

526. In memory of
JERUSHA
Daughter of Chris^r &
Elisabeth Leffingwell
who died
July 29th AD. 1814,
aged 32 years

(footstone)
Jerusha
Leffingwell

527. Sacred
to the memory of
Miss Elizabeth Leffingwell
who died
May 28, 1830,
aged 63 years.

(footstone)
E. L.

528. Here Lyes Buried ye Remains
of Mrs Elizabeth Gookin y^e
Daughter of Mr Edmund &
Mrs Sarah Gookin Who
Dyed February ye 2^d AD 1731½
in ye 16th year of her age.
ye lord gaue & ye lord hath taken away
bleſſed be ye name of ye lord

(footstone)
Mrs Elizabeth
Gookin Dyed
February ye 2^d
A^D 1732

(footstone)
529. 1 7 3 0
Died Mrs Sarah
Leffingwell Wife
to Capt John
Leffingwell

530. HERE LYES Y^e
PRETIOUS DUST
OF DANIEL GOOKIN
SON TO MR EDMOND
& MRS SARAH
GOOKIN BORN
SEP^t ye 28th 1723
& DIED ye 9 of
OCTOBER NEXT

(footstone)
DANIEL
GOOKIN

531. Here Lyes ye Body of
That Worthy, Vartuous
& Moſt jnieneuous
jenteal Woman M^rs
Sara Leffingwell Wife
to Cap John Leffingwell
Who Dyed May y^e
19th 1730 Ageed 39 y
ye Lord Gaue & ye Lord
hath taken away Bleſſe^d
Be ye Name of ye Lord

(footstone)

532. HERE LYES Y^e
BODY OF JAMES
SON OF CAPT
OBADIAH & MRS
MARTHA SMITH
WHO DIED OCTO^r
Y^e 4 1729 IN Y^e 4
YEAR OF HIS AGE

533. ABNER Y^e SON
OF CAP^t OBADIAH
& MRS MARTHA
SMITH DIED
OCTO^r Y^e 1ST
1729 IN Y^e
7 YEAR OF
HIS AGE

534. HERE LYES
Yᵉ BODY OF MRS
BETHIAH ABELL
FORMER WIFE TO
MR JOSHUA ABELL
WHO DIED MARCH
yᵉ 31 1723
IN Yᵉ 63
YEARE OF
HER AGE

(footstone)
MRS
BETHIAH
ABELL

535. HERE LYES
Yᵉ BODY OF MR
JOSHUA ABELL
WHO DEPARTED
THIS LIFE
MARCH Yᵉ 1
1725 & IN Yᵉ
76 YEAR OF
HIS AGE

(footstone)
MR
JOSHUA
ABELL

536. In memory of
Mr Jonathan Starr
who departed this life
at Lisbon Novʳ 21ſt 1793
in the 61ſt year of his
age

(footstone)
Mr
Jonathan
Starr

537. Sacred to the memory of Mrˢ
Sarah, Conſort of Mʳ Jonathan
Starr & the amiable daughter
of Mʳ Benajah Leffingwell
She departed this Life the 26ᵗʰ
day of April 1790 in the 55ᵗʰ
Year of her age.

Hail! happy ſpirit wing'd from
                (toilſome earth;
Lo! the bright Seraphs formed thy
                (Heavenly birth.
Suſpend, ye friends the ſympa
                (thetic ſigh,
Bleſt are the dead who in the
                Saviour die.

538. In memory of
Simeon
Leffingwell
who died March
14ᵗʰ 1803 aged
25 years

(footstone)
Simeon
Leffingwell

539. In memory of
Mr. Phinehas Leffingwell
who died Sepʳ 23ᵈ 1797 in
yᵉ 56ᵗʰ Year of his age
In memory of
Mrs. Eliſabeth conſort to Mr.
Phinehas Leffingwell who died April
21ſt 1796, in yᵉ 51ſt Year of her age.

My lover friends familiar all,
Removed from ſight & out of call,
To dark Oblivion is retired,
Dead or at leaſt to me expir'd.

(footstone)
Mr Phinehas
& Mrs Eliſabeth
Leffingwell

540.
    In memory of
  Mr. Ebenezer Carew
  who died dec^m 30th
  1800 in ye 57th year
     of his age
       Alſo
In memory of two Children
 of Mr Ebenezer and Mrs
   Mehetable Carew
  Maria died dec^m 7th
  1794 aged 7 weeks,
Gardiner died march 21^ſt
   1797 aged 3 weeks.

Death is uncertain yet moſt ſure
ſin is the wound Chriſt is the cure

    (footstone)
      Mr
   Ebenezer
    Carew

541.
In Memory of M^rs
Eunice wife to M^r
Ebenezer Carew
who died Aug^ſt 14th
1785 in ye 38th
year of her Age
Nature's laſt debt
with chearfulneſs I pay
& take my flight to y^e
bright world of day

  (footstone)
   M^rs
  Eunice
   Carew

542.
  In Memory of Mrs Martha Lathrop
 Relict of Col^n Simon Lathrop who
    Died Oct^br 16th AD. 1775
    in ye 80th year of her Age.

How happy they, the happieſt of their kind
Whom gentler ſtars unite & in one fate
Their hearts their fortunes & their beings blend
Till evening comes at laſt ſerene & mild
When after the long vernal day of life
Enamoured more as more remembrance ſwells
With many a proof of recollected love
Together down they ſink in ſocial ſleep
Together freed their gentle ſpirits fly
To ſcenes where love & bliſs immortal reign.

    (footstone)
     M^rs
    Martha
   Lathrop

543. In Memory of Col^n Simon
Lathrop who Died Jan^r 25th
AD 1774 in ye 87th year of
his Age.
His widow whofe Remains are at
his fide furvived a fhort time after.

Why do we mourn departed friends;
   or fhake at Deaths alarms
'Tis but the voice that Jefus fends
   to call them to his arms

The graves of all his faints he Blefs'd;
   and foftened ev'ry Bed
where fhould the dying members reft,
   but with the dying head.

Thence he arofe afcending high
and fhew'd our feet the way;
up to the Lord our flefh fhall fly,
at the great rifing day.

     (footstone)
     Col^n
     Simon
     Lathrop

544. Here lies Intered Mrs Hannah
Lathrop Confort of Rufus Lathrop
Efq^r who departed this life April y^e
18th 1785 In the 46th year of her Age.

"No pain, nor grief nor
               anxious Fear
"Invade thy Bounds No mortal Woes
"Can reach the lovely Sleeper here
"And Angel watch her foft repofe

"So Jefus flept, Gods dying Son,
"Paft through the Grave
              & bleft the Bed
"Reft here fair faint
           till from his Throne
"The morning break and
            pierce the Shade

     (footstone)
     M^Rs
     Hannah
     Lathrop

545. In memory of
Rufus Lathrop Efq
who departed this
life Aug 18th 1805,
in the 75th year
of his age

     (footstone)
     Rufus
     Lathrop Efq

546. In memory of Mrs Zerviah
Lathrop who departed this
life January 4th 1795 in the
57th year of her age.
she was the fecond wife of
Rufus Lathrop Efq^r who
furvives to mourn the lofs
of two amiable companions,
friends in life their deaths
ware marked with circumftances
     of ftrong refemblance.

In faith fhe dy'd; in duft fhe lies
but faith forfees that duft muft rife
when Jefus calls, when hope affumes
and boafts her joy among the tombs.

     (footstone)
     Mrs Zerviah
     Lathrop

547. In Memory of M^rs
Elizabeth Daugh^r to Col^n
Simon Lathrop & M^rs
Martha his wife, who
died of a Confumption
March 6th 1763 in ye 30th
Year of her Age.
   Life how fhort
   Eternity how long

     (footstone)
     M^rs
     Elizabeth
     Lathrop

548. In Memory of Miſs
Hannah Choate, Daughtr
to John Choate Eſqr of
Ipſwich & Mrs Mary his
wife, who Departed this
life June 4th AD 1784 in
ye 18th year of his Age

A graſſy turf o'rſpreads
    my head,
The neighboring Lillies
    dreſs my bed;
And ſhed a ſweet perfume.
Here I put off the Chains
    of Death,
My ſoul too long has worn
Friends I forbid one groan
    ing breath
or tear to wet my Urn

(footstone)
Miſs
Hannah
Choate

549. Here Lyeth the Remains of
Doctor Theophilus Rogers
and of Mrs Elizabeth his Wife
Daughter of Mr William Hide
The Doctr died on the 29th of
Septemr 1753 in the 54th Year
of his age. And his Wife on the
24th of Novemr 1753 in the
54th Year of her age alſo.
Both continued to the ſame Year
of Life, Both died on the ſame
day of the Week, and both
depoſited in this Grave.

(footstone)
Theophilus and
Elizabeth Rogers

550. Lucretia ye
Daughter of
Zabdiel &
Elizabeth
Rogers died
Febry 26th 1763
in ye 3d Year
of her Age

(footstone)
Lucretia
Rogers

551. In Memory of
Miſs Rebeckah
Adgate Daughtr
to Dean Thomas
& Mrs Ruth Adgate
ſhe departed
this Life Sept
9th AD 1781 in
ye 85th year of
her Age.

(footstone)
Miſs
Rebekah
Adgate

552. HERE LIES Ye BODY
OF RVTH EDGERTON
LATE WIFE OF LIEVT
JOHN EDGERTON
WHO DIED FEBRVARY
Ye 23 1729
AGED 36 YEARS

(footstone)
MRS
RUTH
EDGERTON

553. In memory of Mrs.
Sally Snow, conſort
of Mr. Benjamin Snow
& daught of Doctr
Theophilus & Mrs.
Penelope Rogers, who
departed this life April
8th 1788, in ye 27th
Year of her age.
This ſtroke is too great!
  But the curtain drawn
  we then ſhall ſee
The perfect order of Deity

(footstone)
Mrs
Sally
Snow

554. In memory of
Charles Knox Snow
Son of Mr. Benjamin
& Mrs. Sally Snow,
who departed this
life April 7th 1789,
aged 2 Years & 5
months
Is Charles gone too!
God is Juſt

(footstone)
Charles
Knox
Snow

555.
HERE LYES BURIED Yᵉ BODY OF MRᴿ ISRAELL LOTHRUP Yᵉ HUSBAND OF MRˢ REBEKAH LOTHROP WHO LIUED A LIFE OF EXEMPLARY PIETY & LEFT Yᵉ EARTH FOR HEAVEN MARᶜ Yᵉ 28 = 1733 IN Yᵉ 73 YEAR OF HIS AGE

(footstone)
Mr ISRAEL LOTHROP
DYED MARCH Yᵉ 28
1733 IN Yᵉ 73
YEAR OF HIS AGE

556. Here lyeth Interred the Body of
Mrs REBEKAH LOTHRUP
The Beloved Wife & Conſort of
Mr ISRAEL LOTHRUP.
She was the loving Mother of
Many Children & after ſhe had
Serued her Generation by the Will of
GOD Fell aſleep Auguſt the 22ⁿᵈ
1737 in the 74th year of her Age
MEMENTO MORI MORS VINCET OMNIA

(footstone)
AUGUſt THE 22
1737 DIED Mrs
REBEKAH
LOTHROP
IN THE 74 YEAR
OF HER
AGE

557. IN MEMORY
of Mary Yᵉ Wife of
Mr Benjamin Wheat
who died Novemr 2
1753 aged 52 Years.

(footstone)

558. In Memory
of Nathan
ſon to MR
Benjamin
& Mrs Anne
Wheat he
died May
23
Aged

(footstone)

559. IN MEMORY
of Mary Yᵉ Daughter
of Mr Benjamin Wheat
& Mary his Wife
who died Decem 28th
1752 aged
20 Years

(footstone)
Mary Wheat
1752

560. Suſanna yᵉ
Daughter of
Benjamin &
Mary Wheat
died Janry 14
1741 aged
6 Months

(footstone)
S. W.
1741

561. Elizabeth yᵉ
Daughter of
Benjamin &
Mary Wheat
died Febry 19th
1743 aged
4 Years

(footstone)
E. W.
1743

562. Here Lie Interred the Remains of Mr THOMAS ADGATE the son of Deacon Thomas Adgate OF Norwich who died Dec 13 1736 in the 34th

    (footstone)
DECR Y^e 13th
1736 DIED M^r
THOMAS ADGATE
JUN IN Y^e 34th
YEAR OF HIS
AGE

563. HERE LIES Y^e BODY OF MRS RUTH LATE WIFE OF DEACON THOMAS ADGATE WHO DIED AUGUST Y^e 22 1734 & IN Y^e 63 YEAR OF HER AGE

    (footstone)
MRS
RUTH
ADGATE

564. HERE LYES Y^e BODY OF FLAUIUS SON OF MR WILLIAM & MRS ANNE HIDE JUN^rS DIED JUNE 2 1723 AGED ELEVEN DAYS.

    (footstone)
FLAVIVS
HIDE

565. HERE LYES Y^e BODY OF MR JOHN BASSETT OF BOSTON DIED OCTOBER Y^e 2 1723 AGED 31 YEARS

    (footstone)
JOHN
BASSETT

566. In memory of Mrs Balſheba wife to Mr Silas Armſtrong who died ſept 26th 1788 aged 55 Years

The ſweet remembrance of the Juſt ſhall flouriſh when they ſleep in duſt

567. In Memory of Lucretia Hubbard Daugh^tr to William & Lydia Hubbard who died Oct^br 14 AD 1775 Aged 5 years

568. In memory of Capt John Leffingwell who died Auguſt 16th 1773 in ye 85th Year of his age Death is a debt to nature due Which I have paid & ſo muſt you

    (footstone)
Capt
John
Leffingwell

569. Here lies what was Mortal of Mary the wife of Capt John Leffingwell ſhe died April 3^d 1771 in the 68th year of her age.

    (footstone)
Mrs
Mary
Leffingwell

570. 　　　　Sacred
　　　　to the memory of
　　　Capt Hart Leffingwell
　　　& Mrs Eunice Kingsley
　　　　Brother & Sister
　　who were both inter'd
　　　　in this vault
　　　　April 8th 1811,
　　after a virtuous life
　　　resigned in peace
　　　aged 77 & 66 years

Who lov'd them living & lament them dead;
Pay this last tribute to their silent shade

　　　　(footstone)
　　　　　Capt
　　　　　Hart
　　　　Leffingwell
　　　　　& Mrs
　　　　　Eunice
　　　　　Kingsley

571. 　　In memory of
　　　Maria Gardiner
　　Carew, daughr to Mr
　　Ebenezer & Mrs Mehe
　　table Carew ſhe died
　　ſept 25th 1789 aged
　　11 months & 10 D

　　Weep not for me
　　my parents dear
　　I am not dead
　　but ſleeping here.

　　　　(footstone)
　　　　　Maria
　　　　　Carew

572. 　In Memory of Eli
　　zabeth Lathrop Carew
　　daught to Mr Ebene
　　zer & Mrs Eunice
　　Carew ſhe died
　　Augſt 2d 1781, Aged
　　9 months & 27 D.

　　Sleep ſweet babe
　　& take thy reſt
　　God calls the home
　　He ſaw it beſt

　　　　(footstone)
　　　　　Elizabeth
　　　　　Carew

573. 　　In Memory of
　　　　Lydia dau of
　　　Christor & Elizabeth
　　　Leffingwell who
　　　died June 6th 1772
　　　　in ye 4th year
　　　　of her age

574. Two small, broken, unlettered stones.

575. Small, unlettered stone.

576. Small, unlettered stone.

577. 　　In Memory of
　　Doctr Ezekiel Rogers
　　Eldeſt Son of Doctr
　　Theophilus and Mrs
　　Elizabeth Rogers
　　who died Novemr 11th
　　1745 in the 23d Year
　　　　of his Age

　　　A hopefull Yoth

　　　　(footstone)
　　　　　Ezekiel
　　　　　Rogers

578. 　　In Memory of
　　Deacon Thomas
　　Adgate Who Died
　　Dec. the 10 1760
　　in the 92 year
　　　of his Age
　　Help Lord for the
　　Godly man Ceaseth

　　　　(footstone)
　　　　　Deacon
　　　　　Thomas
　　　　　Adgate

579. 　　　HERE
　　　LIES THE BO
　　DY OF MRS ABGA
　　EL TRACY WHO
　　DIED SEPTEM R
　　1711 AGED 51 Y S

　　　　(footstone)
　　　　　A T

580. HERE LIES
      THE BODY OF
      DEACON THOMAS
      ADGET WHO
      DIED JVLY 1707
      AGED 87 YEARs

         (footstone)
           T A

581.   HEAR
      LIES THE B
      ODY + OF + Mrs
      MARY ADGA
      TE WHO DIE
      D MARCH 1713

         (footstone)
           M A

582. HEARE + LI
      ES + THE + BO
      DY + OF + LVC
      Y + ADGATE
      WHO + DIE
      D + IAN Ye 9
      1718 + Ye 4 Y

         (footstone)
           L A

583. In Memory of
      Mr Benjamin
      Allen he depar-
      ted this Life may
           1783
      23d in ye 76th year
      of his Age

         (footstone)
            Mr
         Benjamin
           Allen

584. In Memory of
      Mrs Rebeckah
      Allen wife to
      Mr Benjamin
      Allen ſhe died
      Auguſt 13th 1783
      in ye 62d year
      of her Age

585. Here   y
      Bod   Philip
      Son to mr
      & mrs Ruth adg
      who departed
         fe decm ye 17th
      1764 in ye 7th
      year of his age

         (footstone)
          Philip
          Adgate

586. In Memory of Mr
      Thomas Adgate 3d he
      died in New London
      March 3d 1777 in
      ye 45th year of his
      Age

         (footstone)
          Thomas
          Adgate

587. In Memory of
      Mrs Eunice Adgate
         Relict of
      Mr William Adgate
      who died Oct 13th
      1813 aged 69.

         (footstone)
            Mrs
          E.   A.

588. In Memory   In Memory
     of Lucy daught   of Mr William
     to Mr William   Adgate who
     & Mrs Eunice   departed this
     Adgate who died   life Jan 4th
     June 1ſt 1781   1779 in ye
     in ye 12th year   35th year of
     of her Age   his age

           (footstone)
         Mr   Lucy
       William   Lucy
       Adgate   Adgate

589. (Raised Brick Tomb.)
In Memory of Mr Elijah Adgate
who departed this life April
8th 1775 in ye 36 year of
his age

In Memory of Mrs Abiah wife
to Mr Elijah Adgate who departed this life July   1766
in ye 29th year of her age

In Memory of Phile daught
to Mr Elijah & Mrs Abiah
Adgat who Departed this life
Augft   1766 in ye aged year
of 6 her age months

Place not your hopes on things
For things below are vain
The Father Mother and the Child
Will not return again

590. Mrs ABIGAIL
wife of
Mr Lynde Lathrop,
daughter of Elijah and
Abigail Adgat, died
June 4 1788 AE 27 years
This monument is erected
Aug. 1832, by John Lathrop
Son of the deceased

(footstone)
A. L.

591. Here Lies the
Remains of Jabez
fon to Mr Matthew
Adgate & Hannah
his wife he died
April ye 20th 1764
in ye 23d year
of his Age

(footstone)
Jabez Adgate

592. In memory of Lucy
wife of Mr Matthew
Adgate Junr
Daughr to Mr Afa
& Mrs Lucy Waterman
who died Nov 21ft
1762 in ye 26 year
of her age leaving
an infant 10 days
old who died ye 5th
of Janr following

(footstone)
Probably No. 595.

593. Here lies ye body
of Andrew Adgate
Son to Matthew
& Mrs Hannah Adgate
who died July ye
24 1751 & in the
19 year of his age

(footstone)
Andrew
Adgate

594. Here Lies The Remains
of Hannah the Wife of
Mr Matthew Adgate
Who died May the 28th
1766 in the 62d year
of her age

(footstone)
Mrs
Hannah Adgate

595. (footstone)
Mrs
Lucy
Adgate

596. In Memory of Mr
Matthew Adgate
who departed
this life July 3d
1787 in ye 81ft
year of his age

(footstone)
Mr
Matthew
Adgate

597. Sacred
To the memory of
Mrs Abigail Lord
relict of the late Rev^d
Benjamin Lord D.D.
who departed this
life Octr 4th AD 1792
in the 85th Year of
her age

(footstone)
Mrs
Abigail
Lord

598. In memory of Mr Benja
min Lord, who Died
May 18th 1787, in y^e
60th Year of his age.
he was the eldeſt ſon of
the late Revd Benjamin
Lord D.D.
& left a widow & 8 Children
to lament his death.

Softly his fainting head he lay
Upon his Maker's breaſt
His Maker kiss'd his ſoul away
And laid his fleſh to reſt.

(footstone)
M^r
Benjamin
Lord

599. Anne daughter
of Doctor
Theophilus
Rogers and
Penelope his
Wife died
Oct^or 27th
1770 Aged
8 Months

(footstone)
A   R
1 7 7 0

600. ABISHAI SON
OF CAP BENAIAH
& MRS ZERUIAH
BUSHNELL WHO
DIED JUNE Y^e 6
1720 AGED
16 WEEKS

(footstone)
ABISHAI
BUSHNELL

601. HERE LIES BURIED Y^e MUCH
LAMENTED BODY OF MARY
WATERMAN DAUGHTER OF
Mr JOHN WATERMAN &
M^Rs ELIZABETH WATERMAN
WHO   DEPARTED   THIS
LIFE NOVEM^r 13th A^d 1736
IN Y^e 15th YEAR OF HER AGE
Y^e GOOD LORD GRANT W^e
MAY BE READY AT A CALL

(footstone)
M^Rs MARY
WATERMAN
DIED NOVEM^r
13th 1736 IN Y^e
15th YEAR OF HE
AGE

602. HERE LIES THE
BODY OF MR
EZRA HIDE OF
NORWICH WHO
DYED IVLY 18
1741 IN THE 32
YEAR OF HIS
AGE

(footstone)
HERE LIES
THE BODY OF
EZRA HIDE

603. Frances the Daughter of Zabdiel & Elizabeth Rogers, died Septemr 21ft 1763 Aged 1 Mo & 15 Days

(footstone)
Frances
Rogers
1763

604. HERE LIES Ye BODY OF SAMUELL SON OF MR DANIEL TRACY WHO DIED JULY Ye 1st 1720, AGED 5 YEARS.

(footstone)
SAMUEL
TRACY

605. HERE LIES Ye BODY OF ELIZABETH Ye DAUGHTER OF Mr DANIEL TRACY WHO DIED APRIL Ye 16th 1715 AGED 2 YEARS

(footstone)
TRA

606. RICHARD Ye SON OF MR BENAJAH & MRS JOANNA LEFFINGWELL DIED NOUEMBEr Ye 6 1727 & AGED ONE MONTH & NINE DAYS

(footstone)
RICHARD
LEFFINGWELL

607. HERE LYES Ye BODY OF MR THOMAS LEFFINGWELL DECEST MARCH Ye 5th 1724 & IN Ye 75th YEARE OF HIS AGE

(footstone)
MR
THOMAS
LEFFINGWELL

608. HERE LYES Ye BODY OF ANNE DAVGHTER TO MR JOHN & MRS ANNE WATERMAN WHO DIED MAY Ye 25 1725 AGED THREE YEARS ONE MONTH & 16 DAYS

(footstone)
ANNE
WATERMAN

609. HERE LIES Ye BODY OF ELIAS SON OF MR HEZEKIAH & MRS HANNAH HUNTINGTON WHO DIED MAY Ye 20 1730 AGED 6 MONTHS & 20 DAYS

(footstone)
Elias
HUNTINGTON

610. Beneath this ftone lies deposited the remains of Samuel fon to Capt Elifha Edgerton & Mrs Elifabeth his wife he Died O   4th 1786
of

611. In memory of
Eliſabeth Edgerton
Relict of
Capt Eliſha Edgerton
who departed this life
Decr 5th 1815,
in the 83d year
of her Age

The world recedes it disappears,
Heaven opens on my eyes my ears,
With sounds seraphic ring,
Lend lend your wings I mount I fly,
Oh! grave where is thy victory,
Oh! death where is thy sting.

(footstone)
Elisabeth
Edgerton

612. In Memory of
Capt Eliſha Ed-
gerton Who De-
parted this Life
Auguſt 22d 1782
in ye 56th year
of his Age

The world recedes it
disappears;
Heav'n opens on my eyes
my ears
With founds feraphic
ring,
Lend lend your wings!
I mount, I fly
O Grave where is thy
victory
O death where is thy
fting.

(footstone)
Capt
Eliſha
Edgerton

613. Here is Interred the
Body of Mrs Phebe late
Conſort of Mr John
Edgerton
died July 29th 1763 in
the 63d year of her age

(footstone)
MRS
Phebe
Edgerton

614. Here lies the Body of
Mr John Edgerton of
Norwich who died
Feb. 15, 1768 aged
77 years he left 10
Children & 31 Grand
children
mors omnia vincit

(footstone)
Mr
John Edgerton

615. In Memory of Mr
John Edgerton he
Departed this
Life Febr 28th
1778 in ye 58th
year of his Age

(footstone)
Mr
John
Edgerton

616. In memory of
Mrs Hannah conſort of
Mr Jabez Tracy
who died Sept 22d
1790 in the 38th year of
her age

(footstone)
Mrs
Hannah
Tracy, 90

617. In Memory of M^r
Andrew Leffing
well ſon to M^r
Thomas Leffingwell
he Died Aug^{ft} 12th
1782 in ye 49th
year of his Age

(footstone)
M^r
Andrew
Leffingwell

618. In memory of Mr
Thomas Leffingwell
ſon of Mr Thomas & Mrs
Eliſabeth Leffingwell
born July 29th 1732 &
died Dec 8th 1814
aged 82 years

(footstone)
T. L.

619. In memory of Mr
Thomas Leffingwell
who departed this
life Sept 28th AD
1793 in ye 90th
Year of his age

(footstone)
Mr
Thomas
Leffingwell

620. Here Lyes Mrs
Eliſabeth ye Loving
Conſort of Mr Thom
as Lef   ll & Da
ughter   Benjamⁱⁿ
Lord   ok
Who Dy   April
ye 30th AD 1763
in ye 55th year of her Age

621. In memory of
Mrs LYDIA HART
Relict of the late
Dr Levi Hart
& daughter of
Thomas & Elizabeth
Leffingwell, who died
May 23, 1825
aged 81

(footstone)
L. H.

622. In Memory of
Mr Martin Leffing
well ſon to M^r
Thomas Leffingwell
& Mrs Eliſabeth
his wife he Died
April 6th 1781
in ye 43^d year
of his Age

(footstone)
Mr
Martin
Leffingwell

623. In Memory of
Mr Oliver Lef-
fingwell ſon to
Mr Thomas
Leffingwell, who
died at Sea Dec
11th 1771 in y^e
21^{ft} year of
his age

624. In Memory of M^{rs}
Abigail Wife to M^r
Matthew Adgate
ſhe Died Aug^{ft} 7th
1777 in y^e 58th
year of her Age

(footstone)
M^{rs}
Abigail Adgate

Mr. Thomas Leffingwell, 1724
See Page 78

Mrs. Mary Leffingwell, 1745
See Page 87

Dr. Solomon Tracy, 1732
See Page 86

Ebenezer Backus, Esq., 1768
See Page 58

(Elevated Tomb)

625.
IN Memory of the Revd Benjn Lord D D
Bleſſed with good natural abilities, inprov'd
from a liberal Education, & refined by Grace
he early dedicated himſelf to the ſacred office
tho' incumber'd through life with much bodily
infirmity he executed the ſeveral duties of his
Charge in a manner which was acceptable &
uſefull—— In 1774 he had conferr'd upon him the
higheſt honours of Yale College after having
been the faithfull Paſtor of the 1^ft C^h of Ch^t in
Norwich for 67 years, he departed this life
March 31^ſt 1784 AE 90. tho' now unconſcious in Death may
the living hear (or ſeam to hear) from him the following address

think, Chriſtians, think!
You ſtand on vaſt Eternity's dread brink
Faith and Repentance, Piety and Pray'r!
Deſpite *this* World, the *next* be all *your* care
Thus while my Tomb the ſolemn ſilence breaks
And to the eye this cold dumb marble ſpeaks
Tho' dead I preach, if e're with ill ſucceſs
Living I ſtrove the important truths to preſs
Your *precious, your immortal fouls* to ſave
Hear me, at leaſt O hear me from my *Graue*

626. Here Lies the Body of M^rs
Anne Late Conſort of the Rev^d
Benjamin Lord of Norwich
(Daughter of the late Rev^d
Edward Taylor of Weſtfield)
who after an illness of 16
years died on the 5th Day
of July 1748 in the 52^d
year of her age.

627. HERE LYES Y^e
REMAINS OF BEN
JAMIN SON OF Y^e
REUEREND BENIA
MIN LORD & MRS
ANNE LORD WHOSE
LIFE EXPIRED IN Y^e
5th YEAR OF HIS AGE
JULY 25 A D 1726.

(footstone)
BENIAMIN
LORD

628. In Memory of Lucre
tia Abel Daugh^tr to
Capt Iſaac Abel &
Hannah his wife ſhe
died Octr 31^ſt 1780
in ye 6th year
of her Age
Like a ſweet flower ſhe
Bloom'd but O how nipt

(footstone)
Lucretia
Abel

629. Here is deposited
the Body of Joseph
Lord A M Son to
the Reverend M^r
Benjamin Lord
who died march
the 12 1762 in
the 31^ft year
of his age

(footstone)
M^r
Joseph
Lord

630. HERE LIES Ye BODY
OF MRS ELIZABETH
LATHROP LATE WIFe
TO MR JABEZ LA=
THRUP WHO DIED
APRIL Ye 14 1730
AGED 19 YEARS 6
MONTHS & 5 DAYS

  (footstone)
  ELIZABETH
  LATHRUP

631. In Memory of Mrs
Anne wife to Mr
Iriger Sanger who
died Octr 10th 1789
in ye 31ſt Year of
her age

Death is uncertain
  yet moſt ſure
ſin is the wound
Chriſt is the cure

632. In Memory of Capt
Joſeph Winſhip who
was ſuppoſ'd to be
loſt at ſea Decr 1765
in his 39th year

Alſo was loſt at the
ſame time Joſeph
Winſhip 3rd Age'd
11 years

Octbr 19th 1753 died
Joſeph Winſhip Jnr
in his 2d year.
whoſe remans are
here inter'd

both ſons of Capt Joſeph
Winſhip & Mrs Eliza-
beth his wife

  (footstone)
  Joſeph
  Winſhip Junr

633. Here lyes what was
Mortall of cap William Mr
Hide Eſqr Junr who
Departed this life ye
7 of IVNE = 1738
Aged 36 years. As
Envmerable are Gon
Before So All are
Drawing after

  (footstone)
  Mr William
  Hide Eſqr

634. HERE LIES Ye BODY
OF CAPt RICHARD
BVSHNELL ESQVIRE
WHO DIED AVGVST
Ye 27 1727 & IN Ye
75 YEAR OF HIS AGE

AS YOU ARE
SO WAS WE
BUT AS WE ARE
YOU SHALL BE

  (footstone)
  CAPT
  RICHARD
  BUSHNELL
  ESQUIRE

635. HERE LYES WHAT
WAS MORTALL OF
THAT WORTHY GENTIL
MAN CAPT CALEB BUSH
NELL SON TO CAPt
RICHARD BUSHNELL
ESQVIRE WHO DIED
FEBRUARY Ye 18 1724/5
AGED 46 YEARS & 8 MON
THES & 23 DAYS

  (footstone)
  CAPt
  CALEB
  BUSHNELL

636. Small, broken, unlettered stone.

637. Small, broken, unlettered stone.

638. Small, broken, unlettered stone.

639. HERE LYES Ye BODY
OF HEZEKIAH SON
OF MR THOMAS &
MRS LYDIA LEF
FINGWELL WHO
DIED MAY Ye 30th
1725 AGED 13
YEARS 16 DAYS

(footstone)
HEZEKIAH
LEFFINGWELL

640. JOANNA Ye DA
VGHTER OF
MR BENAJAH
& MRS JOANNA
LEFFINGWELL
WHO DIED JAN
VARY Ye 25 1730
AGED 10 MONTHS
LACKING 4 DAYS

(footstone)
JOANNA
LEFFINGWELL

641. HERE LIES Ye
BODY OF BE
NAJAH SON
OF MR BENAJA
& MRS JOANNA
LEFFINGWELL
WHO DIED
MAY Ye 5 1731
AGED 6 MONth

(footstone)
BENAJAH
LEFFINGWELL

642. HERE LIES INTARRED
Ye REMAINS OF REBECK
AH Ye DAUGHTER OF
Mr ISAAC & MRs REBECK
AH HUNTINGTON
WHO DIED JUNE Ye 5
1725 IN Ye 8 YEAR
OF HER AGE
MEMENTO MORI

(footstone)
643. SAMUEL
HUNTIN
GTON

644. Here lies interr'd the Body
of Mrs Hannah first born to
Colln Hez Huntington Esqr
And Hannah his Wife
she lived beloved and died
lamented March 23, A. D.
1744,5, aged 24 years

An intimate friend of hers begs leave to add
Whilst Many Would Let to their Longing Arms
christ only had her Heart And Death her Charms
Death Must at last the Sacred Dust Resign
of Every Saint all glorious and divine
But this so lovely can we ask for more
than that the Tyrant sho'd his Prey resore
in all her Beauty as she was Before

(footstone)
No. 672

645. Here Lies ye Bodys of Matthew
Gideon & Araunah ye Sons of
Mr Benjamin & Mrs Mary
Lothrup Mattew Dyed the
2 of December 1732 in ye
8 year of his Age Gideon dyed
December 5 1732 in ye 6
year of his Age Aaraunah
Dyed December 9 1732
in ye 10 Mon^h of his Age

(footstone)
1732
DYED
MATTHEU LOT^RP
GIDEON LOTHR^P
& ARAUNAH

646. Here Lies Buried ye
Body of Eunice ye
Daughter of Mr Hez
And Mrs Hannah
Huntington who
Died octob^r ye 30th
1732 in ye 8th year
of her Age

647. (footstone)
Elijah
Huntington

648. C H L O E
1 8 5 4
C. MOORE

649. Memory of
Mr JAMES BURNHAM
who departed this life
April 27th 1803
in the 73 year
of his age

This truth how certain
when this life is o'er
Man dies to live
and lives to die no more

(footstone)
M^r
James
Burnham

650. Memory of
Mrs SARAH confort
of Mr James Burnham
who departed this life
Sep 24th 1792
in the 62^d year
of her age

Farewell my friends
dry up your tears
I sleep in death
till Chrift appears

(footstone)
M^rs
Sarah
Burnham

651. Granite stone—no visible inscription.

652. Two small, unlettered, granite stones.

653. In Memory of M^r
Silas Armftrong he
died fept 10th AD
1786 in ye 62^d
year of his age

Death is a debt
to nature due
Which I have paid
& fo muft you

(footstone)
M^r
Silas
Armstrong

654. In memory of Mrs
Temperance Brown
Late confort of John
Brown who died
April 4th 1814 in the
49th year of her age

(footstone)
Mrs
T. B.

655. In memory of Mrs.
Lorinda, wife of
Mr Eleazer Mather,
who died April 1ft
1800 in ye 23d
year of her age

(footstone)
Mrs
Lorinda
Mather

656. In Memory of Mrs Lydia
wife to Mr Hezekiah
Leffingwell & daught to
Doctr Jofeph Wetherell
of Taunton who died
July 7th 1785 aged 44 Years
And of her brother
Jeremiah Wetherell
who died at fea July
29th 1766 aged 22 Years.

(footstone)
el

657. In memory of
Deacn Nathaniel
Shipman
who departed this
life Sept 8th 1805,
in the 83d year
of his age

(footstone)
Deacn
Nathaniel
Shipman

658. In memory of
Mrs. Elisabeth
wife of
Mr Nathl Shipman
and daughter of
Mr Thos Leffingwell
who died Jan 8th
AD 1801 in the 71ft
year of her age

(footstone)
Mrs
Elisabeth
Shipman

659. IN
MEMORY OF
ABIGAIL SHIPMAN
Wife of
NATHANIEL SHIPMAN Jun
& daughter of
BENJAMIN COIT ESQ
who deid
July 31, 1800,
Aged 31 Years.

(footstone)
A. S.

660. NATHANIEL SHIPMAN
Born   May   17   1764
Died   July   14   1853

(footstone)
N.   S.

661. IN
MEMORY OF
LYDIA L. SHIPMAN
daughter of
NATHANIEL & ABIGAIL
SHIPMAN
Born Dec. 17, 1795
Died Jan. 18, 1851
Aged 55 Years

(footstone)
L. L. S.

662. Here is interd ye
Body of William
fon to Mr Benjamin
Lord Junr who died
Decb 21 1760 in
ye 3d year of
his age

(footstone)
William
Lord

663. HERE LYES Ye BODY
OF MR DANIEL
TRACY WHO
DIED JVNE Ye
29 1728 AGED
76 YEARS

(footstone)
MR
DANIEL
TRACY
THIS WORTHY IN
A GOOD OLD AGE
DIED BY A FALL
FROM A BRIDG

664. In Memory of
Daniel Son to Mr
Samuel and Mrs
Sybel Tracy who
died June
A D 1753 aged
2 years & 8 days

(footstone)
Daniel Tracy

665. HERE LYES Ye
BODY OF ABIGAIL
TRACY DAUGHTER
OF MR DANIEL &
MRS ABIGAIL TRA
CY WHO DIED
MAY Ye FOURTH
1725 AGED
8 YEARS &
TEN MONTHS

(footstone)
ABIGAIL
TRACY

666. Two small, sunken, unlettered stones.

667. Two small, sunken, unlettered stones.

668. IN THIS SPOT OF
EARTH IS INTERRD
Ye EARTHY PART OF MR
SOLOMON TRACY
WHO DIED JVLY Ye 9th
1732 & IN Ye 82d
YEAR OF HIS AGE

THE DEAD IN SILENT
LANGUAGE SAY
TO LIUING THINKING
READER HEARE
O LOUING FRINDS
DOE NOT DELAY
BUT SPEEDILY FOR
DETH PREPARE

(footstone)
MR
SOLOMON
TRACY

669. THIS Monument Sacred
to the memory of Mrs
Anne Wetmore the Wife
of Mr Prosper Wetmore
and Daughter of the
Honouble Hez Huntington
Esq who deceased the 12th of
August 1754 in the 31 year
of her age

(footstone)
Mrs
Anne
Wetmore

670. HERE LIES Yᵉ BODY OF MR RICHARD EDGERTON WHO DIED JUNE Yᵉ LAST DAY 1729 & IN Yᵉ 64 YEAR OF HIS AGE

(footstone)
MR RICHARD
EDGERTON

671. IN MEMORY of MRS Hannah the virtuous and loving Confort of Colⁿ Hez. Huntington Efqʳ who Departed this life September 4ᵗʰ A. D. 1746 and in the 46ᵗʰ year of her age.

Ah! Lavifh Death to fill this Narrow fpace
In yonder Dome Made a Vaft empty Place

(footstone)
Mʳˢ
Hannah
Huntington
Aetatis Suaeˢ 24
1744

672. Footstone of 644.
Mʳˢ
Hannah
Huntington Aetatis
Suae 24
1744

673. HERE LYES INTERR'D Yᵉ REMAINˢ OF DEACᴺ CHRISTOPHER HUNTING TON OF NORWICH BORN NOVᴱMBER Yᵉ=1=1660=& Yᵉ FIRST BORN OF MALES IN Yᵉ TOWN HE SERVED NEAR 40 YEARS IN Yᵉ OFFICE OF A DEACON & DIED APRILL Yᵉ 24=1735= IN Y 75 Yᴿ OF HIS AGE
MEMENTO=MORI

(footstone)
HEAR LIES Yᵉ BODY OF
DEACᴺ CHRISTOPᵗ HUNTON

674. unice yᵉ daughter Ebenezer & Mary Fitch died Aug. yᵉ 1753 Aged 17 Months

Sleep lovely Babe
And take your Reft
God cald you hence
Because he faw it' beft

675. EUNICE STRONG
BORN
Jan 25, 1800
DIED
March 2, 1852

(footstone)
E. S.

676. IN MEMORY of an aged nurfing Mother of Gods Newenglifh-Ifrael Viz. Mrs. Mary Leffingwell, wife to Enfign Thomas Leffingwell Gentᵗ who died December yᵉ 2ᵈ A.D. 1745 aged 91 years

(footstone)
Mrs
Mary
Leffingwell

677. Here Lies Buried the Body of Deacon Thomas Leffingwell the Hufband of Mʳˢ Lydia Leffingwell & Son to Mʳ Thomas Leffingwell Deceafeed & Mʳˢ Mary Leffingwell & Aftaʳ he had Sarueed God & His people fell Afleep in Jefuf July 18 1733 in yᵒ 60 yeaɪ of his Age O Remember Death judgment & Eternity

(footstone)
DIED DEACON
THOMAS
LEFFINGWELL
1733

678. Here Lyeth Interred
What was mortal of yᵉ
Widow Lydia Leffingwell
Relick to Deacon
Thomas Leffingwell
Deceaſt who died Nov
yᵉ 28th 1757 in yᵉ 81ſt
year of her Age

(footstone)
Lydia
Leffingwell

679. Two sunken, granite stones.

680. Here Lies the Body
of Mʳ Joſeph Turnner
Son to Mʳ Joſeph &
Mʳˢ Eliſabeth Turnner
who died April yᵉ
24 A. D. 1747 in
the 20 year of his age

(footstone)
Joſeph
Turnner

681. Here Lyes yᵉ Body
of Sarah Huntington
the Late virtovs &
Loving Conſort of
Mʳ Jeremiah Hunting
ton of Norwich who
died Aprill yᵉ 5
A D 1747 in the
22ᵈ year of her
age

682. In memory of
Capᵗ Joseph Carew
who died
Janʸ 18th 1818,
in the 80th year
of his age

(footstone)
Capᵗ J.
Carew

683. In Memory of Mʳˢ
Eunice wife of Mʳ
Joſeph Carew Daught
er of Mʳ John Edger
ton who died March
16 A. D. 1772 in the
36 year of her age

(footstone)
Mʳˢ
Eunice
Carew

684. In Memory of Mʳˢ
Betſey Wife to Mʳ
Amaziah Weſton
ſhe Departed this
Life Febʳʸ 1ſt 1780
in yᵉ 24th year of her
age

(footstone)
Betſey Weſton

685. Sunken, granite stone.

686. In Memory of
           to Mʳ
Daniel and Mʳˢ
Sarah Abbott
who died   June
              ged

687. SACRED
TO
the MEMORY of
MARY
Relict of
Wᴹ Billings
WHO DIED
Jan. 22, 1805,
Aged 73.

(footstone)
M. B.

688. Here Lies the Body of Mrs
Hannah Huntington wife to
Mr Simon Huntington only
Daughter to Mr Daniel Tracy
And Mrs Abigail his wife,
The 15th Child out of 16
Buried, was Born Sept 2nd
1727 and Departed this
Life July 30th 1753 in ye 26
Year of her age

All flefh is grafs & all the
Goodliness thereof as the
Flower of ye field

(footstone)
Mrs
Hannah
Huntington

689. Here Lies Interred the
Body of Mrs Elizabeth
Tracy the loving and
Well-Beloved Confort
of Mr John Tracy
Who Departed this Life
October the 25 A D 1737
in the 61 year of her

MEMENTO MORI
MORS UINCET OMNIA

(footstone)
Mrs Elisabeth
Tracy Dieb
October the
25 A D 1737

690. Small, unlettered granite stone.

691. HERE LYES Ye
BODY OF MR JOHN
TRACY WHO
DIED MARCH Ye
27 1726 AGED
53 YEARS &
2 MONTHS &
8 DAYS

(footstone)
MR
JOHN
TRACY

692. Sacred to the memory of
Mr John Huntington
who departed this life
August 19th 1794 in the
85th year of his age

They who the longeft leafe enjoy
have told us with a figh,
that to be born feems little more
than to begin to die.

(footstone)
Mr John
Huntington

693. In Memory of Mrs
Civil Wife of Mr
John Huntington
who died Febry
ye 13th 1748/9 in
ye 37th Year of
her Age

(footstone)
Mrs Civil
Huntington
1748 9

694. IN MEMORY OF Mr JOSEPH
BUSHNELL WHO DEPARTED
THIS LIFE DECEMB
THE 23 A D 1746
AND IN THE = 96
YEAR OF HIS AGE

A man of truth & Faithfulness
He long did perfect love profess

(footstone)
Mr JOSEPH
BUSHNELL

695. IN MEMORY OF MRs
MARY BUSHNELL WHO
DEPARTED THIS LIFE
MARCH THE 31 A D
1745 AND IN
THE 92d YEARE
OF HER AGE

A virtuous Woman A loving wife
It was the habit of her life

(footstone)
MRS MARY
BUSHNELL

696.   Mrs Abigail Leffingwell
Relict of
Samuel Leffingwell Eſq
died Nov. 23, 1811,
aged 84

(footstone)
Mrs Abigail
Leffingwell

697.   Sacred
to the memory of
Samuel Leffingwell Eſq^r
who departed this life
March 24th 1797 in the
75th year of his age

(footstone)
Samuel
Leffingwell Eſq

698.   In Memory of M^r
Daniel Leffingwell
Ju^r the loving Con
ſort to Mrs Betſey
Leffingwell his
wife who depart-
ed this life Sept
15th 1778 in ye 27th
year of his Age

(footstone)
M^r
Daniel
Leffingwell

699.   ELIZABETH
LEFFINGWELL
relict of
Daniel Leffingwell
Died Dec. 23, 1831,
aged 81

(footstone)
E. L.

700.   Here lieth what was
mortal of Mrs Hannah
the loveing Conſort of
Capt Samuel Leffingwell
and Daughter of M^r
Daniel Buck who died
March 29th A.D. 1761
in the 37th
of her Age

(footstone)
Hannah
Leffingwell

701.   here lyeth what was
mortall of mrs Sarah
the 2nd loveing conſort
of cap^t Samuell Leffingwell
& daut^r of Joseph ruſſell
eſq^r of briſtol who depar
ted this life october ye 22
1763 in the   year of
her age

(footstone)
Mrs
ſarah leffingwell

702.   Here is Interred the
Body of Iſaac Huntingto^n
Eſq^r born in Norwich Feb
5th 1688 died Feb^r 23 17
64 in y^e 77 year of his
age a man of various Pu
blic Caracters very Uſeful
in them all Eſpecially as a
Judge of y^e County Court
Remarkable for his bod
ily infirmities thro the
Course of life & firmneſs
of mind & judgment
to y^e Laſt.

(footstone)
Iſaac
Huntington
Eſq =

703.
    (footstone)
    Mr David
    Bushnell

704. To the Memory of
MR ELEAZER LORD
born at Saybrook
Decbr 23d 1699, died
Norwich March 7th
1786 in the 87th Year
of his Age, relict of
Mrs Zerviah Lord, his
loving Consort who
died May 3rd 1751
He that dwelleth in ye secret
place of ye Most High shall
abide under the shadow
of the Almighty
    (footstone)

705. Here lies the Body of
Mrs Anne the Beloved
Consort of Capt Richard
Hide who died ye 20th
of April 1762 in the
54th year of her age
Mors omnia vincit
    (footstone)
    Mrs
    Anne Hyde

706. In memory of Richard
Hyde Esquire, who
died Decr 22d AD
1785, in the 79th
Year of his age
Death is a debt
to nature due
Which I have paid
& so must you
    (footstone)
    Richard
    Hyde Esqr

707. Here Lies ye Body
of Hr ISAAC
Tracy who De-
parted this Life
on the 25th day
of Janr AD. 1779
in ye 73d year
of his Age
    (footstone)
    Mr
    Isaac
    Tracy

708. Asa Lord Decd Decbr ye
18th 1766 in the 31st year
of his age
He survived his fair &
Beloved Wife 4 years &
5 months. Active in life
but soon Cut of & flyes
a way to the regions of
Light & Love
    (footstone)
    Mr
    Asa Lord

709.
    (footstone)
    Mrs
    Abigail Lord

710. IN MEMORY OF
Mrs Abigail ye Wife
of Mr Asa Lord &
Daughter to Mr Thomas
Mumford & Mrs Abigail
his Wife of Groton who
Departed this Life July
ye 16th A D 1762 in ye 25th
year of her Age
    (footstone)
    Mrs
    Abigail
    Lord

711. Sunken, unlettered granite stone.

712. Sunken, unlettered granite stone.

713.
IN MEMORY of
Elizabeth the Wife
of Mr Christopher
Leffingwell, and
Daught'r of Mr John
Harris who died
July 31st AD 1762
in the 25th Year
of her Age

(footstone)
Elizabeth
Leffingwell
1762

714.
In Memory
of Cp^t Richard
Leffingwell who
died at au Mole, ee
in Hifpaniola April
20th 1768: in the
23^d Year of his
Age

715.
Here Lies the Body of
Mrs Zerviah Late Con
fort of Mr Eleazer Lord
(Daughter of Mr Thomas
Leffingwell & Lydia
his Wife) who died
the 3^d Day of May
1751 in the 41
year of her age

(footstone)
Zerviah
Lord

716.
In memory of Mrs.
Abigail Lord, relict
of Mr. Eleazer Lord,
who departed this
life Novr 30th AD
1786 in ye 77th Year
of her age
Memento mori fugit hora

(footstone)
Mrs
Abigail
Lord

717.
(footstone)
M^r
Eleazer
Lord

718. Sunken, unlettered, granite stone.

719. Sunken, unlettered, granite stone.

720. Small, uninscribed, granite stone.

721. Two uninscribed, granite stones, probably one grave.

722. Two uninscribed, granite stones, probably one grave.

723. Small, unlettered stone.

724. Small, unlettered, granite stone.

725. Small, unlettered, granite stone, prone.

726. Small, unlettered, granite stone, prone.

727.
In Memory of
Rodifa Zibbero
who Died may
17th 1781 in y^e
15th year of
her Age

728.
(footstone)
M^rs
Eunice
Bufhnell

729.
In Memory
of Mr Benajah
Leffingwell who
died June 8th 1756
Aged 63 Years

(footstone)
Benajah
Leffingwell

730. In Memory of Mrs Joanna Dyar Relict of Col^o John Dyar formerly the wife of Mr Benajah Leffingwell and daughter of The Hon^m Richard Chriſtophers Eſq^r who died Dec^b 7th 1784 in ye 78th year of her Age

    (footstone)
    M^rs
    Joanna
    Dyar

731. Elizabeth the Daughter of Chriſtopher & Elizabeth Leffingwell died Nov 20th 1760 Aged 6 Weeks & 3 Days

    (footstone)
    E. L.
    1760

732. Betſey Daught^r of Chriſtopher & Elizabeth Leffingwell died Jan^ry 10th 1762 Aged 3 M^o & 2 Days

    (footstone)
    Betſey
    Leffingwell
    1762

733. Richard Leffingwell Billings ſon of William & Mary Billings Born Aug 24 & died ſept 26 1768

    (footstone)
    Richard
    Leffingwell
    Billings

734. Abigail ye Daughter of William & Mary Billings died March 26th 1761 Aged 9 M^o

735. In Memory of Lucretia Daug^t to Capt Henry Billings & Lucretia his Wife ſhe died Feb 1^ſt 1778 in ye 2 Year of her Age

736. In Memory of Mary Daugh^t to Capt Henry Billings & Lucretia his Wife. ſhe Died Nov, 6th 1777 Aged 1 month

737. In Memory of Charles Son to Capt Henry Billings & Lucretia his Wife he Died May 7 1778 in ye 4th year of his Age

738. Here Lies ye Body of Dyar Son to Mr Eliſha Leffingwell & Allis his wife who died Oc^t ye 5th 1770 Aged 3 years & 5 month^s

739. Sunken, unlettered, granite stone.

740. Sunken, unlettered, granite stone.

741.
In memory of
JOHN MEAD
who died Aug 14, 1871
aged 88
and of
CHARLOTTE
his wife
who died May 5, 1869,
aged 89

(footstone)
J. M.
C. M.

742.
In Memory of
Dezenah Zibbero
ſhe died Octr
17th 1781 in
ye 12th year
of her age

No. 727
(footstone)
743.
Rodiſa
Zibbero

(footstone)
744.
Charles
Billings

745.
In Memory of
Mrs Eunice Daught
to Mr David
Bushnell & Mrs
Mary his wife
ſhe Died ſept
10th 1783 in ye
28th year of her Age
(footstone No. 728)

746.
In Memory of
Boſton Trow trow
Govener of ye Affri
can Trib he Died
May 28th 1772
AEt 66

(The Enclosed Huntington Lot.)
747.
Here Lies Interred
The Body of Mr
Zechariah Hunting-
ton who departed
this life Sept ye 8th
1761 in the 30th
Year of his age
Mors omnia vincit

748.
IN MEMORY OF
three Sons of Mr Ep
hraim & Mrs Lydia
Bill SILVESTER
LYNDE & GORDEN
who died Auguſt
Ye 1ſt 7th & 11th 1753
in ye 7th 5th & 2d year
of their Ages

(footstone)
Silveſter
Lynde
Gordon Bill
1753

749.
MRS SARAH
LATE WIFE OF
DEACON SIMON
HUNTINGTON
WHO DIED
JANUARY Ye 4
1 7 2 1 &
IN Ye 88
YEAR OF
HER AGE

(Tomb)
HUNTINGTON

750 to 767.

JABEZ HUNTINGTON AUG. 7, 1719. OCT. 5, 1786.
ELIZABETH BACKUS, HIS WIFE FEB 21, 1721. JULY 1, 1745.
HANNAH WILLIAMS HIS WIFE JULY 23, 1726. MAR. 25, 1807.
JEDIDIAH HUNTINGTON AUG. 4, 1743. SEPT. 25, 1818
ANDREW HUNTINGTON JUNE 21, 1745. APR. 7, 1824.
LUCY COIT, HIS WIFE JULY 2, 1746. MAY 9, 1776.
HANNAH PHELPS, HIS WIFE DEC. 16, 1760. JULY 30, 1838.
JOSHUA HUNTINGTON AUG. 16, 1751. FEB. 1, 1821
HANNAH HUNTINGTON, HIS WIFE NOV. 3, 1750. APR. 23, 1815.
HANNAH HUNTINGTON JULY 3, 1753. SEPT. 27, 1761
EBENEZER HUNTINGTON DEC. 26, 1754. JUNE 17, 1834
SARAH ISHAM, HIS WIFE NOV. 23, 1771. DEC. 3, 1793
MARY McCLELLAN HIS WIFE MAY 15, 1773. Nov. 5, 1819.
LOUISA M. HUNTINGTON FEB. 20, 1798. DEC. 6, 1877
GEO. WASHINGTON HUNTINGTON NOV. 23, 1799. MAY 13, 1870.
EMILY L. HUNTINGTON AUG. 6, 1801. DEC. 26, 1871
NANCY L. HUNTINGTON APR. 6, 1803. MAR. 21, 1878
SARAH I. HUNTINGTON MAY 1, 1806. OCT. 22, 1885

768.
DEACON
SIMON HVN
TINGTON DY
ED IVNE 28 1706
AGED 77 YEARS

769.
Sacred
to the memory of Mrs.
Anne Huntington,
confort of
Gurdon Huntington
& daughter of
Andrew Perkins Efq.
who died April 21ft AD.
1802, aged 34 years

(footstone)
Mrs Anne
Huntington

(Elevated Tomb)
770. In memory of Mrs Anne Hunt
ington the virtuous confort of
Benjamin Huntington Efq^r
She was the daugh^t of Col
Jabez Huntington of Windham
was born Jan^r 20th 1740 and
died Octr 6th 1790 in the
51^ft Year of her age
In memory of the Honble Benj
amin Huntington who was born in
this town the 19th of April 1736
He held various important offices
in this ftate with reputation and
finifhed a well fpent life in
Rome in the ftate of New York
the 16th of Oct 1800 in the 65th
year of his age

771.
SIMON
HVNTINGTON
DYED JVLY
29 1707
AGED 21
YEARS

772. In Memory
Mrs Susannah Huntington
the virtuous Consort of
Mr Gurdon Huntington
and Daughter of
Jared Tracy Esqr
who died Augt 21st AD. 1793
in the 23d year of her age

(footstone)
Mrs
Susannah
Huntington

773. HERE
IS INTERRED
the Body of Capt Joshua
Huntington Esqr who Departed
this Life, on the 26th day of
August 1745 in the 47th year
of his age and very Justly
Lamented by the Surviving
Made by Benjamin Collins Lebanon

(footstone No. 776)

774. Rough, unlettered, granite stone.

775. (footstone)
S   H

776. (footstone)
IN
MEMORY
of Capt Joshua
Huntington Esq
O B Aug 26
1745 Atatis
Suae 47
(May be associate of 773)

777. (footstone)
D   H

778. (footstone)
MRS
SARAH
HUNTINGTON
(May be associate of 386)

779. In memory of
Robert son of
Gurdon & Anne
Huntington who
died May 13th
AD 1801 aged 1 year
& 7 months

(footstone)
R. H.

780. Here lyes interred the Remains
of Deacon Simon Huntington who
was born in Saybrook in Feb 6
1659 And Succeeded his Father
in the office of a Deacon in Nor
wich Served therein about 30
years and then Died in the 2 of
Novem 1736 in the 77th year of his age

(footstone)
1736 NOVEM 2D DIED DEACON SIMON HUNTINGTON

781. Here lyes interred the Body of Lydia
the Wife of Deacon Simon Huntington
Deceased who was born in Norwich
in august 1663 lived with him 55
years Survived him 9 months and
Died on the 8th Day of August in
the 74th year of Her age

(footstone)
MRS LYDIA HUNTINGTON DIED AUGUST 8th 1663

782. In Memory of M^rs
Sibel the wife of M^r
Daniel Huntington
Who died October 12
1744 and in the
25 year of her Age
it is appointed unto
Man once to die
We have Hope to
wards God that thare
Shall be a Resurrection
of the Dead

(footstone)
Mrs SIBEL
HUNTING
TON

783. In Memory of Da
niel ſon to Benja
min Huntington
Eſq^r & M^rs
Anne his wife
who died dec^r
30th 1781.

(footstone)
Daniel
Huntington

784. Here Lies interred the
Remains of Mrs Abigal
The Wife of Mr Daniel
Huntington of Norwich
Who Died Dec^br 25 1734
& in the 56 year of her Age
MEMENTO MORI
MORS VINCET OMNIA

(footstone)
MR^s ABIGAL
HUNTINGTON Y^e
Wife of Mr DANIEL
HUNTINGTON
of Norwich died
Dec^br 25th
1734

785. Here lie interred the Remain^s
of Diadema & Lucretia Daughter^s
of Mr Thomas & MR^s Abigal
Carew of Norwich the first
of which Died Nou^br 24 1736
& in ye 4th year of her Age Y^e other
on ye 29th Day of y^e ſame Nou^br
& in ye 11th Month of her Age
MEMENTO MORI

(footstone)
DIADEMA & LUCRETIA
DAUGHTERS TO
Mr THOMAS CARE^w

786. JEDADIAH
SON OF OF JO
SHUA & MR^s HAH
NAH HUNTING
TON WHO DIED
MAY Y^e 12th 1725
AGED 3 YEARS
3 MONTHES
& 10 DAYS

787. Here Lyes ye Body
of Mr Daniel Hun-
tington Who Depart
ed this Life Sep^t
13th AD 1741 in y^e,
67th year of his
Age.

(footstone)
M^r
Daniel
Huntington

788. In Memory of Daniel
Huntington Efqr
deceaf'd: He had a
liberal Education
was an excellent Schol
lar, a found Reafoner,
fagacious, Juft & much
efteemed in civil life,
was a plain Chriftian,
kind Husband
 tender Parent
 faithful friend,
 a good Neighbour,
 an honeft man,
& Died in peace July
26th AD: 1753: in ye
43d year of his Age

(footstone)
Daniel
Huntington
Efqr

789. HERE LYES INTERRED THE
BODY OF ANDREW SON TO
Mr JOSHUA HUNTINGTON
WHO WAS BORN IN NORWICH
THE SECOND DAY OF OCTOBr
1724 AGED 15 YEARS THRE
MONTHS AND 12 DAYES
AND DIED THE 14 DAY
OF JANUARY ANoD 1739/40

(footstone)
ANDREW
HUNTINGTON
DIED
JANVARY
14 1739/40

790. HERE
IS INTERRED
the Body of Mrs Elifabeth
Huntington wife to Mr Jabez
Huntington who Departed
this Life July the jft AD 1745
in the 24th year of her age

791. HERE LYES Ye
BODY OF ENSIGN
JAMES HUNTING
TON DIED SEPt
Ye 3 1727 AGED
47 YEARS 3 MON
THES & 14 DAYS

(footstone)
ENSIGN
JAMES
HUNTINGTON

792. In Memory of Charlotte
daught to Mr Felix & Mrs.
Anne Huntington who
died Novr 3d 1786
aged 1 year & 2 months

793. To the memory of Mrs prifcila
Huntington the wife of Mr
James Huntington who
After a patient & pios
Life fell afleep in Jefus
January the 19 1742/3
In the 67 year of her age

(footstone)
Mrs prifcila
Huntington

794.   y of

  in
year his
 Age

(footstone)
Mr
peter
Huntington

795. In memory of Edward and
Martha fon & daught to Capt
Simeon Huntington & Mrs
Frelove his wife, Edward died
June 7th 1792, in ye 9th Year
of his age
Martha died Auguft 16th 1791,
in ye 6th Year of her age.

796. CHESTER P. HUNTINGTON,
DIED
March 13, 1836,
Aged 55.

CHARLES E. HUNTINGTON,
was lost at sea
Nov. 1839, Aged 25.

(footstone)
C. P. H.

797. In memory of
Capt
Simeon Huntington
who died Aug. 10th
1817 aged 77.

(footstone)
Capt
S. H.

(This ends the records of the enclosed Huntington Lot)

(The enclosed Townsend Lot)

798. JOHN H. TOWNSEND
DIED
Oct 4th 1858,
Aged 80 years

(footstone)
J. H. T.

799. In
Memory of
FANNY
the daughter of
Nathaniel & Hannah
Townsend
who died March 29, 1836,
Aged 59.

(footstone)
F. T.

800. Sacred to the memory
of Capt John Hughes
who was industrious &
ufefull in life untill
debilitated by age &
infirmity who died decr
29th 1803, aged 84 years.

(footstone)
Capt
John
Hughes

801. Sacred to the memory
of Mrs Zipporah
Hughes confort of
Capt John Hughes fhe
departed this life Janr
23d 1799, in ye 75th
year of her age

Lend lend your wings
I mount! I fly!
O Grave! where is thy victory
O Death! where is thy sting?

(footstone)
Mrs
Zipporah
Hughes

802. In fure & certain
hopes of the refurrec
tion to eternal life,
is here deposited
the remains of Mrs
Hannah wife to Mr.
Nathaniel Townsend
& daught of Capt John
& Mrs Zipporah
Hughes who died of
a confumption Decr
21ft 1801 aged 42
years & 6 months

(footstone)
Mrs
Hannah
Townsend

803. In
Memory of
NATHANIEL TOWNSEND
who died
Nov. 15, 1834,
Aged 86.

(footstone)
N. T.

(The end of records in the enclosed Townsend Lot)

804. In Memory of
Thomas Baldwin
who died Sept^mb
ye 10th 1741 in y^e
80th Year of
his Age

(footstone)
Thomas
Baldwin
1741

805. Jabez ye Son
of John & Luce
Baldwin died
Aug^ft ye 6th 1753
in ye 2^d Year
of his Age

(footstone)
Jabez Baldwin
1753

806. In Memory of
Abigail ye Wife of
Thomas Baldwin
who died Octo^r
ye 9th 1753 in y^e
80th Year of
her Age

(footstone)
Abigail Baldwin

807. Bethiah Daughtr
of Ebenezer &
Bethiah Baldwin
died Jan^ry 2^d
1741/2 Aged
1 Month

(footstone)
Bethiah
Baldwin

808. IN MEMORY OF
Mrs Bethiah ye Wife
of Capt Ebenezer
Baldwin who De
parted this Life
January ye 28th
1762 in ye 43^d
year of her Age

(footstone)
M^rs
Bathiah Baldwin

809. In memory of
CAP^t EBENEZER BALDWIN,
who departed this life May
2^d AD 1792, aged 82
A reputable Citizen,
A kind hufband, a tender parent
An amiable cheerful neighbour
A good man
Supported by Chriftian fortitude
He bore with singular Philofophy
the peculiar calamities of his life
during nine years of blind-
nefs & Infirmity
and the extreme Pains of
his laft lingering ficknefs
in the fure hope of a long wifhed
for Eternity of happinefs

(footstone)
Capt
Ebenezer
Baldwin

810. CHARLES
fon of Dudley &
Caroline Hosford
died
May 22, 1826

(footstone)
C. H.

811. IN MEMORY OF
SAMUEL CALKINS
WHO DIED
DEC. 21, 1815,
AGED 46

ALSO
SALLY CALKINS
HIS WIFE
WHO DIED
JULY 5, 1859
AGED 93

812. Sacred
to the memory of
Mrs Lovisa Tracy
Wife of
Mr Dorastus Tracy
Who died
March 9, 1816,
AE. 46

(footstone)
L. T.

813.   Sacred
to the memory of
Mr Dorastus Tracy
who died
Octr 16, 1815,
Aged 49.

(footstone)
D. T.

814.   Alass poor human nature!
In memory of
Eunice, wife of
William Clegg,
who died
Oct. 11, 1819,
aged 28 years.
Also
of Phillip their Son
who died Oct. 28th 1819
aged 1 year.

(footstone)
E. C.

814a.   Henry B. son to
Mr. Henry & Mrs
Esther Starkwea
ther who died
April 20th 1815
in the 5th year
of his age

(footstone)
H. B. S.

815.   WILLIAM H. BLISS
DIED
March 4, 1868,
aged 48.

(footstone)
W. H. B.

816.   ELIAS BLISS
DIED
Sept 25, 1833,
Aged 83.

(footstone)
E. B.

817.   In
MEMORY OF
WILLIAM BLISS
WHO DIED
Oct. 19, 1844,
aged 78.

To thy holy care and keeping,
We this sacred spot entrust,
Keep thy vigil o'er the sleeping—
Father guard this hallowed dust

(footstone)
W. B.

818.   Sufan, daughter
of Wm & Margaret
Cleveland died
Feb. 6th 1805 aged
2 years.

Suffer little
children to come
unto me and for-
bid them not.

(footstone)
Sufan
Cleveland

819.   HARRIET S.
daughter of
Francis Cleveland
Granddaughter of
Wm. & Margaret
died Nov. 29, 1834
aged 12 yrs & 4 mo.

"The parting groan
Gave back to dust it's dust
To Heaven its own."

(footstone)
H. S. C.

820.
In memory of
Zachariah Lathrop
who died
Dec. 26, 1817,
in the 76th year
of his age

(footstone)
Z. Lathrop

821.
SACRED
TO THE MEMORY OF
Mrs. ELIZABETH
relict of
Mr. John Morse
WHO DIED
Sept 6, 1847
AEt. 75 Yr's.

A friend to all, sincere and true
Our heart felt sorrows are thy due
And tho' we now thy loss deplore,
Soon may we meet to part no more.

(footstone)
E. M.

822.
SACRED
TO THE MEMORY OF
MR. JOHN MORSE,
WHO DIED
July 22, 1843,
AEt. 68 Yr's

He was a kind husband and an affectionate
Father, and we trust a sincere christian.

(footstone)
J. M.

823.
SACRED
to the memory of
Miss JULIA MORSE,
daugh of
John and Elizabeth
Morse who died Sept
2, 1827, Aged 27 yrs.

She sleeps in Jesus' kind embrace,
In Heaven, she views his smiling face:
Surviving friends, for death prepare,
And meet her happy spirit there.

(footstone)
J. M.

824.
In
Memory of
Miss SUSANNA AMANDA,
daughter of
John and Elizabeth Morse,
who died
August 1st. 1841,
AEt. 31.

In the hope of a blessed Immortality beyond the grave.
Behold dear youth as you pass by,
This stone informs you where I lie,
Remember then you soon will have,
Like me, a mansion in the grave.

(footstone)
S. A. M.

825.
In
memory of
MRS. Susanna Morse,
wife of
Mr. John Morse,
who died
Jan. 5, 1828,
aged 78 years.

(footstone)
S. M.

826.
In
memory of
Mr. John Morse
who died
Oct. 14, 1837,
aged 87 years.

(footstone)
J. M.

827. In
Memory of
DANIEL MORSE
who died
Feb 13, 1839,
AEt. 54

The grave will close o'er those we love,
Yet in our hearts still love remains,
It rises to their home above
And cold forgetfulness disclaims.

(footstone)
D. M.

828. In
Memory of
SOPHIA
wife of
Daniel Morse,
WHO DIED
Aug. 26, 1854,
aged 66.

Oh for the death of those
Who slumber in the Lord!
Oh be like theirs my last repose,
Like theirs my last reward.

(footstone)
S. M.

829. In memory of
PARMENAS JONES
who died
at Albany, N. Y.
Feb. 21, 1839,
Aged 86.
and his wife
ROSANA
who died at Norwich, Ct.
April 22, 1815,
Aged 64.

The dead in Christ shall rise first.

(footstone)
P. J.
R. J.

830. EBENEZER JONES,
died Dec. 1813,
AEt 70.
ELIZABETH
Relict of
Ebenezer Jones,
died Nov. 1815,
AEt 76.

(footstone)
J.
E.   E.

831. Sacred
to the memory of
Mrs. ELIZA C.
relict of
Edward W. Wyyman
WHO DIED
May 10, 1831,
Ae 41 years & 11 mo.

(footstone)
E. C. W.

832. HENRY JOSEPH
COOLIDGE
died in Savannah, Ga.
Sept. 7, 1803,
AEt. 37,
LUCY,
Relict of
Henry Joseph
Coolidge
died Jan. 26, 1844,
AEt. 76.

(footstone)
H. J. C.
L. C.

833. FRANCES JANE COOLIDGE
Jan. 24, 1874.
Born at New Haven
Oct. 14, 1791.

834. In memory of
Mr. Levi Lathrop,
son of Mr. Zepha
niah Lathrop and
Mrs. Hannah his
wife who died
Jan. 6th 1814, in
the 26th year
of his age

(footstone)
Mr Levi
Lathrop

835. In memory of
Mr. Zephaniah Lathrop,
who died Oct 25th
1815
in the 69th year
of his age

(footstone)
Mr Zaphaniah
Lathrop

836. In
Memory of
ANDREW GRISWOLD
WHO DIED
Sept. 28, 1825,
Aged 72.
ALSO
ANNA GRISWOLD
His Wife
WHO DIED
Nov. 23, 1842,
Aged 74.

(footstone)
A. G.

837. Sacred
to the memory of
Mr. Carpenter Morse
who died
Novr 2d 1815,
in the 41ft year
of his age.

Respected by all his acquaintance
and much lamented.

(footstone)
Mr
Carpenter
Morse

838. In memory of
Capt. Timothy Morse,
who died
June 19th 1816,
in the 36th year
of his age

Beloved by all who knew him
His hope was in GOD.

(footstone)
Capt
Timothy
Morse

839. In
memory of
Avery Morse
who died
2, 1826,
aged 44 years.

(footstone)
A. M.

840. Here lies the body of
Henry Hunter,
who died Nov. 19th in the
year of our Lord 1810
in the 85th year of his
age.

Mark the perfect man,
and behold the upright for
the end of that man is peace.

(footstone)
Henry Hunter

841. In memory of
Miss Sally Daught of
Mr. Joseph &
Mrs Lucy Winship
who died
Novr 5th 1819
aged 17 years.

(footstone)
S. W.

DEACON CHRISTOPHER HUNTINGTON, 1735
First born of males in ye town of Norwich
SEE PAGE 87

FOOTSTONE

842. ELIZABETH GRIFFIN
died
Oct. 6, 1857,
aged 84

(footstone)
E. G.

843. In
memory of
Jeremiah Griffin
who died
March 12, 1825, aged
52 years

(footstone)
J. G.

844. Eliza Ann
daughter of
Daniel Leach
Jun & Lydia his
wife died Sep
18th 1820 aged
19 months
& 17 days

(footstone)
E. A.
L.

844a. Mary Ann
daughter of
Stephen & Mary
Remington
died Sept 7th
1822, aged 1
year & 15 days

(footstone)
M. A. R.

845. In memory of
THE
REV. DAVID AUSTIN,
who was born at New Haven,
March 19, 1759,
died at Norwich
February 5, 1831.

For him to live was Christ, and to die was gain.

(footstone)
D. A.

846. In memory of
Mrs Lydia Austin,
consort of the
Rev'd David Austin,
daughter of Deacn Joshua
& Mrs. Mercy Lathrop,
she died 25th Oct 1818
aged 54 years

Beneath this stone death's prisoner lies
The stone shall move, the prisoner rise
When Jesus, with almighty word
Calls his dead saints to meet their Lord.

(footstone)
Lydia
Austin

847. In Memory of
Mrs. JERUSHA PERIT
Wife of
P. Perit of New York
and DAUGHTER OF
the late
THOMAS LATHROP
who died the 18th Oct.
1821,
aged 32 years, and 8 months.

(footstone)
J. P.

848. In
Memory of
Mr. WILLIAM LATHROP
WHO DIED
Sept 13, 1825,
aged 24 years

(footstone)
W. L.

849. HANNAH,
widow of
THOMAS LATHROP
died Jan. 28, 1862,
aged 92 years.

asleep in Jesus.

Her children rise
up and call her blessed.

(footstone)
H. L.

850.   In
memory of
Thomas Lathrop
who died
Dec. 20th 1817,
aged 55 years.

Blefsed are the dead who die in the Lord.

(footstone)
T. L.

851.   In memory of
Mrs. Margaret Porter
of East Hartford,
who died
Oct. 13th 1814,
aged 76.

(footstone)
M. P.

852.   LUCERTIA HUNTINGTON
wife of
Epaphras Porter,
born
July 31, 1783,
died
Nov. 12, 1850.

"Made perfect through sufferings."

(footstone)
L. H. P.

853.   EPAPHRAS PORTER,
died Oct. 19, 1861,
aged 82 years.

(footstone)
E. P.

854.   JESSE HUNTINGTON,
BORN
April 17, 1774,
DIED
Dec. 21, 1851.

(footstone)
J. H.

(The inscribed marble slab which formed a portion of the Hubbard family table-tomb in the old burial ground has disappeared, but from the inscription list in the Pastoral library of the First Church, the following is presented:

Here lye the Remains of Lydia
Hubbard, daughter of Joseph & Lydia Coit,
& wife of William Hubbard, who died
Nov. 2, 1778, aged 37 years.
Also the Remains of 4 children of William
& Lydia Hubbard: Lydia, wife of Thomas
Lathrop, died Dec. 26, 1790, aged 25.
William died Sept. 10, 1789, aged 22.
Joseph died May 25, 1790, aged 20.
Lucretia died Oct. 14, 1775, aged 5.

Each humane virtue their mild eyes expressed,
And a young heaven was opened in their breasts.
In the last hour their triumph shone complete,
And death disarm'd sat smiling at their feet.
And now, thou faithful stone, proclaim aloud,
A Christian is the noblest work of God.

855.   In memory of
Mr. Rufus Backus Abel
who died
Aug. 19th 1812,
aged 56 years

The well attested virtues of departed worth, need not the indiscriminating pen of Eulogy.

(footstone)
R. B. A.

856. In memory of
Mrs. Abigail
wife of
Mr. John Huntington,
who died
April 3rd 1814,
aged 62 years

(footstone)
Mrs A
Huntington

857. In memory of
Mr. John Huntington
who died
Sep. 30th 1815,
aged 70 years

(footstone)
Mr. J.
Huntington

858. Sacred
to the memory of
Nancy, daughr of Jabez
& Anna Armstrong,
who died May 5th 1814,
in the 34th year
of her age

Farewell all sublumary things,
I go to see the King of Kings.

(footstone)
N. A.

859. IN
Memory of
MARY
wife of
Abel P. Whitley
who died
Sept. 9, 1838,
AEt. 39.

(footstone)
M. W.

860. PRUDENCE FELLOWES
wife of
NATHAN MINER
died Dec. 27, 1860,
aged 83.

Gone, but not forgotten.

(footstone)
P. M.

861. This Monument is
Erected to the memory
of
SAMUEL AVERY
WHO DIED
Dec. 15, 1844,
in the 92nd year
of his age

(footstone)
S. A.

862. This monument is
erected in memory of
Candace wife of
Samuel Avery
who died
Aug 31ft 1816,
in the 68 year
of her age

(footstone)
Candace
Avery

863. In memory of
Miss Anne Tracy
daughter of
Fredk & Deborah Tracy
who died
Sept 30, 1823,
aged 45 years.

(footstone)
A. T.

864. In memory of
Mrs. Deborah Tracy,
who died
July 27th 1820,
aged 71 years
Also
of Mr Fredk Tracy
who died
June 21ft 1803,
at Cape Francois
aged 54 years

(footstone)
D. T.

865.	In memory of
Miſs Sarah Grant
daughter of Capt'
James & Mrs Hannah
Grant who died
Jan. 16th 1808 aged
80 years

(footstone)
Miſs Sarah
Grant

(Brick Tomb)
866. SAMUEL HUNTINGTON Eſqr

Governor of Connecticut
having ſerved his fellow Citizens
in various important Offices
died the 5th day of January AD. 1796,
in the 65th year of his age.
His Conſort
MRS. MARTHA HUNTINGTON
died June 4th AD 1794 in the 57th
year of her age

This Tomb contains their Relicts

867.	In
memory of
Mrs. HANNAH TRACY,
wife of
Benjamin Tracy Esq.
who died
Oct 9, 1822,
aged 52 years

(footstone)
H. T.

868.	In
memory of
Benjamin Tracy Esq.
who died
May 5, 1832,
in the 76th year
of his age

(footstone)
B. T.

869.	In memory of
Mrs Sarah
wife of
Stephen Gifford
who died
Oct 20, 1825,
aged 88 years.

(footstone)
S. G.

870.	Sacred
to the memory of
Mr. Stephen Gifford,
who died April 8, 1809,
aged 82 years

(footstone)
Mr. Stephen
Gifford

871.	SUSAN H. GIFFORD
DIED
April 19, 1871,
aged 75 years

(footstone)
S. H. G.

872.	POLLY DOUGLASS
DIED
MARCH 1848
AGED 71

"She hath done what she could."

(footstone)
P. D.

873.	In memory of
Mr. John Keeney
ſon of Mr. Edward & Mrs.
Patience Keeney, who
was born at Newport Aug.
29th 1768, & died June 16th
1809, aged 40 years

Good when he gives,
ſupremely good,
Not leſs when he denies,
Even croſſes from his sove-
reign hand
Are bleſſings in diſguiſe

874. Consider Sterry,
aged 56,
Died Nov. 15, 1817,
When
the world lost
A genius for Mathematics & Astronomy
seldom equal^d, rarely surpass^d.
This monument
is erected
by the society of Freemasons
of which he was an ornament,
by whose lustre
the path to that high eminence
which he attained
is made plain to those who strive
for equal excellence.

(footstone)
C. S.

875. Mr.
CHARLES CHARLTON
DIED
Nov. 8, 1818,
aged 62 years.

Mrs
SARAH CHARLTON
his wife died
Sept. 22, 1812,
aged 66 years

(footstone)
C. C.
S. C.

876. LUCRETIA CAREW,
relict of
ELIPHALET CAREW,
died July 5, 1858,
aged 90 y'rs & 6 mos.

(footstone)
L. C.

877. ROSWELL MORGAN
DIED
JULY 12, 1853,
Aged 77

(footstone)
R. M.

878. ANN H.
WIFE OF
ROSWELL MORGAN,
BORN
FEB. 15, 1792,
DIED
MAY 15, 1876.

(footstone)
A. H. M.

879. ABBY W. LATHROP
died Sept. 22, 1861,
aged 47 years.

"Blessed are the dead which die in the Lord."

(footstone)
A. W. L.

880. Augustus Frederick
Son of Augustus
& Mary Lathrop^e
died Novr 7th 1818,
aged 7 years.
& 23 D^s

(footstone)
A. F. L.

881. MARY
Wife of
Augustus Lathrop,
Died
July 4, 1833,
Aged 54.

(footstone)
M. L.

882. Sacred
to the memory of
Capt
Augustus Lathrop
who died Oct. 7th 1819,
in the 34th year of his
age.

(footstone)
Capt.
A L

883.
IN
Memory of
MR.
GARDNER CARPENTER,
DIED
April 26, 1815,
Aged 66.

(footstone)
G. C.

884.
IN
Memory of
MRS. MARY
Relict of
Gardner Carpenter
DIED
March 17, 1838,
Aged 70.

(footstone)
M. C.

885.
In memory of
Mrs. Hannah, wife of
Mr. Harcoless Phillips
who died
Oct. 12, 1822,
aged 26.
Also
their child Hannah
who died
Feb. 24, 1823,
aged 5 months.

(footstone)
H. P.

886.
CORAL E. RICHMOND
BORN
APRIL 10, 1868,
DIED
NOV. 11, 1891.

(footstone)
C. E. R.

887.
IN
Memory of
Mrs. LUCRETIA,
wife of
Capt. Thomas Miller,
who died
Aug. 9, 1850,
Aged 70.

Let me go; my heart hath tasted
Of my Saviour's wondrous grace,
Let me go; where I shall ever
See and know him face to face.

(footstone)
L. M.

888.
In
Memory of
Capt. Thomas Miller
who died
July 29, 1826,
aged 51 years.

889.
In memory of
John Saniford
Son of Thomas &
Lucretia Miller
who died
Nov. 22, 1815,
aged 3 years
& 4 months.

(footstone)
J. S. M.

890.
In Memory of
MARK ANTHONY DEOLPH
WHO DIED
in Demorara Dec. 16, 1783.
Also his wife
MRS. PRISCILLA DEOLPH
WHO DIED
March 10, 1826
AE. 84

I know that my Redeemer liveth.

(footstone)
M. A. D.
P. D.

891. IN
MEMORY
OF
MISS
Mary Ann Billings
WHO DIED
Oct. 1, 1831,
Aged 24

(footstone)
M. A. B.

892. In
Memory of
RUFUS DARBY,
who died July 29, 1830,
aged 57 years.

MARY,
a daughter of Rufus and
Mary Darby, died Oct.
24, 1819, aged 16 years.

HENRY,
son of Rufus & Mary
Darby, died Nov. 7, 1819,
aged 20 years.

(footstone)
R. D.
M. D.
H. D.

893. MARY,
wife of
Rufus Darby,
DIED
May 18, 1858,
aged 85 yrs.

(footstone)
MOTHER

894. IN
Memory of
MRS. ALICE
Wife of
WM. BALDWIN
WHO DIED
Dec. 10, 1833,
Aged 60.

(footstone)
A. B.

895. Sacred
to the memory of
Mr William Baldwin,
who died Oct. 12th 1818,
aged 57 years.

(footstone)
W. B.

896. In memory of
Margaret Baldwin
WHO DIED
April 1810,
Aged 80 years

(footstone)
M. B.

897. In memory of
ASA LATHROP
WHO DIED
March 26, 1835,
Aged 79.

(footstone)
A. L.

898. Sacred
to the memory of
Mrs. Elizabeth Lathrop,
wife of Mr. Asa Lathrop,
and daughter
of Mr. Eleazer Lord who
died Aug. 23d 1805,
aged 48 years.

God unerring gives and
takes the Vital Spark.

(footstone)
E. L.

899. In memory of Mrs
Elifabeth Lord,
confort of
Mr. Eleazer Lord, &
the youngeft daughtr
of the late
Rev. Dr. Lord
fhe died Oct. 22d
1803, in the 75th
year of her age

(footstone)
Mrs
Elifabeth
Lord

900. In memory of
Mr. Eleazer Lord,
who died on the
16th of Jan. 1809 in
the 80th year of
his age

(footstone)
Mr. Eleazer
Lord

901. In memory of
MARY
Wife of
WM. BINGHAM,
who died
March 7, 1816,
aged 87.

Erected by her Son
DAVID NEVINS

(footstone)
M. B.

902. In memory of
David ſon to
David & Mary
Nevins who
died Auguſt
17th 1782
Aged 11 months.

(footstone)
David
Nevins

903. Sacred
to the memory of
Mary Nevins,
daughter of David &
Mary Nevins who
departed this life
Oct. 23d AD. 1800
aged 22 years.

(footstone)
Mary Nevins

904. IN MEMORY
of
MARY NEVINS,
Eldest daughter of
Henry & Lucretia Nevins.
She died February 28, 1819,
Aged 13.

Remembrance oft shall thee restore
For thee the tear be daily shed,
Belov'd till life shall charm no more
And mourn'd till memory's self
be dead

(footstone)
Mary Nevins

905. In memory of
MARY,
wife of David Nevins,
who died
Septr 23d 1820,
aged 64 years.

Also
of David, son of
David & Mary Nevins,
who was lost at sea,
Augt 1806, aged 23 years.

(footstone)
M. N.

906. In
Memory of
LUCRETIA,
wife of
Henry Nevins,
WHO DIED
March 28, 1835,
Aged 51.

(footstone)
L. N.

907. FELIX HUNTINGTON
died
Sept. 1822.

(footstone)
E. H.

908. ANNIE
wife of
Felix Huntington
died 1806,
aged 50.

(footstone)
A. H.

909. This monument is affectionately dedicated to the memory of Mary Brown Huntington, daughter of Felix & Anne Huntington, who died July 24th 1801, in the 21ſt year of her age. Happy through faith in the proſpect of a bleſſed immortality.

O death where is thy ſting?
O grave where is thy victory?
The ſting of death is ſin; and the ſtrength of ſin is the law.
But thanks be to God, who giveth us the victory,
through our Lord Jeſus
Chriſt.

(footstone)
Mary B
Huntington

910. CHARLOTTE HUNTINGTON
born
Oct. 28, 1787,
died
May 28, 1867.

(footstone)
C. H.

911. In
Memory of
DEBORAH MANWARING
WHO DIED
May 29, 1844,
Aged 71.

A partaker of the glory that shall be revealed.

(footstone)
D. M.

912. SACRED
TO THE MEMORY OF
NANCY ROGERS,
relict of
DENISON ROGERS,
WHO DIED
Aug. 1, 1857,
aged 85 years.

"The righteous shall be
in everlasting remembrance."

(footstone)
N. R.

913. SACRED
TO THE MEMORY OF
MR. DENISON ROGERS,
WHO DIED
May 29, 1846,
aged 73 years.

(footstone)
D. R.

914. (Raised Tomb)
Dedicated
to the memory of
ASA SPALDING ESQR
who was born
on the 20th day of May 1757,
and died (very suddenly)
on the 13th day of Aug. 1811,
of a disease called by the
Medical faculty
Angina Pectoris.

All flesh is graſs.

915.	Miſs
Maria Elizabeth Spalding,
the only child of
Asa Spalding Esqr
and Lydia his wife,
born September 1ſt 1797,
she was friendly and
pleasing in her life,
and died of the spotted
fever, August 4th 1809
Greatly lamented.

(footstone)
Miſs
Maria Elizabeth
Spalding

916.	To
the memory of
MARY TRACY
daughter of
Doct. Elisha &
Elizabeth Tracy.
DIED
Feb. 28, 1838,
aged 74.

(footstone)
M. T.

917.	DEBORAH D. TRACY,
daughter of
Doctor Elisha &
Elizabeth Tracy,
a sensible amiable
& accomplished Woman,
deseased June 1824,
aged 52.

(footstone)
D. D. T.

918.	This Monument is
erected ſacred to the
memory of Maſter
Francis Tracy, the
much beloved ſon
of Doct. P. & Mrs A
Tracy, who died
April 23d 1802
aged 5 years.

(footstone)
F. T.

919.	CHARLOTTA M. TRACY,
daughter of Doct. Elisha
& Elizabeth Tracy
deceased July 1820,
aged 59.

She was early devoted
to piety & during a
distressing disease of
many years, she practised
a patience & fortitude
unparalleled.

(footstone)
C. M. T.

920.	In memory of
Mrs. Lucy
relict of
Mr. Simon Edgerton
who died
Dec. 15, 1823,
aged 56 years.

(footstone)
L. E.

921.	In memory of
Mr. Simon Edgerton
who died
Febr 3d 1820,
aged 66 years.

(footstone)
S. E.

922.	Sacred
to the memory of
Mr. Daniel Huntington,
ſon of Deacn Simon &
Mrs. Zipporah Huntington,
who died ſuddenly, Dec. 3d
AD. 1805, aged 43 years.

(footstone)
Mr. Daniel
Huntington

923.	In memory of Mrs.
Mary, Consort of Mr.
Daniel Huntington
who died Dec. 6th 1815,
in the 55th year of
her age

(footstone)
M. Huntington

924.
LUCY H.
Wife of
CYRUS MINER,
DIED
Nov. 17, 1845,
AE. 47

The memory of the just is blessed.

(footstone)
L. H. M.

925.
CYRUS MINER,
DIED
Dec. 14, 1848,
AE. 58

(footstone)
C. M.

926.
ELISHA,
Son of
Simon Edgerton
&
Lucy Griswold
his Wife,
Born Nov. 26, 1802,
Died
May 12, 1850.

(footstone)
E. G.

927. In memory of Zenas L.
fon of Capt Zenas Whiting
and Mrs. Phebe his wife,
died Dec^m 3^d 1801, in
his 22^d year.

Ebenezer fon of Mr. Ebe
nezer and Mrs. Phebe
Raymond died in Charlef
ton South Carolina Sept
16th 1802, aged 23 years.

Thefe happy youths refigned
   their breaths
Prepar'd to live & ripe for death
Ye blooming youth who fee this
   ftone
Learn early death to be your own.

(footstone)
Mr.
Zenas L.
Whiting

928.
SACRED
TO
the memory of
STEPHEN DAVIS
WHO DIED
May 27, 1827,
Aged 54.

(footstone)
S. D.

929.
SACRED
TO
the memory of
ELIZABETH,
relict of
Stephen Davis,
WHO DIED
Feb. 12, 1832,
Aged 56.

(footstone)
E. D.

930. In affectionate
remembrance of
Elisha Hyde Esqr
who died Decr 16th 1813,
in the 63^d year of his age.
Sacred Also to the
memory of Zebulon
P. Burnham who sailed
for Tenerieffe March 10th
1810, and is supposed to
have been lost at sea,
aged 44 years.

(footstone)
Elisha
Hyde
Esqr

931.	Sacred
to the memory of
Nancy Maria Hyde,
daugh^r of Elisha &
Nancy Hyde,
who died
March 26th 1816,
aged 24 years.

(footstone)
Nancy
Maria
Hyde

932.	MARY HARLAND
died
January 15, 1859,
aged 79.

FANNY HARLAND
died
March 30, 1859,
aged 72.

(footstone)
M. H.
F. H.

933.	In memory of
Mr. HENRY HARLAND,
who died
June 1, 1841,
aged 52 years

(footstone)
H. H.

934.	In memory of
Hannah, relict of
Thomas Harland,
who died
March 6th 1816,
aged 62 years.

(footstone)
H. Harland

935.	This monument perpetuates the memory of
Thomas Harland, &
Thomas Harland; jun.
Thomas Harland departed
this life March 31st 1807,
aged 72 years.
Thomas Harland jun.
died Nov. 27th 1806,
aged 25 years.
Here age & youth a common doom have found,
And both be mingled in
this hallow'd ground.

(footstone)
Thomas
Harland
& Thomas
Harland jun.

936.	In memory of
HALLY HARLAND
who died
Aug. 13, 1842,
aged 2 years.

(footstone)
H. H.

937.	In memory of
EDWARD
HARLAND
who died
Sept. 12, 1824,
aged 1 year.

(footstone)
E. H.

938.	In memory of
HARRIET & HANNAH
HARLAND, who died
April 24th & Sept. 8th
1837,
Aged 12 & 2 years.

(footstone)
H. H.
H. H.

939.
In memory of
Mrs. LUCY CAREW,
relict of
Mr. Daniel Carew,
WHO DIED
Aug 6, 1832,
aged 74 years.

(footstone)
L. C.

940.
In memory of
Mr. DANIEL CAREW,
WHO DIED
Nov. 5, 1813,
aged 66 years

(footstone)
D. C.

941.
DANIEL CAREW
DIED
Sept. 30, 1838,
aged 57.

LUCY CAREW
DIED
at Providence, R. I.
Aug. 27, 1800,
aged 17.

(footstone)
D. C.

942.
IN
Memory of
Mr
Joseph Coit
who
died April 21ſt
1807
Aged 52 years.

(footstone)
J. C.

943.
In memory of
three infant child-
ren two ſons and
one daughter of
Gurdon & Laura
Edgerton, who
died Sept. 1804
July 1809
& Dec. 1812.

(footstone)
Infants

944.
IN
Memory of
GURDON EDGERTON,
who died
March 5, 1849,
Aged 77.
also his wife
LURAH EDGERTON
who died
Nov. 7, 1843,
Aged 63.

(footstone)
G. E.
L. H. E.

945.
Frances H. Leffing
well died Dec. 17
1814, aged 6 years.
Lucretia Leffing
well died Dec. 11
1814, aged 9 months
Daughters of
Eliſha & Frances
Leffingwell.

946.
Sacred
to the memory of
Mrs. Alice Leffingwell
consort of
Mr. Eliſha Leffingwell,
who departed this life
Jan. 4th 1807, aged 61
years

(footstone)
Mrs. Alice
Leffingwell

947. Sacred
to the memory of
Mr. Eliſha Leffingwell
who departed this life
June 4th 1804, aged
61 years.

(footstone)
Mr. Eliſha
Leffingwell

948. Louiza M.
daughter to Mr.
Andrew L. Wattles
& Mrs Margery
his wife died
April 3rd 1818,
aged 7 months.

(footstone)
L. M. W.

949. AUGUSTUS C. TRACY   JULIET TRACY   JOSHUA P. TRACY

Born   Born   Born

Feb. 13, 1812,   Dec. 30, 1810   March 31, 1816,
Died Dec. 19, 1814,   Died Feb. 21, 1815,   Died Nov. 14, 1816,
aged 2 yrs. 10 mos.   aged 4 yrs. 2 mos.   aged 7 mos.

"Suffer little children and forbid them not to
come unto me; for of such is the kingdom of heaven."

(footstone)
A. C. T.   J. T.   J. P. T.

950. HANNAH HYDE,
widow of
JOSHUA TRACY,
born in Norwich, Conn.
May 7, 1786,
died in Salem, Mass.
Sept 23, 1874,
aged 88 yrs. 4 mo.

(footstone)
H. T.

951. JOSHUA TRACY,
Born in Lisbon
Jan. 3, 1776,
Died in Norwich
Aug. 10, 1816,
aged 40 years
& 7 mos.

(footstone)
J. T.

952. Mrs. DEBORAH E.
wife of
Mr. Henry Welch
DIED
Aug. 17, 1821,
AE 29.

(footstone)
D. E. W.

953. Mrs. HANNAH
wife of
Mr. Henry Welch,
DIED
Nov. 24, 1835,
AE 42

(footstone)
H. W.

954. CATHARINE,
wife of
Jonathan Crocker,
DIED
Nov. 25, 1834,
AE. 67

(footstone)
C. C.

955. In memory of
Eliphalet Carew Jr
who died
Feby 16th 1817,
aged 53 years.
Also of Doct.
Azor Carew,
who died Jany 18th
1800, on his passage
from England
to New York,
aged 31 years.

(footstone)
E. C.

956.   In memory of
Mrs. Mary, wife of
Eliphalet Carew,
who died
March 24th 1814,
in the 75th year
of her age.

(footstone)
M. C.

957.   In memory of
Mr. Eliphalet Carew
who died
April 8, 1822,
aged 82 years.
Also
Daniel son of Azor
& Nancy Carew,
who died in Augusta
Georgia July 24, 1824,
aged 30 years.

(footstone)
E. C.

958.   In memory of
John H.
son of Abel &
Lois Edwards
who died
Oct. 26, 1824,
aged 14 years

(footstone)
J. H. E.

959.   AMY E.
daughter of
Stephen & Amy
Willcox
died
June 8, 1848,
AE. 11 yrs.

This lovely bud so young & fair,
Called home by early doom;
Just came to show how sweet a flower
In paradise might bloom.

960.   HANNAH
Wife of
Stephen Wilcox
DIED
Aug. 3, 1853,
aged 60.

(footstone)
H. W.

961.   IN
Memory of
Capt John Doane
who died
April 29, 1818,
in the 45 year
of his age

(footstone)
J. D.

962.   IN
Memory of
Eunice Howes,
relict of
Capt. John Doane
who died
Aug. 9, 1855,
aged 80 years.

(footstone)
E. H. D.

963.   In
Memory of
Eunice H. Doane,
who died
Dec. 25, 1826,
aged 22 years.
Also
of John G. Doane,
who died
at New Orleans,
July 27, 1824,
aged 19.

(footstone)
E. H. D.

964.
In
Memory of
Emily C. Doane,
who died
Nov. 7, 1827,
aged 14 years.

(footstone)
E. C. D.

965. BETSIE H. DOANE
DIED
Oct. 19, 1895,
AGED 85 YRS.

"I have put my trust in the Lord God."

966.
IN
memory of
GUSTAVUS ADOLPHUS
Son of
Mulford & Dorcas
Howes
Born in New-York
29th June 1830,
died 22, April 1832,
Aged 1 year 9 months
and 24 days.

(footstone)
G. A. H.

967.
MARY A.
daughter of
Azariah &
Jane F. Lathrop
died Feb. 28, 1841,
aged 2 yrs. & 7 mos.

Suffer little children to come unto me and forbid them not for of such is the kingdom of Heaven.

(footstone)
M. A. L.

968. ABEL EDWARDS
died Oct. 2, 1853,
aged 76.
LOIS MIX
wife of
ABEL EDWARDS
died Nov. 4, 1868,
aged 96.

(footstone)
A. E.
L. M.

969.
JOHN M.
son of
J. & M. DURR,
died Apr. 14, 1864,
aged 1 day.

970.
JOHN CRYER,
Born in Rochdale,
England,
1781,
died Oct. 25, 1850.

In his old age he left his Native land, enjoyed for a few months the society of his children; but how soon he left us.

(footstone)
J. C.

971. WILLIAM EDWARDS
DIED
FEB. 5, 1813
AGED 47

ALSO HIS WIFE
ANNA EDWARDS
DIED
JULY 11, 1857,
AGED 86 YEARS

(footstone)
W. E.
A. E.

972.
IN
MEMORY OF
WILLIAM EDWARDS,
DIED
July 20, 1849,
AE. 45

(footstone)
W. E.

973.
In
MEMORY OF
CLARRISSA E.
WIFE OF
Charles Pitcher
WHO DIED
Aug. 24, 1847
Aged 52

(footstone)
C. E. P.

974.
LEVERETT B.
Eldest son of
Charles & Clarissa
PITCHER
DIED
Sept. 15, 1852,
AE. 26

(footstone)
L. B. P.

975.
WILLIAM H.
Son of
William S. &
Frances T. Cooley,
died
July 7, 1831,
Aged 4 years.

Oh! Lightly, lightly tread
Upon these early ashes, ye that weep
For him that slumbers in the dreamless sleep
of the eternal bed!

(footstone)
W. H. C.

976.
ELEAZOR
SON OF
John & Betsy
MAPLES,
DIED
Feb. 28, 1829,
AE 2 ms. & 3 ds.

977.
In
Memory of
Doct.
JUSTIN WALSWORTH
OF
ALABAMA
formerly of this Town,
who died at Norwich,
Aug. 10, 1834,
aged 30 years.

(footstone)
J. W.

978.
EDWIN H. MASON
CO I 22 REGT.
CONN. VOLS.
DIED
JAN. 19, 1878.

979.
ANDREW MASON
DIED
JAN. 4, 1883,
AGED 79 YEARS
EMILY F. ROSS
WIFE OF
ANDREW MASON,
DIED
JUNE 5, 1883,
AGED 74 YEARS

Gone but not forgotten.

(footstone)
A. M.
E. F.   R. M.

980.
In
memory of
ERASMUS D. AMES,
died Feb. 1, 1847,
aged 43 years.

(footstone)
E. D. A.

981.   In
memory of
SARAH ANN,
wife of
E. D. Ames
died Feb. 28, 1836,
aged 30 years.

Here to the dreary grave confin'd,
She sleeps in death's dark gloom,
Until the eternal morning wakes,
The slumbers of the tomb.

(footstone)
S. A. A.

982.   LYDIA HYDE,
daughter of
the late
Mr. Eliab Hyde,
DIED
Sept. 10, 1853,
aged 48.

(footstone)
L. H.

983.   JANE E.
Daughter of
John A. & Emeline
Burdick,
DIED
Feb. 6, 1837,
AE 5ms. & 9 ds.

984.   Thomas Bradbury
died July 23, 1830,
aged 32.

Mr. B. was a native of
Mossley, near Manchester
Eng. and emigrated to
This country with his wife
Sept. 1826.
Here lie the loving Husband's dear remains
The tender Brother, and the generous friend.

Far from my friends and kindred dear,
I'm called to lay my body here;
Till God my judge shall bid me rise
And meet my kindred in the skies.

(footstone)
T. B.

985.   ISABELLA,
daughter of
Andrew & Isabella
Hogan,
died Dec. 20, 1848,
AE 5 yrs. & 9 mos.

986.   MERIAL
WIFE OF
Daniel Huntington,
of Windham, deceased,
DIED
March 7, 1857,
AE. 91

It is well

(footstone)
M. H.

987.   ELIZABETH ANDERSON,
BORN
April 11, 1765,
DIED
March 29, 1849.

(footstone)
E. A.

988.   Edwin R.
son of
Edwin &
Eliza Hewlit
died Sept. 5, 1830,
aged 15 months.

(footstone)
E. R. H.

989.   SAMUEL CHARLTON
died July 8, 1868,
aged 83 yrs.
DOLLY,
his wife
died Sept. 22, 1882,
aged 92 yrs.

Beloved, respected in life
Hopes one, in Christ they shall
Rest together, waiting for the
Resurrection of the just.

(footstone)
S. C.
D. C.

990.   MARIA,
died Sept. 8, 1821
aged 4 years.

DWIGHT,
died Dec. 28, 1829,
aged 1 year.

HOWARD,
died Jan. 13, 1830,
aged 4 years.

Children of Samuel
& Dolly Charlton.

(footstone)
M. C.
D. C.
H. C.

991.   ELIZA ANN CHARLTON,
DIED
Oct. 12, 1851,
AE. 32.

Every tear is wiped away,
Sighs no more shall heave the breast;
Night is lost in endless day,
Sorrow, in eternal rest.

(footstone)
E. A. C.

992.   IN
MEMORY OF
ZACHARIAH HUNTINGTON
BORN
NOVEMBER 2, 1764,
DIED
JUNE 23, 1850.

993.   IN
MEMORY OF
THOMAS M. HUNTINGTON
DIED
Sept. 11, 1851.

"There shall be no death neither shall there be any
more pain; for the former things are passed away."

994.   MARY B. CAMPBELL,
March 28, 1832.

THO's Z. B. HUUTINGTON,
Son of
Mary B. & Tho's M. Huntington
July 4, 1827,

And they shall walk
In soft white light
with Kings & Priests abroad.

995.   IN
MEMORY OF
SALLY ANN,
WIDOW OF
HON. JABEZ W. HUNTINGTON
BORN MAY 18, 1811,
DIED JUNE 26, 1861.

"Blessed are the dead who die in the Lord."

996.   IN
MEMORY OF
JABEZ W. HUNTINGTON
BORN NOV. 8, 1788.
FROM THE YEAR 1829
TO HIS DECEASE, NOV. 2, 1847,
JUDGE OF THE SUPREME COURT
OF THE STATE OF CONNECTICUT,
&
REPRESENTATIVE & SENATOR
IN THE CONGRESS OF
THE
UNITED STATES.

997. GEORGE W. HUNTINGTON, M.D.
NOV. 6, 1858.

HE GIVES HIS BELOVED SLEEP

998. TIMOTHY CHILDS, M.D.
SEPT. 3, 1865.
HE SHALL RISE AGAIN.

999. ETTA
daughter of
Washington H. & Julia E.
Havens,
Died Nov. 25, 1857,
aged 2 y'rs. 3 mos.

"And Jesus called a little child unto Him."

(footstone)
E. H.

1000. TO
the memory of
CAPT.
DANIEL HAVENS,
BORN
in Sag Harbor, L. I.
May 1, 1783.
After a life of great
industry, and strict
integrity in the
discharge of all
public and private
Duties, he fell
asleep in Jesus
June 19, 1852,

"Them also which sleep
in Jesus, will God bring
with him."

(footstone)
D. HAVENS

1000a. DESIRE HOWES,
WIFE OF
DANIEL HAVENS,
BORN
in Chatham, Mass.
March 1, 1786,
DIED
in Norwich Town
Nov. 11, 1876.

(footstone)
D. H. HAVENS

1000b. WASHINGTON H.
HAVENS,
DIED AT
MONTICELLO, ILL.
APRIL 14, 1857
AGED 31 YS.

Asleep in Jesus!
Far from thee
Thy kindred and
Their graves may be
But thine is still
a Blessed sleep,
From which none ever
wake to weep.

(footstone)
W. H. HAVENS

1000c. ANTOINETTE H.
HAVENS
DIED
APRIL 10, 1858,
AGED 34 YS.

He giveth his beloved
sleep

(footstone)
NETTIE H. HAVENS

1000d. HARRIET D.
HAVENS
DIED
FEB. 8, 1861,
AGED 42 YS.

Asleep in Jesus O how
sweet.

(footstone)
HARRIET D. HAVENS

1001. GEORGE D. FULLER,
Born Sept. 8, 1804,
Died April 17, 1883.
HANNAH M. HAVENS,
wife of
GEORGE D. FULLER,
Born Feb. 22, 1817,
Died Dec. 25, 1853.

(footstones)
G. D. FULLER
H. M. FULLER

1002.   SUSAN SOPHIA,
wife of
GEORGE D. FULLER
DIED
May 30, 1838,
aged 29.

"Absent from the body, and present with the Lord."

1003.   MARIA ANTOINETTE,
daughter of
JONATHAN C. & PATIA
HAVENS,
of Saint Louis, M°
Born Sept. 23, 1835,
Died Oct. 30, 1853.

"For what is your life; It is even a vapour that appeareth for a little time, and then Vanisheth away."

(footstone)
M. A. H.

1004.   JONATHAN COLLINS JR
SON OF
Jonathan C.
& Patia Havens,
of Saint Louis, M°
Born Jan. 26, 1849,
Died July 5, 1854.

"He shall gather the lambs with his arm, and carry them in his bosom."

(footstone)
J. C. H.

(footstone)
1005.   DANIEL
(Note: Daniel Havens Fuller)

(footstone)
1006.   ANNA
(Note: Anna Havens Fuller)

1007.   In memory of
ERASTUS COOLEY,
who died
May 19th 1830,
Aged 55 Yrs.

ABBY	GEORGE A.
wife of	son of
ERASTUS COOLEY	ERASTUS & ABBY
DIED	COOLEY
Nov. 28, 1821,	died Jan. 22, 1808,
aged 47 yrs.	aged 9 mo's.

1008.   In memory of
Mifs
Sally Morris
of Colchester
who died Sept.
11th 1805, in the
25th year of her
age.

(footstone)
Mifs Sally
Morris

1009.   In Memory of
Miss Lucy daughr to Mr
John Bushnell & Mrs Lucy his
wife who died Decr 22d AD
1805 In the 17th year of
her age. Also Fanny her
sister died Jan. 2d AD 1806,
In the 10th year of her
age.
                                    by
When you our friends are passing
And this informs you where we Lie
Remember you ere long must have
Like us a mansion in the grave.

(footstone)
Miss Lucy Bush
nell and Fanny
Bushnell

1010.   In Memory of Mʳ
John Bushnell who
died Jan. 16ᵗʰ AD
1806. In the 47ᵗʰ
year of his Age

Lie here & slumber in the ground
Till the last trumpet joyfull sounds
Then burst the band with sweet sur
  prise
And in thy Saviours image rise.

(footstone)
Mʳ John
Bushnell

1011.   In Memory of Mʳ
John son to Mʳ John
Buſhnell & Mʳˢ Lucy
his wife who died
Jan. 20ᵗʰ AD 1806
In the 21ˢᵗ year of his
age.

Remember youths as you paſs by
You in the grave may shortly lie.
Death call'd for me at twenty
  one
But shorter age may call you
  home

1012.   MARY ANN
daugh of James
Lucinda Bush
nell died Oct 2
1822 aged 1 year
and 8 months.

(footstone)
M. A. B.

1013.   In memory of
Mrs.
HANNAH MEEKER
who died Dec. 1, 1824,
in the 64 year of
her age.

(footstone)
Mrs
HANNAH MEEKER

1014.   IN MEMORY OF
LUCY BUSHNELL,
relict of
John Bushnell,
WHO DIED
Dec. 6, 1840,
Aged 83.

(footstone)
L. B.

1015.   In memory of
William ſon of
Thomas & Free-
love Marſhall
who died Oct.
14ᵗʰ 1808 in the
16ᵗʰ year of his
age.

(footstone)
William
Marſhall

1016.   Broken, uninscribed, granite stone.

1017.   JAMES BUSHNELL
DIED
June 27, 1872,
AE. 80.

(footstone)
J. B.

1018.   SINDA,
wife of
James Bushnell
died Sept. 17, 1862
aged 72.

(footstone)
S. B.

1019.   Mr. John Bliſs
died March 25ᵗʰ
1815, aged 66.

(footstone)
John Bliſs

1020.   Mr. John Bliss died
April 15th 1809 aged 92.
Mrs. Sarah Bliss wife of
Mr. John Bliss died
Jan. 25th 1806, aged 85.

(footstone)
John and
Sarah Blifs

1021.   In memory of
Miss Anna L. Bliss
who died
Nov. 5, 1822,
aged 21 yrs.

(footstone)
A. L. B.

1022.   In memory
of
CHARLES L. HUNTINGTON
Son of
E. & A. HUNTINGTON
who died
Feb. 3, 1832,
in the 23rd year
of his age.

(footstone)
C. L. H.

1023.   Sacred
to the memory of Mrs.
Nabby Huntington
confort of
Eraftus Huntington Efq.
& daughter of Mr. Abiel &
Mrs. Mary Hyde
who died on the firft day
of July AD. 1811, AE. 25

(footstone)
Mrs. Nabby
Huntington

1024.   IN
memory of
ERASTUS HUNTINGTON, Esq.
WHO DIED
Feb. 10, 1846,
Aged 76.

(footstone)
E. H.

1025.   Sacred
to the memory of
Mr. Jofeph Hyde
who departed this life
Feb. 23d 1811,
aged 22.

(footstone)
Mr. Jofeph Hyde.

1026.   Sacred
to the memory of
Mifs Nancy Hyde
daughter of Mr. Abiel
& Mrs. Mary Hyde
who died Auguft 16th
AD. 1808 aged 24 years.

(footstone)
Mifs
Nancy Hyde

1027.   In memory of
Mrs. Martha Hyde
relict of
Capt James Hyde
who died
May 18th 1823,
aged 67 years.

GOD is the strength of my heart,
and my portion forever.

(footstone)
M. H.

1028.   This monument
is erected to the memory
of Capt. James Hyde who
departed this life
univerfally lamented
April 9th 1809,
aged 54 years.

(footstone)
Capt.
James Hyde

1029. In memory of
Fanny B. Hyde,
daughr of
Erastus & Fanny
Hyde, who died
Octr 8th 1816,
aged 18 years.

In her last moments she said
Prepare to follow me, farewell.
Jesus receive my spirit, Amen.

(footstone)
Fanny B.
Hyde

1030. In memory of
Eliza M. Hyde
daughter of
Erastus & Fanny Hyde,
who died
Jan. 26th 1819, aged 18 years.
She liued and died in the faith
of the Gospel.

(footstone)
E. M. Hyde.

1031. In memory of
Erastus N. Hyde
Son of Erastus
& Fanny Hyde
who died April 8th 1821,
aged 18 years.

Precious in the sight of the Lord
is the death of his saints.

(footstone)
E. N. H.

1032. JOSEPH
Son of
John & Rebecca Kinsman
of the Town of
Kinsman, Ohio,
member of the
Senior Class in
Yale College
died
June 27, 1819,
Aged 24.

(footstone)
J. K.

1033. Sarah L. Starr,
Eldeſt daughter
OF
Christopher Starr,
died Oct. 8, 1819,
aged 25.

(footstone)
S. L. S.

1034. Mary L. Starr,
Relict of
Christopher Starr,
Died
Sept. 5, 1843,
Aged 67.

1035. Sacred
to the memory of
Olive Starr, Consort of
Christopher Starr,
& Daught of
Simon Perkins,
who died
Decr 8th 1815,
aged 46 years.

(footstone)
Olive Starr

1036. In memory of
Christopher Starr,
WHO DIED
Dec. 16, 1827,
aged 61 years.

(footstone)
C. S.

1037. FATHER
ABIEL B. SHERMAN
BORN
in Hopkington, R. I.
DIED
in Norwich, Ct.
Aged 87.

Resurgam.

(footstone)
A. B. S.

GENERALS HUNTINGTON TOMB, 1852
"The Family Tomb of the Honorable Jabez Huntington, Esq., who died Oct. 5, 1786, aged 67 years"
SEE PAGE 95

GENERALS HUNTINGTON TOMB, 1933
SEE PAGE 95

1038.
MOTHER
JULIA HAZARD
WIFE OF
A. B. SHERMAN,
Born in Newport, R. I.
Died in Norwich, Ct.
Aged 72.

"Blessed are the pure in heart for they shall see God."

(footstone)
J. H. S.

1039. Entered into rest
ALMIRA J. HAZARD
daughter of
Carder & Sarah Hazard
Feb. 16, 1884.

"Until the day break and the shadows flee away."

(footstone)
A. J. H.

1040. SACRED
to the memory of
SARAH ELIZA,
daughter of
Carder & Sarah Hazard
who died
July 3, 1858,
aged 45 years.

(footstone)
S. E. H.

1041. In memory of
JOANNA R.
daughter of
Abial B. & Julia S.
SHERMAN
who departed this life
Sept. 6, 1835,
Aged 18 months.

(footstone)
J. R. S.

1042. (Tablestone)
In memory of
Mr. CARDER HAZARD,
late of
Newport, Rhode Island,
who died
March 18, 1823,
aged 43 years.

1043. (Tablestone)
In memory of
Mrs. SARAH HAZARD
wife of
Mr. Carder Hazard
and daughter of the late
William Coggeshall Esqr
of Bristol, Rhode Island,
who died 29th Nov. 1817,
in the 34th year of her age

1044. Carder
Son of Carder
& Sarah Hazard
died June 16th
1815, aged 9
months & 13 D^s

(footstone)
C. H.

1045. SACRED
to the memory of
GEORGE CARDER
third Son of
Carder & Sarah Hazard
who died
March 5, 1840,
Aged 22 years.

ALSO
In memory of
WILLIAM COGGESHALL
First Son of
Carder & Sarah Hazard
who died
in Middletown, R. I. Nov. 6, 1807,
Aged 3 months.
Buried in Newport.

(footstone)
G. C. H.

1046. In memory of
Capt. Joſeph Hoſmer
who departed this
life July 23ᵈ 1803 in
the 39ᵗʰ year of
his age

(footstone)
Capt. Joſeph
Hoſmer

1047. In memory of
Mr. Henry Culver,
who departed this
life Sept. 29ᵗʰ 1808
aged 24 years.

(footstone)
Mr
Henry Culver

1048. ORRIN H. BILL
only Son and child of
Chester & Mira Bill
who died
Sept. 5, 1840,
AEt 25.

O happy dead in Christ that sleep
While o'er their smouldering dust we weep.

(footstone)
O. H. B.

1049. CHESTER BILL
DIED
Aug. 29, 1867,
aged 79 years.

(footstone)
C. B.

1050. MIRA
wife of
Chester Bill,
died Dec. 13, 1863,
aged 71 years,
10 mos. & 20 days.

(footstone)
M. B.

1051. Sacred
to the memory of
Miss Betsey Lathrop
who died
Octʳ. 13, 1822,
aged 64 years.

The sweet remembrance of the just
Shall flourish when they sleep in dust.

(footstone)
B. L.

1052. Sacred
to the memory of
Mʳ Jonathan Lathrop
who died
Dec. 14, 1817,
aged 83 years.

your fathers, where are they?
and the prophets do they live forever?

(footstone)
Mʳ Jonathan
Lathrop

1053. Sacred
to the memory of
Mrs. Thede Lathrop,
Consort of
Mʳ Jonathan Lathrop
who died
Decʳ 22, 1816,
aged 80 years.

Farewell my friends and children dear
Prepare for Death while I sleep here.

(footstone)
Mʳˢ Thede
Lathrop

1054. BELA PECK,
died Dec. 15, 1850,
aged 92 years.

(footstone)
B. P.

1055. SACRED
to the Memory of
BETSEY
the wife of
Bela Peck
died Nov. 24, 1818,
Aged 54 years.

How exemplary her life how unshaken
her faith, how peaceful her death,
how glorious her immortality.
Who would not die the death of the righteous.

(footstone)
B. P.

1056. In memory of
Wm Peck Williams,
Son of W^m &
Harriet Williams,
who died
February 27th 1815,
aged 1 year
& 9 months.

(footstone)
W. P. W.

1057. SACRED
to the memory of
LYDIA
the wife of
BELA PECK
died August 18, 1835,
Aged 68 years.

(footstone)
L. P.

1058. SACRED
to the memory of
Mrs. Lydia Lathrop
Consort of
Mr. Darious Lathrop,
who died
March 22^d AD. 1814,
aged 55 years.

(footstone)
Mrs
Lydia
Lathrop

1059. Sacred
to the memory of
DARIUS LATHROP
who died
Sept. 15, 1827,
aged 67 years.

(footstone)
D. L.

1060. In memory of
Mrs. Rebecca Lathrop,
wife of
Mr. Ezra Lathrop,
& daugh^r of Elijah
Huntington Esqr of
Bozrah. She died
May 25th 1812,
aged 39 years.

(footstone)
Mrs.
Rebecca
Lathrop

1061. memory of
hilip Huntington
who died
Feb. 4, 1825
aged 54.

(footstone)
P. H.

1062. In memory of
Mrs. Phila
wife of
Philip Huntington
who died
Nov. 30, 1806,
aged 38.

(footstone)
P. H.

1063. In memory of Mr.
untington,
fon of
ntington, Efq
ary his wife
ied Oct. 12th
e 30th year
age.

(footstone)
Mr. Daniel
Huntington

1064. Tho Jefferson
son of
Eleazer &
Lucy Rogers
died May 15, 1810,
aged 3 years & 1 mo.
take thy rest;
Sleep on sweet babe and
shalt be blest.
For God hath said thou

(footstone)
T. J. R.

1065. In memory of
M Lu ers
daughter of Mr. James
& M ers
who died April 1803
in the 35th year of her
age

(footstone)
Mifs Lucy
Rogers

1066. In
memory of
Mrs. Hannah, consort
of Mr. Jabez Bushnal
& daugtr of Mr. James
Rogers, who died Janry
21st 1815, in the 39th
year of her
age.

(footstone)
H. B.

1067. In
memory of
Mrs Zilpah, consort of
Mr. James Rogers, who
died March 10th 1814
in the 77th year of
her age.

(footstone)
Z. R.

1068. In memory of
Mr. JAMES ROGERS
WHO DIED
Sept. 28, 1821,
aged 82 years.

(footstone)
J. R.

1069. SARAH,
daughter of
Eleazer Rogers
& Lucy Edgerton;
born Sept. 27, 1793,
died July 16, 1859.

"I know that my Redeemer liveth."

(footstone)
S. R.

1070. LUCY,
Wife of
Eleazer Rogers,
DIED
Feb. 28, 1851,
in the 89th year
of her age.

Rest in hope.

(footstone)
L. R.

1071. SACRED
to the memory of
ELEAZER ROGERS Esq.
WHO DIED
June 24, 1843,
in the 80 year
of his age.

(footstone)
E. R.

1072. Mary
daugr of Ezra
& Rebecca
Lathrop died
May 17th 1802,
aged 1 year.

(footstone)
M. L.

1073. Jane E.
daugr of Ezra
& Rebecca
Lathrop died
Jan. 14th 1810,
aged 6 months.

1074. MARIA
daughter of
Henry C. &
Maria Rogers,
DIED
Aug 6, 1832,
AE. 3 months.

(footstone)
M. R.

1075. CORNELIA J.
only Child of
Wm. L. & Mary P.
KINGSLEY
DIED
Dec. 7, 1831,
AGED
2 Ys. & 24 ds.

This little bud so young and fair
Called home by early doom
Just came to show how sweet a flower
In Paradise will bloom.

(footstone)
C. J. K.

1076. In memory of
Hannah daughter
of Jeremiah & Ly
dia Lathrop who
died Feb. 13th 1802,
aged 12 years &
5 months

(footstone)
Hannah
Lathrop

1077. In memory of
Mr.
Jeremiah Lathrop,
who died
Dec. 30th 1816,
aged 69 years.

(footstone)
Mr.
Jerh
Lathrop

1078. In memory of
Mrs. Lydia, relict of
Mr. Jeremiah Lathrop,
who died
March 24th 1819,
aged 69 years.

(footstone)
L. L.

1079. In memory of
Mrs. Lydia Fox, wife
of Mr. Ezekiel Fox of
Montville, who died
Jan. 29th 1805, aged 24
years.

Eunice C. Fox daughter of
Mr. Ezekiel & Mrs. Lydia
Fox, died Aug. 12th 1804,
aged 15 weeks.

(footstone)
Mrs. Lydia
Fox

1080. Mr. Ebenezer Lord departed this life July 3d 1800, aged 70 years.

(footstone)
Mr. Ebn Lord

1081. Mrs. Temperance, relict of Mr. Ebenezer Lord, departed this life March 26th 1804 aged 64 Years.

(footstone)
Mrs. Tempe
Lord

1082. SAMUEL HUNTINGTON,
died June 23, 1812,
aged 65.
PHILURA TRACY,
his wife
deid Aug. 30, 1816,
aged 65.

(footstone)
S. H.
P. T. H.

1083. In memory of
ABBY L. LATHROP
WHO DIED
March 2, 1835,
Aged 46.

(footstone)
A. L. L.

1084. In
Memory of
Burrel Lathrop
Who died
Sept 17, 1840,
Aged 45.

God is just.

(footstone)
B. L.

1085. MARGARET F. LATHROP
died
Aug. 24, 1863,
aged 76.

(footstone)
M. F. L.

1086. BETSY LATHROP
BORN
Sept. 12, 1784,
DIED
March 9, 1870.

LUCY L. LATHROP
DIED
Dec. 5, 1874,
aged 93.

(footstone)
B. L.

1087. HENRY B. HARRIS,
BORN
Nov. 12, 1814,
DIED
Nov. 30, 1855.

(footstone)
H. B. H.

1088. RUFUS
HUNTINGTON,
DIED
Sept. 21, 1832,
AGED 69.

(footstone)
R. H.

1089. LUCRETIA
HUNTINGTON
DIED
Sept. 2, 1826,
AGED 77.

(footstone)
L. H.

1090. CHARLES,
son of
Thomas & Mary
Thomas died
Aug. 19, 1825,
aged 1 year.

(footstone)
C. T.

1091. GURDON,
son of Thomas
& Mary Thomas
died Oct. 16th 1820,
aged 1 year
& 6 Mos

I take these little lambs said he
And lay them on my breast;
Protection they shall find in me
In me be ever blest.

(footstone)
G. T.

1092. JOHN AUSTIN
son of
Thomas & Mary
Thomas died
Nov. 26, 1824,
aged 20 mos.

(footstone)
J. A. T.

1093. CAROLINE EUNICE,
died Jan. 7, 1827,
aged 5 years.
CAROLINE,
died April 29, 1827,
aged 1 month.
Children of Thomas
& Mary Thomas.

(footstone)
C. E.

1094. Sacred to the memory of
Thomas L. Thomas,
who died May 17, 1829, in
the 70th year of his age.
Also Annie his wife who
died Aug. 5, 1825, in the
60th year of her age.
Blessed are the dead which die
in the Lord, from henceforth: yea
saith the spirit, that they may
rest from their labours; and
their works do follow them.

(footstone)
T. L. T.
A. T.

1095. Harriet L. Strong,
daughter of
Joseph H. and
Lucretia Strong,
born June 26th 1811,
died January
23d 1820.

(footstone)
H. L. S.

1096. George A. Strong,
son of
Joseph H. and
Lucretia Strong
born February
6th 1816, died
July 2d 1820.

(footstone)
C. A. S.

1097. In
memory of
CHARLES H. STRONG,
who was born
Nov. 30, 1808,
and died
Sept. 16, 1839.

(footstone)
C. H. S.

1098. ANNE GOODELL
Born
Dec. 23, 1787,
Died
Sept. 6, 1874.

(footstone)
A. G.

1099. In
Memory of
MRS MARY STRONG,
Widow of
REV. JOSEPH STRONG, D. D.
Born
March 24, 1760,
Died
May 14, 1840.
"Mary hath chosen that good part, which shall
not be taken away from her."

(footstone)
M. S.

135

1100. In
Memory of
REV. JOSEPH STRONG, D. D.
Pastor of the first
Congregational Church in Norwich,
who died Dec. 18, 1834,
in the 82nd year of his age
and the 57th year of his ministry.

"Blessed are the dead which die in the Lord
from henceforth: Yea, saith the spirit, that
they may rest from their labours; and
their works do follow them."

(footstone)
J. S.

1101. WILLIAM GOODELL
Born
May 21, 1795,
Died
Dec. 20, 1871

(footstone)
W. G.

1102. In memory of
SARAH
wife of
Silas Goodell
who died Dec. 11, 1822,
aged 65 years.

(footstone)
S. G.

1103. In memory of
Capt. SILAS GOODELL
who died
March 20, 1825,
aged 77 years.

(footstone)
S. G.

1104. GERARD F. CARPENTER,
DIED
Aug 6, 1861,
Aged 82.

"I know that my Redeemer liveth."

(footstone)
G. F. C.

1105. REBECCA E.
wife of
GERARD F. CARPENTER,
DIED
Feb. 8, 1867,
aged 77 years.

In hope eternal life.

(footstone)
R. H. C.

1106. ANNE
daughter of
JOSEPH & EUNICE CARPENTER,
Born
May 15, 1782,
Died
April 10, 1852.

"I have put my trust in the Lord God."

(footstone)
A. C.

1107. SARAH GOODELL
Born
Feb. 25, 1793,
Died
Feb. 4, 1879.

(footstone)
S. G.

1108. IN MEMORY OF
ABEL GRISWOLD
WHO DIED
Feb. 14, 1839,
AEt. 76.

(footstone)
A. G.

1109. IN MEMORY OF
Mrs. ESTHER
wife of
Mr. ABEL GRISWOLD
WHO DIED
March 11th 1840,
AEt. 71.

(footstone)
E. G.

1110. Mrs. Lydia Fosdick
wife of
Mr. Alvan Fosdick
born Dec. 26, 1749
died Nov. 28, 1825

(footstone)
L. F.

1111. In memory of
HARRIET
wife of
Henry Holt
of Spring Gardens,
Rochdale, Lancashire, England,
died in Yantic Vill.
July 15, 1853,
aged 22.

Our Sister the haven hath gained,
Out plying the tempest and wind,
Her rest she hath sooner obtained
And left her companions behind.

(footstone)
H. H.

1112. LYDIA L. BLISS
BORN
Jan 12, 1807,
DIED
Feb. 18, 1884.

(footstone)
L. L. B.

1113. In
Memory of
Mr. Zephaniah Bliss,
WHO DIED
Aug. 7, 1827,
aged 74 years.

(footstone)
Z. B.

1114. In
Memory of
Mrs. TEMPERANCE
relict of
Mr. Zeph. Bliss,
WHO DIED
Sept. 7, 1830,
aged 66 years.

(footstone)
T. B.

1115. GEORGE BLISS,
BORN
November 25, 1804,
DIED
September 12, 1857.

(footstone)
G. B.

1116. SARAH BLISS
BORN
May 4, 1798,
Died
October 12, 1875.

(footstone)
S. B.

1117. SARAH,
daughter of
John & Abby W.
Bliss,
died July 31,
1837,
aged 2 years
& 51 days.

(footstone)
S. B.

1118. DR. DAVID ROGERS,
SURGEON IN THE ARMY OF THE
REVOLUTION.
BORN IN NORWALK.
DIED IN NORWICH
JUNE 21 1829,
AGED 89 YRS.

ERECTED BY HIS GRANDSON
WILLIS R. AUSTIN

(footstone)
D. R.

1119. ELIAS VAN BUREN,
SON OF
Henry H. and
Almira Shepard,
died Jan. 8, 1838,
aged 16 months.

I take these little lambs said He
And lay them on my breast
Protection they shall find in me
In me be ever blest.

(footstone)
E. S.

1120. IN
Memory of
Miss SALLY G.
daughter of
Elias & Sally Shepard
DIED
May 1, 1850,
AE. 45.

(footstone)
S. G. S.

1121. IN
Memory of
Miss HARRIET K.
SHEPARD,
who died Jan. 10th,
1837.
Aged 34 Yr's.

(footstone)
H. K. S.

1122. IN
Memory of
Mrs. SALLY SHEPARD,
Consort of
Mr. Elias Shepard,
who died
June 10, 1838,
Aged 62.

(footstone)
S. S.

1123. In memory of
MR
ELIAS SHEPARD
who departed this life
June 25, 1835,
in the 58th year
of his age.

Now he resides where Jesus is
Above this dusty sphere
His soul was ripened for that bliss
While yet he lingered here

(footstone)
E. S.

1124. Wm. GREEN,
died Nov. 8, 1881,
aged 80 Yrs. 20 ds
Also his wife
SARAH GREEN
born Mar. 30, 1818.

A present.

(footstone)
W. G.

1125. IN
Memory of
GEORGE THOMAS
Son of
Ebenezer Thomas,
who died
Feb. 2, 1841,
Aged 53.

1126. IN
Memory of
Doct.
Joseph Thomas,
who died
April 20, 1840,
AEt. 68 y's.

(footstone)
J. T.

1127. In memory of
PHEBE THOMAS
consort of
Doct. Joseph Thomas,
who departed this life
Jan. 1, 1827,
in her 44 year.

(footstone)
P. T.

1128. IN
MEMORY OF
CHARLES THOMAS,
Born Feb. 14, 1783,
died Sept. 5, 1835.

(footstone)
C. T.

1129. NANCY CAREW
was born
Feb. 13, 1772,
DIED
Aug. 26, 1851.

(footstone)
N. C.

1130. CHARLES CAREW,
WAS BORN
July 2, 1774,
DIED
June 10, 1842,
Aged 68.

(footstone)
C. C.

1131. THOMAS CAREW,
was born
Feb. 28, 1793,
DIED
Dec. 29, 1851.

(footstone)
T. C.

1132. MARY ANN STRONG,
Wife of
O. E. HUNTINGTON,
daughter of
JOSEPH H. & LUCRETIA
STRONG,
died 23 Nov. 1840,
Aged 33.

Looking for the mercy of our Lord Jesus Christ unto eternal life.

(footstone)
M. S. H.

1133. Miss Abigail
Gardiner
died
Jan. 19, 1823,
aged 75 years.

(footstone)
A. G.

1134. Mrs. MEHITABLE,
relict of
Mr
EBENEZER CAREW
Who died
Aug. 28, 1841,
in her 89 year.

(footstone)
M. C.

1135. To the
memory
of
DANIEL CARPENTER
who departed this life
June 11, 1837,
aged 43 years.

When ling'ring pains his bosom tore
Resign'd he kiss'd the chast'ning rod
Each mortal pang with meekness bore
And smil'd in death to meet his God.

1136. In memory of
WALTER R. LESTER
Son of
Walter & Mary Ann
LESTER,
WHO DIED
Oct. 14, 1831, in the
20th year of his age.

Them also which sleep in Jesus
Will God bring unto him.

(footstone)
W. R. L.

1137. Ann G.
daughter of
Walter &
Mary Ann Lester,
died April 12, 1829,
aged 5 years.

(footstone)
A. G. L.

1138. Ann,
daughter of
Walter &
Mary Ann Lester,
died Oct. 4, 1823,
aged 2 years.

(footstone)
A. L.

1139. Sarah Eliza,
daughter of
Walter &
Mary Ann Lester,
died Sept. 10, 1824,
in the 12 year
of her age.

(footstone)
S. E. L.

1140. Joseph Carpenter,
son of
Walter &
Mary Ann Lester,
died Sept. 20, 1824,
in the 10 year
of his age.

(footstone)
J. C. L.

1141. Harriet,
daughter of
Walter &
Mary Ann Lester,
died Sept. 26, 1824,
aged 5 years.

(footstone)
H. L.

1142. Sacred
to the memory of
Mary Ann
wife of
Walter Lester,
& daughter of the late
Mr. Joseph Carpenter,
who died Oct. 17, 1828,
aged 43 years.

Heaven waits not the last moment; owns her friends
on this side death, and points them out to men.

(footstone)
M. A. L.

1143. WALTER LESTER,
BORN
March 29, 1782,
DIED
Feb. 26, 1851.

Into thine hand I commit my spirit: thou hast
Redeemed me, O Lord God of truth.

(footstone)
W. L.

1144. STEPHEN D. JOHNSON
DIED
June 12, 1849,
aged 28.

Sweet is the scene where Christians die,
Where holy souls retire to rest,
How mildly beams the closing eye,
How gently heaves the expiring breast.

(footstone)
S. D. J.

1145. ANN MARIA
Wife of
Stephen D. Johnson,
DIED
June 16, 1880,
Aged 58.

"Come unto Me all ye that
Labor and are heavy laden
And I will give you rest."

(footstone)
A. M.

1146. DAVID A.
SON OF
Thomas & Julia Ann
BILLINGS,
DIED
Oct. 12, 1833,
AE. 6 years.

So fades the lovely blooming flower,
Frail smiling solace of an hour;
So soon our transient comforts fly,
And pleasure only blooms to die.

(footstone)
D. A. B.

1147. In
Memory of
Mifs Anne Tracy,
who died
July 8, 1825,
in her 74 year.

(footstone)
A. T.

1148. In
Memory of
Mifs Lois Tracy,
who died
Dec. 13, 1825,
aged 70 years.

(footstone)
L. T.

1149. WM. GEORGE TRACY,
DIED
Oct. 28, 1834,
Aged 38.

(footstone)
W. G. T.

1150. DEDICATED
TO
the memory
of
URIAH TRACY,
WHO DIED
Sept. 12, 1832,
Aged 79.

(footstone)
U. T.

1151. In
Memory of
Mr. ELIAB HYDE,
who died
Sept. 22, 1829,
aged 69 years.

(footstone)
E. H.

1152. In
Memory of
Mrs. LYDIA HYDE,
relict of
Mr. Eliab Hyde,
who died
Oct. 26, 1833,
aged 65 years.

(footstone)
L. H.

1153. In
Memory of
LUCY ANN HYDE,
who died
Sept. 18, 1852,
aged 41 years.

(footstone)
L. A. H.

1154. In memory of
Mrs. ANNA,
relict of
Dea. Caleb Huntington,
who died Sept. 17, 1851,
aged 89.

(footstone)
A. H.

1155. DEACON
CALEB HUNTINGTON,
DIED
March 1, 1842,
Aged 93.

"The Righteous hath hope in his death."

(footstone)
C. H.

1156. In memory of
SOPHIA HUNTINGTON,
who died June 9, 1853,
aged 56.
Also of
LOUISA E. HUNTINGTON,
who died Aug. 6, 1854,
aged 52.
Children of
Rev. Lynde Huntington,
of Bradford, Conn.

(footstone)
S. H.
L. E. H.

1157. In memory of
Mrs. ELIZABETH
relict of
Mr. Ebenezer Hyde,
who died
Sept. 1, 1825,
aged 71 years.

(footstone)
E. H.

1158. Wm HENRY
son of
Orrimille &
Anna Mabrey,
died Sept. 20, 1823,
aged 2 years
& 6 mos.

(footstone)
W. H. M.

1159. ANNA
wife of
Oramel Mabrey
died May 8, 1876,
aged 80 years.

(footstone)
A. M.

1160. ORINELL MABREY
Died Nov. 18,
1867,
aged 71.

(footstone)
O. M.

1161. ANNA
LANCASTER,
died
Sept. 22, 1831,
AE. 77.

(footstone)
A. L.

1162. Mrs. THANKFULL S.
MABREY,
E
Feb. 24, 1848,
aged 82.

(footstone)
T. S. M.

1163. In
Memory of
Mr. Simon Backus,
who died
April 25, 1823,
in his 31 year.

(footstone)
S. B.

1164. Sacred
To the memory of
Mr. Asa Backus,
who died
Dec. 26, 1829,
aged 67 years.

(footstone)
A. B.

1165. Sacred
To the memory of
Mrs. Parthena,
wife of Asa Backus,
who died
Oct. 25, 1807,
aged 40 years.

(footstone)
P. B.

1166. In
Memory of
ASA BACKUS,
WHO DIED
June 5, 1836,
Aged 33.

(footstone)
A. B.

1167. Sarah Jane
daughter of
Asa &
Caroline Backus
died Sept. 7, 1830,
aged 16 months.

(footstone)
S. J. B.

1168. LUCY ANN,
daughter of
Lewis &
Mary Hyde
died Oct. 9, 1825,
aged 10 months.

(footstone)
L. A. H.

1169. NANCY
WIDOW OF
JOS. S. HUNTINGTON

1170. In
MEMORY OF
ERASTUS WATERMAN,
WHO DIED
March 16, 1850,
aged 77 years.

(footstone)
E. W.

1171. In
MEMORY OF
EBER BACKUS ESQ.
WHO DIED
May 30, 1845,
in his 77th year.

(footstone)
E. B.

1172.　　　　In
MEMORY OF
EUNICE BACKUS,
relict of
Eber Backus Esq.
WHO DIED
Sept. 3, 1846,
in her 82d year.

(footstone)
E. B.

1173.　　　SACRED
TO THE MEMORY OF
OUR FATHER
WILLIAM D. LEE,
DIED
JAN 23, 1861,
AGED 45 YRS.

(footstone)
W. D. L.

1174.　　GEORGE W. LEE,
Born
4th July 1776,
Died
29th 1850.

ROBERT M.
Son of
George W. & Susan Lee,
Died in Texas,
20th Oct. 1838,
Aged 21.

(footstone)
G. W. L.

1175.　　　SACRED
TO THE MEMORY OF
GEORGE W. LEE,
WHO WAS BORN
SEPT. 30, 1807,
DIED
AUG. 5, 1865.

(footstone)
G. W. L.

1176.　　　Asa Fitch,
son of
George W. &
Susannah Lee,
died
Aug. 25, 1825,
aged 12 years.

(footstone)
A. F. L.

1177.　　　James E.
son of
George W. &
Susannah Lee,
died
July 23, 1824,

7 months.

(footstone)
J. E. L.

1178.　　　In memory of
Harriet F. Tracy
only daughter of
Doct. P. & Mrs. A. Tracy,
who was born Sept. 3, 1788,
and died universally lamented,
April 25, 1830.

She sure has gone to realms above,
Where Joy, eternal reigns,
To join in praise of Saviour's love,
In songs of Seraph strains.

(footstone)
H. F. T.

1179　DR. RICHARD P. TRACY,
Born March 21,
1791,
Died March 17,
1871.

(footstone)
R. P. T.

1180. DR. PHILEMON TRACY,
died
April 26, 1837,
aged 80 years.

A good man out of the good treasure of the heart bringeth forth good things.

(footstone)
P. T.

1181. MRS. ABIGAIL TRACY
relict of
Doct. Philemon Tracy
died
Aug. 20, 1838,
Aged 79 years.

"Blessed are the pure in heart for they shall see God."

(footstone)
A. T.

1182. LYDIA TROTT,
died
August, 1828,
Aged 70 years.

(footstone)
L. T.

1183. In
Memory of
SARAH TRACY,
daughter of
Jared and Margaret
TRACY,
Born Feb. 10, 1767,
Died
Oct. 27, 1838,
Aged 71.

(footstone)
S. T.

1184. In
Memory of
JOSEPH W. TRACY,
BORN
March 9, 1773,
DIED
April 3, 1845,
Aged 72.

(footstone)
J. W. T.

1185. In
Memory of
WEALTHY,
Widow of
Joseph W. Tracy,
BORN
January 8, 1780,
DIED
July 14, 1849,
Aged 69.

1186. In
Memory of
SARAH G.
daughter of
JOSEPH W. & WEALTHY
TRACY,
who died 25 May 1838,
in the 19 year
of her age.

(footstone)
S. G. T.

1187. DINAH PALMER,
Wife of
Cory K. Lewis
DIED
March 2, 1844,
AE. 41 yrs.
& 5 m's.

(footstone)
D. P.
L.

1188. CORY K. LEWIS,
DIED
Nov. 28, 1842,
AE. 47.

(footstone)
C. K. L.

1189. EUNICE
daughter of
Asa H. &
Emily Birchard
died Aug. 25, 1829,
aged 15 months.

(footstone)
E. B.

1190. In memory of
Mr. John Birchard,
who died
Nov. 14th 1822,
aged 56 years.

God is just, supreme his power:
Mortals be silent, and adore.

(footstone)
J. B.

1191. In
Memory of
Mr. Joseph W. Birchard,
who died
Nov. 27, 1826,
aged 27 years.

(footstone)
J. W. B.

1192. ADALINE J.
daughter of
Thomas T. &
Emily T. Willcox
died
July 26, 1832,
aged 7 weeks

1193. In
Memory of
John W. Birchard
who died
Dec. 20, 1828,
aged 21 years.

(footstone)
J. W. B.

1194. Mrs. EMILY T.
Wife of
Mr. Thos. T. Willcox,
died July 30,
1833,
aged 24 years.

(footstone)
E. T. W.

1195. In memory of
Mrs. Judith Lord,
wife of Mr.
Hez. Lord,
who died
Jan. 28, 1824,
aged 84 years.

(footstone)
J. L.

1196. In memory of
Mr. Hezekiah Lord,
who died
Nov. 11, 1824,
aged 84 years.

(footstone)
H. L.

1197. HENRY EDWIN LORD,
Son of
Henry & Sarah B. Lord,
DIED
September 5, 1849,
Aged 22 years.

Not lost—but gone before.

(footstone)
H. E. L.

1198.
In
Memory of
SARAH B. LORD,
relict of
Henry Lord,
who died
June 5, 1843,
Aged 44.

(footstone)
S. B. L.

1199.
In
Memory of
HENRY LORD,
who died
Nov. 3, 1838,
Aged 48.

(footstone)
H. L.

1200.
In memory of
Thos. J. Huntington,
who died
Oct. 1, 1824,
aged 23 years.

Life is uncertain death is sure
Sin is the wound but Christ is the cure.

(footstone)
T. J. H.

1201.
In
memory
of
MARY COOK
wife of
SILAS BABCOCK,
who died
Nov. 21, 1882,
aged 97.

(footstone)
M. C. B.

1202.
In
memory
of
SILAS BABCOCK
who died
Aug. 13, 1838,
aged 75.
Formerly of Westerly, R. I.

(footstone)
S. B.

1203.
GEORGE F. PERKINS,
born
Aug. 3, 1828,
died
May 29, 1877.

(footstone)
G. F. P.

1204.
In
Memory of
REV. GEORGE PERKINS,
who died
Sept. 17, 1852,
aged 69.

"The rightious hath hope in his death."

(footstone)
G. P.

1205.
In
Memory of
BETSEY H.
wife of
Rev. George Perkins,
and daughter of
Dr. John Turner, deceased
who died
Nov. 18, 1838,
aged 45.

(footstone)
B. H. P.

1206. In
Memory of
DR. JOHN TURNER,
WHO DIED
May 7, 1837,
Aged 73.

The righteous hath hope in his death.

(footstone)
J. T.

1207. In
Memory of
HANNAH TURNER
Relict of
Doct. John Turner,
WHO DIED
May 7, 1845,
Aged 80.

(footstone)
H. T.

1208. HANNAH H.
Daughter of
George & Marionette
PERKINS,
BORN
May 1, 1820,
DIED
May 12, 1842,
Aged 22.

(footstone)
H. H. P.

1209. MRS. ABIGAIL
Relict of
Mr. John Pierce,
DIED
Dec. 5, 1845,
Aged 85.

(footstone)
A. P.

1210. ANN M. LATHROP
DIED
Oct. 14, 1839,
AE. 39.

(footstone)
A. M. L.

1211. FRANK T. LATHROP,
DIED
May 13, 1832,
AE. 34.

(footstone)
F. T. L.

1212. CORNELIA S. WILLIS,
DIED
June 20, 1849,
AE. 44.

(footstone)
C. S. W.

(Table Tomb)
1213. DANIEL LATHROP
Born
October 13, 1769,
Died
July 13, 1825,
BETSY LATHROP
Wife of
DANIEL LATHROP
Born
May 15, 1774,
Died
October 10, 1850.

1214. JAMES T. RICHARDS,
DIED
Dec. 13, 1838,
Aged 31.

"Justified by faith."

(footstone)
J. T. R.

1215. ANN T. RICHARDS,
relict of
James T. Richards
DIED
Sept. 5, 1843,
Aged 37.

"Saved by Grace."

(footstone)
A. R.

1216. ELIZABETH T. RICHARDS
only daughter of
James T. & Ann T. Richards,
BORN
Feb. 12, 1837,
DIED
Jan. 29, 1845

For of such is the kingdom of Heaven.

(footstone)
E. T. R.

1217. THOMAS TRACY RICHARDS,
only Son of
James T. & Ann T.
RICHARDS,
born 28 Sept. 1835,
Died
25 December 1851.

All these died in faith.

(footstone)
T. T. R.

1218. SACRED
To
the memory of
MARGARET
daughter of
the late Fred^k
& Deborah Tracy
who died
Sept. 30, 1832.
Aged 45.

(footstone)
M. T.

1219. SACRED
To
the memory of
ELIZABETH,
daughter of the late
Fred^k & Deborah
TRACY,
who died Aug. 14,
1841, Aged 57.

"Blessed are the dead
Who die in the Lord."

(footstone)
E. T.

1220. IN
MEMORY OF
MRS. ALICE
Wife of
HENRY TRACY,
WHO DIED
Dec. 12, 1848,
aged 73 years.

"Her children rise up and call her blessed."

(footstone)
A. T.

1221. IN
MEMORY OF
HENRY TRACY
WHO DIED
May 21, 1846,
Aged 73.
ALSO
FRANCIS C. TRACY,
who died at Guayama, Porto Rico,
Feb. 27, 1846,
Aged 42.

(footstone)
H. T.

1222. MARY E. TRACY,
daughter of
Henry & Alice
TRACY,
Died Nov. 1, 1840,
Aged 42.

"Blessed are the dead who
die in the Lord."

(footstone)
M. E. T.

1223. HARRIET S.
daughter of
Abner &
Harriet S. Bassett,
died Sept. 6, 1828,
aged 4 months
& 4 days

(footstone)
H. S. B.

1224. SARAH G.
DAUGHTER OF
STEPHEN AND NANCY
ALLEN
DIED JAN. 2, 1889,
AGED 58 YRS.

ASLEEP IN JESUS

1225. OUR MOTHER
NANCY ALLEN,
Born June 4, 1791,
Died Aug. 10, 1864.
In my father's house are
many mansions.

(footstone)
N. A.

1226. OUR FATHER
STEPHEN ALLEN,
Born April 20, 1791,
Died July 24, 1864.
I know that my Redeemer
liveth.

(footstone)
S. A.

1227. In
Memory of
RACHEL
wife of
George S. Lincoln,
who died
Nov. 10, 1852,
aged 32.

Jesus can make a dying bed
Feel soft as downy pillows are,
While on his breast I lean my head
And breath my life out sweetly there.

(footstone)
R. L.

1228. George W. Potter
Died Jan. 27, 1824,
aged 25.

        down
In youthful bloom death laid me
There to wait the trumpets sound
When God has call'd I must arise
To meet my Saviour in the skys.

(footstone)
G. W. P.

1229. Mrs. AMY CROCKER
Died
May 12, 1828,
aged 57 years.
"Blessed are the dead
Which die in the Lord."

(footstone)
A. C.

1230. Mrs. Mary Williams,
Died
April 15, 1831,
Aged 90 years.

(footstone)
M. W.

1231. IN
Memory of
MISS
MARY WILLIAMS
WHO DIED
Aug. 12, 1835,
Aged 71.

(footstone)
M. W.

1232. In
Memory of
VASHTI WILLIAMS,
who died
July 19, 1851,
aged 76.

(footstone)
V. W.

1232a. OUR DARLING
BARCKEVE LEVONIAN
MARCH 20, 1894,
SEPT. 3, 1898.

1233. CHARLES A.
son of
Chas T. & Catherine C.
Hopkins,
died Aug. 1, 1852,
AE. 6 weeks & 4 d'ys

Sleep on sweet babe
And take thy rest
God called thee home
He thought it best.

(footstone)
C. A. H.

1234. CATHERINE C.
wife of
Chas T. Hopkins,
DIED
June 20, 1852,
aged 24.

Early in life she sought the Lord,
And found salvation sweet,
But now she's gone to heaven above
To bow at Jesus' feet.

(footstone)
C. C. H.

1235. HARRIET E.
daughter of
Gilbert H. & Hannah
Tanner
died Aug. 26, 1851,
aged 11 mos.

She died to sin, she died to care
But for a moment felt the rod
Then rising on the viewless air
Spread her light wings & soared to God.

(footstone)
H. E. T.

1236. MARGARET
daughter of
Gilbert H. & Hannah
Tanner,
died Sept. 9, 1855,
aged 8 mo's & 15 d's.

Ere sin could blight or sorrow fade
Death came with friendly care;
The opening bud to heaven conveyed,
And bade it blossom there.

(footstone)
M. T.

1237. IN MEMORY OF
MARTHA
Wife of David Wright, Esq
Late of New London, died
Mar. 7, 1836, aged 70.

RUSSELL H. WRIGHT,
Lost at Sea
Sept. 1810, aged 18.

WILLIAM H. WRIGHT,
died in New York
June 13, 1832, aged 38.
Sons of David & Martha
WRIGHT.

MARY ANN WRIGHT
daughter of Wm. H. Wright
died in Norwich Dec. 13,
1833, Aged 11 years.

(footstone)
WRIGHT

1238. OUR SISTER
NANCY E.
WIFE OF
YLDEFONSO V. LARRAZA
AND DAUGHTER OF
STEPHEN AND NANCY
ALLEN,
DIED MARCH 12, 1884,
AGED 65 YRS 9 MS.

"She sleeps in peace."

"God giveth his beloved sleep."

(footstone)
N. E. L.

1239. YLDEFONSO S.
SON OF
Yldefonso V. &
Nancy E. Larraza
DIED
Aug. 15, 1842,
AEt 14 Months
& 17 days.

"Suffer this little one to come to me
Forbid it not
These opening flowers I need
To beautify the Paradise above."

(footstone)
Y. S. L.

1240. HARRIET A.
DAUGHTER OF
Jonathan W. & Delia A.
BROOKS
died Sept. 2, 1847,
AE 3 yrs & 10 ms.

Sweetly sleep.

(footstone)
H. A. B.

1241. In
Memory of
ELIZABETH A.
Wife of
Doct. Jonathan Brooks,
who died
June 6, 1839,
Aged 27.

(footstone)
E. A. B.

1242. ELIZABETH COIT,
Wife of
Daniel L. Coit,
Born
May 14, 1767,
Died
March 8, 1846.

Whose life evinced the sincerity of her Christian profession: and whose death was cheered with an unwavering trust in a blessed immortality.

(footstone)
E. C.

1243. DANIEL L. COIT,
Born
September 20, 1754,
Died
November 27, 1833.

"Death bursts the involving Cloud
And all is day."

(footstone)
D. L. C.

1244. LUCRETIA F. RICHARDS,
wife of
WILLIAM B. FARLIN,
BORN
Feb. 25, 1805,
DIED
May 25, 1876.

"SO HE BRINGETH THEM
UNTO THEIR DESIRED HAVEN."

(footstone)
L. F. F.

1245. EUNICE C.
wife of
Thomas S. Williams,
DIED
March 11, 1839,
Aged 26.

(footstone)
E. C. W.

Samuel Huntington, Esq., 1796
Governor of Connecticut, Signer of the Declaration of Independence

Mrs. Martha Huntington, 1794
See Page 108

Tomb of Rev. Benjamin Lord
See Page 81

1246. JOANNA LEFFINGWELL,
Wife of
Dea. Charles Lathrop,
Born
October 28, 1771,
died at New York,
May 15, 1851.

Four of her daughters were Missionaries to India.

I shall be satisfied when I awake with thy likeness.   Ps. 17. 15.

(footstone)
J. L.

1247. In memory of
Dea. Charles Lathrop,
who died
Jan. 17, 1831,
aged 61 years.

Mr. L. was 21 years Clerk of Courts in New London County.

(footstone)
C. L.

1248. Commemorative
of
Doct. Rufus Spalding
WHO DIED
Aug. 22, 1830,
aged 70 years.

(footstone)
R. S.

1249. Ferdinand C.
Son of
Samuel &
Philura P.
Claghorn,
Died
Feb. 23, 1831,
AE 5 Ys. & 9 Ms.

(footstone)
F. C. C.

1250. Wm. Quinby
Son of
Samuel &
Philura P.
Claghorn,
Died
Feb. 10, 1831,
AE 1 Yr. & 10 M.

(footstone)
W. Q. C.

1251. In memory of
Caroline Philura S.
daughter of
Samuel &
Philura P.
Claghorn,
who died
Sept. 28, 1824,
aged 15 months.

(footstone)
C. P. S. C.

1252. MARTHA T.
daughter of
Lyman W. &
Mary L. Lee,
died Oct. 21, 1850,
aged 4 y'rs.
& 5 mo's.

Ere sin could blight or sorrow fade
Death came with friendly care,
The opening bud to Heaven conveyed
And bade it blossom there.

(footstone)
M. T. L.

1253. Miss ELLEN A. ROSS,
died at New Haven
Jan. 14, 1863,
aged 17 yrs,
3 months.

"We which have believ'd do enter into rest."

(footstone)
E. A. R.

1254. MR. DAVID M. ROSS,
native of Scotland
DIED
Nov. 18, 1847,
aged 34 years.

(footstone)
D. M. R.

1255. MRS. ALICE,
wife of
David M. Ross,
native of Scotland,
died March 30, 1859,
aged 42 Yrs.

Sweetly sleep thou dearest Mother
Lovely follower of the lamb
Soon we rejoice together
See his love and praise his name.

(footstone)
A. R.

1256. Mrs. Mercy
wife of
Isaac Barnes,
died
April 4, 1825,
aged 25 years.

(footstone)
M. B.

1257. Erected to the
memory of
WILLIAM M. CAREW,
who died June 3, 1860,
aged 78 years.
and
MARY CAREW,
his widow
who died Aug. 1, 1860,
aged 78 years.

(footstone)
W. M. C.　　M. C.

1258. ERECTED
IN
Memory of
MRS.
EMMA CONVERSE,
Wife of
AUGUSTUS CONVERSE,
who departed this life
March 20, 1836,
Aged 53.

(footstone)
E. C.

1259. IN MEMORY OF
AUGUSTUS CONVERSE,
who departed this life
May 12, 1862,
Aged 90 Years.

(footstone)
A. C.

1260. SACRED
TO
the memory of
CHARLES REYNOLDS
died in Richmond, Ohio,
Nov. 29, 1823, Aged 44.
And of his wife
MARY REYNOLDS
DIED
Feb. 25, 1837,
Aged 51.

(footstone)
M. R.

1261. SACRED
TO
the memory of
MISS
SARAH REYNOLDS
WHO DIED
Feb. 4, 1843,
Aged 79.

(footstone)
S. R.

1262. SACRED
to the memory of
ABIGAIL REYNOLDS,
the loveing & beloved wife of
GILES L'HOMMEDIEU,
who died
April 23, 1851,
in the 77 y'r
of her age.

(footstone)
A. R. L.

1263. GILES L'HOMMEDIEU,
Died
Sept. 14, 1859,
aged 94 y'rs.

(footstone)
G. - L'H.

1264. SARAH MARIA THROOP,
DIED
July 8, 1844,
Aged 32.

CARY THROOP JR.
died at Dublin, Ga.
Sept. 15, 1821,
Aged 25.

(footstone)
S. M. T.

1265. In memory of
Mr. CARY THROOP,
WHO DIED
Nov. 25, 1830,
Aged 65 years.

As y   are now
So once was I;
As I am now
So you must be
Prepare for death
And follow me.

(footstone)
C. T.

1266. In memory of
ELIZABETH
Wife of
CARY THROOP
WHO DIED
Feb. 27, 1834,
Aged 65.

How happy are the saints above
From sin and sorrow free;
With Jesus the are now at rest
And all his glory see.

(footstone)
E. T.

1267. WILLIAM C.
DIED
May 7, 1843,
AE 4 yrs & 5 mos.
SOPHRONIA A.
DIED
May 11, 1843,
AE 1 yr & 10 mos.
CHILDREN OF
Thomas L. & Sophronia H.
THROOP.

(footstone)
W. C. T.
S. A. T.

1268. SELAH E.
daughter of
Thomas L. &
Sophronia
THROOP,
died May 5, 1835,
AGED
5 ys. & 7 ms.

(footstone)
S. E. T.

1269. SOPHRONIA S.
daughter of
Thomas & Sophronia
THROOP
DIED
Sept. 11, 1834
Aged 10 Weeks & 2 ds.

(footstone)
S. T.

1270.   In memory of
         Mr. Abiel Roath,
            who died
         Nov. 16, 1829,
         in the 62ᵈ year
           of his age.

The years of affliction are o'er,
The days and nights of distress,
We see him in anguish no more
He's gained his happy release.

         (footstone)
           A. R.

1271.   In memory of
         Mrs. Mary Roath,
             relict of
         Mr. Abiel Roath
            who died
         Dec. 5, 1829,
         aged 61 years.

The rising morning can't assure
That we shall end the day;
For death stands ready at the door,
To take our lives away.

         (footstone)
           M. R.

1272.   IN MEMORY OF
         MISS ELIZA ANN
         ONLY DAUGHTER OF
         Benjamin & Sarah
             A Gorton
         died Aug. 31, 1845,
             AE 20.

Twas the Eternal God that call'd
Eliza, thou was forced to go,
Just to obey her makers call,
And leave all earthly things below.

         (footstone)
           E. A. G.

1273.   IN MEMORY OF
         BENJAMIN F.
            son of
         Benjamin & Sarah
            A. Gorton,
         died Sept. 4, 1845,
         AE 1 y'r & 5 m's.
            & 2 days.

To us for seventeen anxious months
   His infant smiles were given;
And then he bade farewell to earth
   And went to live in heaven.

         (footstone)
           B. F. G.

1274.   Milton
            son of
          John M. &
         Cyntha Fuller,
         of Kent, died
         July 26, 1825.

         (footstone)
           M. F.

1275.   EDWARD L,
            SON OF
         Aaron & Adaline
            STEVENS,
         Born July 5, 1849,
         Died March 24, 1858.

         (footstone)
           E. L. S.

1276.   CHARLES,
             SON OF
         Aaron & Adaline
            STEVENS,
              DIED
           May 6, 1848,
         AE 9 mos & 16 ds.

         (footstone)
           C. S.

1277. MARY ANN,
daughter of
Wm. & Sally
Bayley, died
Aug. 3, 1825,
aged 1 year
& 3 months

(footstone)
M. A. B.

1278. CELINDA CORDELIA
daughter of
Zep^h & Mary
Bennett died
Sept. 7, 1825,
aged 1 year 10 mos.
& 23 days

(footstone)
C. C. B.

1279. TO
the memory of
GEORGE SPALDING,
Son of
Luther & Lydia Spalding,
born March 16, 1797,
died Nov. 22, 1858,
aged 61 years.

(footstone)
G. S.

1280. TO
the memory of
LUTHER SPALDING,
who died
Feb. 3, 1838,
Aged 76 years.

(footstone)
L. S.

1281. TO
the memory of
LYDIA SPALDING,
wife of
Luther Spalding,
who died
June 1, 1847,
Aged 70 years.

(footstone)
L. S.

1282. TO
the memory of
ELIZA ANN SPALDING,
daughter of
Luther & Lydia Spalding,
who died
Jan. 12, 1838,
aged 24 years.

(footstone)
E. A. S.

1283. TO
the memory of
MARY,
daughter of
Luther & Lydia
SPALDING,
who died
June 25, 1803,
AE 8 months.

(footstone)
M. S.

1284. Miſs
Zerviah Greenslit
Died
Dec. 27, 1831,
aged 70 years.

(footstone)
Z. G.

1285. GEORGE F.
Son of
Joseph H. & Ellen F.
HUNTINGTON
died April 30, 1855,
Aged 16 years.

"Jesus Christ is my all."

(footstone)
G. F. H.

1286. JOSEPH H. HUNTINGTON
BORN
JULY 19, 1811,
DIED
JUNE 2, 1865.

"Blessed are the dead which die in the Lord."

(footstone)
J. H. H.

1287. ELEANOR FOSTER
WIFE OF
JOSEPH H. HUNTINGTON
DIED
MARCH 22, 1866.

"He that believeth in me, though he were dead, yet shall he live."

(footstone)
E. F. H.

1288. OUR MOTHER
LUCRETIA G. HYDE,
WIFE OF
JAMES MAPLES,
DIED
May 9, 1872,
aged 74 years.

(footstone)
L. M.

1289. OUR FATHER
JAMES MAPLES,
DIED
Nov. 5, 1855,
aged 67 years.

(footstone)
J. M.

1290. Cynthia States,
daughr of
E. & E. Wentworth
died Sept. 19th 1819,
aged 1 year
& 6 Mos

(footstone)
C. S. W.

1291. CYNTHIA S.
daughter of
Erastus & Esther
Wentworth,
died Aug. 10, 1829,
aged 5 years
& 9 months

(footstone)
C. S. W.

1292. ESTHER,
Wife of
Erastus Wentworth,
Died
Jan. 11, 1841,
Aged 46.

(footstone)
E. W.

1293. SACRED
TO
the memory of
LUCY,
wife of
Peleg Armstrong,
who died
April 3, 1831,
Aged 41.

(footstone)
L. A.

1294. IN
MEMORY OF
ELIZABETH
WENTWORTH,
WHO DIED
April 2nd 1836,
Aged 51.

(footstone)
E. W.

1295. CORNELIA E.
DAUGHTER OF
EBENEZER & EUNICE W.
HUNTINGTON
DIED
MARCH 14, 1893,
AGED 84 YRS.

(footstone)
C. E. H.

1296. MARY ANN HUNTINGTON
DIED
Sept. 18, 1869,
aged 61 y'rs.

DAUGHTER OF
EBENEZZER & EUNICE W.
HUNTINGTON

1297. WILLIAM L.
died Aug. 10, 1825,
aged 9 years.
SAMUEL T.
died Aug. 11, 1825,
aged 6 years.

children of Ebenezer
& Eunice Huntington

1298. EUNICE W.
wife of
Ebenezer Huntington
Died
July 15, 1857,
Aged 78.

(footstone)
E. H.

1299. EBENEZER HUNTINGTON,
DIED
Feb. 27, 1853,
aged 88.

(footstone)
E. H.

1300. JANE G.
wife of
Alexander H. Lester,
died May 2, 1845,
aged 29 years.

(footstone)
J. G. L.

1301. SOPHIA
wife of
Jacob Kahr
died Jan. 10, 1869,
aged 85.

CAROLINE
Daughter of Jacob & Barb. Miller,
aged 6 m.

Jacob Kahr,
Died Oct. 17, 1852.
Aged 70.

1302. JACOB KEHR
Co F 13, REGT.
CONN. VOLS.
DIED
OCT. 8, 1871.

1303. CLARA ELIZA,
daughter of
James N. &
Mary A. Hyde,
DIED
May 27, 1826,
aged 15 months.

(footstone)
C. E. H.

1304. HARRIET D. THOMAS
Born Aug. 19, 1800,
Died April 12, 1861.

"Blessed are the dead which die in the Lord."

(footstone)
H. T.

1305. In memory
OF
SIMEON THOMAS Esq.
WHO DIED
July 2, 1834,
Aged 81

(footstone)
S. T.

1306. In memory of
LUCRETIA THOMAS
Wife of
SIMEON THOMAS
WHO DIED
Sept 17, 1846
Aged 85

They sleep in Jesus

(footstone)
L. T.

1307. ELIZABETH
daughter of
Simeon & Lucretia
Thomas
died June 29, 1851,
Aged 63.
"Victory through our Lord Jesus Christ."

(footstone)
E. T.

1308. IN
Memory of
MISS
CLARINA THOMAS
who died
Aug. 21, 1838,
Aged 87.

(footstone)
C. T.

1309. In
Memory of
CHARLOTTE B.
Wife of
JAMES HOXIE
and daughter of
David & Mary
PITCHER,
WHO DIED
May 3, 1843,
Aged 27.

(footstone)
C. B. H.

1310. In
Memory of
EUNICE C.
Wife of
JAMES HOXIE
and daughter of
David & Mary
PITCHER
Died Sept. 22,
1839,
Aged 28.

(footstone)
E. C. H.

1311. In memory of Emily &
Adelina Pitcher, daughters
of Mr. Ephraim & Mrs. Defire
Pitcher.
Emily died Sept. 22d 1811,
aged 3 years.
Adeline died Aug. 4th 1811,
aged 7 months.

(footstone)
A. P.   E. P.

1312. Oliver E.
SON of
David & Mary
Pitcher died
Dec. 4, 1832,
aged 13 years
and 8 months.

(footstone)
O. E. P.

1313. MARY PITCHER,
Wife of
David Pitcher,
DIED
May 8, 1834,
aged 54 years.

(footstone)
M. P.

1314.   Sacred
to the
Memory of
DAVID PITCHER
Died March 10, 1857,
Aged 79.

(footstone)
D. P.

1315.   MARY B. PITCHER,
died Feb. 7, 1859,
Aged 64 years.

Wife of David Pitcher.

There is sweet rest in heaven.

(footstone)
M. B. P.

1316.   SACRED
to the memory of
JOSHUA YEOMANS,
who died
Aug. 8th 1835,
Aged 83 years.

(footstone)
J. M.

1317.   Miss LUCY ANN
daughter of
Adonijah &
Betsey Perkins,
died Feb. 14, 1831,
in the 20th year
of her age.

Her months of affliction are o're,
The days and the nights of distress;
We see her in anguish no more:
She's gained her happy release.

(footstone)
L. A. P.

1318.   SACRED
TO THE MEMORY OF
OLIVER COATS,
WHO DIED
July 24, 1847,
AE. 78.

"And as we have borne the image of
the earthy, we shall also bear the image of
the heavenly."

(footstone)
O. C.

1319.   SACRED
TO THE MEMORY OF
LUCY COATS
WIFE OF
Oliver Coats,
WHO DIED
May 14, 1841,
AEt. 65.

Her life was exemplary and her faith
that which was counted unto Abraham
for righteousness. Romans 4ch 3, 5, 20, 21, &
22.

Blessed are the pure in heart for they shall see God.

(footstone)
L. C.

1320. MATILDA,
DAUGHTER OF
Oliver C. Coats
AND WIFE OF
Lemuel Smith,
March 12, 1800,
May 21, 1880.

In thy presence is
Fulness of Joy.

(footstone)
M. C. S.

1321. In memory of
MRS. MATILDA,
wife of
David Pitcher
who died
Oct. 31, 1828,
aged 25 years.

(footstone)
M. P.

1322. In memory of
Mrs. OLIVE,
wife of
George S. Armstrong,
WHO DIED
July 31, 1833,
aged 32 years.

Also of their two sons
George A. died
July 6, 1835,
aged 6 years.

Edward A. died
Aug. 19, 1835,
aged 3 years.

1323. WILLIAM A. BROWN
Died
April 14, 1845,
Aged 28.

(footstone)
W. A. B.

1324. SARAH ANN,
Wife of
Wm. A. Brown,
DIED
May 14, 1843,
AEt. 23.

This friend in whom my soul delighted,
We shall meet no more below,
Let us prepare to be united
With her where joys forever flow.

(footstone)
S. A. B.

1325. SALLY R. CASWELL,
DIED
April 30, 1851,
Aged 75.

(footstone)
S. R. C.

1326. HENRY H. ARMSTRONG,
Born
March 28, 1797.
Died
May 26, 1843,
Aged 46.

THOMAS ARMSTRONG
died in Leith, Scotland,
Dec. 8, 1810,
Aged 26.

(footstone)
H. H. A.
T. A.

1327. CATHARINE H.
daughter of
Edward & Ace
ARMSTRONG
DIED
Dec. 12, 1832,
Aged 19.

(footstone)
C. H. A.

1328. JESSE COTTRELL,
Born Dec. 23, 1787,
died in Guadaloupe, W. I.,
Jan. 13, 1816.

His Wife
MARY ARMSTRONG,
Born March 23, 1786,
Died April 11, 1860.

(footstone)
J. C.
M. C.

1329. FRANCIS PITCHER
BORN
Feb. 20, 1808,
DIED
May 5, 1837.

(footstone)
F. P.

1330. ASHER PITCHER
DIED
May 6, 1870,
Aged 81.

My flesh also shall rest in hope.

(footstone)
A. P.

1331. BETHIAH,
wife of
ASHER PITCHER
died Feb. 19, 1863,
aged 73.

I know whom I have believed.

(footstone)
B. P.

1332. In
MEMORY OF
CORNELIA ANN,
daughter of
Asher and
Bethiah Pitcher,
WHO DIED
June 11, 1845,
AE. 25.

Blessed are the dead who die in the Lord.

(footstone)
C. A. P.

1333. LOUISA,
daughter of
Asher & Bethiah
PITCHER,
died Aug. 15, 1852,
aged 37.

To die is gain.

(footstone)
L. P.

1334. NANCY LOUISA,
daughter of
John A. &
Lucy L. Lathrop,
DIED
Oct. 5, 1843,
Aged 4 months.

Sweet one, we gave thee to thy God,
We would not call thee back to earth
Thy body rests beneath the sod,
Thy spirit was of heavenly birth.

(footstone)
N. L. L.

1335. LUCRETIA,
daughter of
Asher & Bethiah
PITCHER,
died Dec. 18, 1879,
aged 47 years.

Entered into rest.

(footstone)
L. P.

1336. RACHEL T.
died Sept. 9, 1863,
aged 64.

MARY M.
died April 12, 1861,
aged 52.

daughters of
JOHN & SARAH R. HYDE.

(footstone)
R. T. H.
M. M. H.

1337.   In memory of
JOHN HYDE
who died Mar. 16, 1848,
aged 74 years.

Also in memory of his wife
SARAH R.
who died June 8, 1865,
aged 86 years.

(footstone)
S. R. H.

1338.   SARAH R. HYDE
daughter of
JOHN & SARAH R. HYDE
DIED
Sept. 25, 1841,
aged 36 years.

(footstone)
S. R. H.

1339.   JANE LEE HYDE,
daughter of
JOHN & SARAH R. HYDE,
DIED
July 18, 1830,
aged 11 years.

(footstone)
J. L. H.

1340.   POTTER SMITH,
aged 70.

ANNA
his wife
died Dec. 25, 1857,
aged 84.

(footstone)
P. S.
A. S.

1341.   In memory of M^{rs}
Efther wife to M^r
David Lamb who
died dec 29th 1788,
in ye 88th Year of
her age

(footstone)
1342.   Anne
Sanger

(May be companion of 631.)

1343.   In Memory of
Afhahel fon to
Capt Edward &
Mrs Afenath Slocum
who died Oct
3rd 1787 aged
1 month

1344.   In mem
Charles W t   a or o
Trapp fon to Ca
Caleb Trapp &
Mrs Efther his
wife he died fep
1ft 1781 in ye 6th
Year of his age

1345.   In memory of two daughters
of Mr. Samuel Woodbridge &
Mrs. Elizabeth his wife.
Harriet died June 19th 1794
aged 20 months
Harriet died Feb^r 10th 1796
aged 6 months & 9 days

Suffer little Children to come
unto me for of fuch is the
Kingdom of Heaven

Inscriptions contained in the Pastoral Library of the First Congregational Church in Norwich of gravestones which have disappeared.

1346. Theo E. daughter of Stephen and Maria Allen, died Dec. 7, 1852, aged 15 months.

1347. Lucy Ann, wife of Hiram P. Arms, died July 3, 1837, 29.

1348. John Backus died Sept. 11, 1814. 54.

1349. Richard, son of William and Mary Billings, died March 21, 1767, aged 10 days.

1350. Mary Ann, daughter of Thomas and Julia Ann Billings, Sept. 23, 1832. 2.

1351. John Birchard 1777. 73.

1352. Elizabeth, wife of Peabody Clement, died April 8, 1834. 76.

1353. Jane T. Fanning, aged 22 years, Died Nov. 6, 1856.

1354. Mr Origin Ford died March 20, 1841. 39.

1355. Daniel Gifford died Oct. 16, 1822. 33.

1356. Daniel D. son of Daniel Gifford was drowned at Norwich Falls, Aug. 17, 1833. 17.

1357. Experience, wife of Francis Griswold.

1358. Philemon Havens, a native of Wrentham, Mass., died Nov. 12, 1819, 48. (In pencil, 50).

1359. Philemon, son of Philemon and Fanny Havens. July 7, 1816, aged 6 years.

1360. Jonathan Hunn died 1790.

1361. Gilbert Huntington died Aug. 21, 1841. 45.

1362. Lucy, consort of Daniel Huntington, died Dec. 6, 1815. 55th.

1363. CHARLOTTE (LATHROP) HUNTINGTON.

1364. JOSEPH HUNTINGTON.

1365. EUNICE (CAREW) HUNTINGTON.

1366. BENJAMIN FRANKLIN HUNTINGTON.

1367. GEORGE FREDERICK HUNTINGTON.

1368. LYDIA COIT HUNTINGTON.

1369. ABBY LATHROP HUNTINGTON.

1370. MARY STRONG HUNTINGTON.

1371. WILLIAM STUART HUNTINGTON.

1372. LYDIA COIT HUNTINGTON.

1373. CHARLES STUART HUNTINGTON.

1374. JOSEPH ELLSWORTH HUNTINGTON.

1375. HARRIET LUCRETIA HUNTINGTON.

1376. LYDIA COIT HUNTINGTON.

1377. CHARLES ELLSWORTH HUNTINGTON.

1378. Issacher, son of Eleazer Hyde. Sept. 16, 1746. 1 year, 3 months.

1379. In Mem
the loving
Mr Nathan
of Capt. Be
Ingraham of
died April y
years & one month
She died in faith &
that tho' she died yet
& that her soul would
& dwell with Christ above.

1380. Miss Martha Jenks, daughter of John and Martha Jenks of Salem, Mass., died Sept. 9, 1827. 37.

1381. Hannah, daughter of Jeremiah and Lydia Kingsley, died Feb. 13, 1802, 12 years, 5 months.

1382. John B. Lathrop died in the hope
of a glorious
immortality Sept. 11, 1854, aged 54

Oh death, where is thy sting!
Oh grave, where is thy victory!

1383. Mary L. daughter of Eleazer L. & Jerusha T. Lathrop, died May 17, 1850. 23.

1384. Burrel, son of Eleazer L. and Jerusha T. Lathrop, died Aug. 8, 1837, aged 1 year, 8 months.

1385. Jane Eliza, daughter of Eleazer L. and Jerusha T. Lathrop, died Oct. 1, 1845. 7.

1386.
HERE
LIES THE BO
DY OF NATHAN
IEL LEFFINGW
ELL WHO DIED JAN
VARY 9, 1710
AGED 24 YEARS.

1387. Joseph, son of Mr Benajah and Mrs Joanna Leffingwell, died Nov. 17, 1746. 4 years, 4 months, 19 days.

1388.
DAVID
LOW DIED
FEBERVRY 10
1709 AGED 23
YERS

1389. Peter Morgan died Aug. 14, 1786. 76.

1390. Zilpah, consort of James Rogers, died March 10, 1814. 77th.

1391. Charles Robinson died Oct. 17, 1838. 39.

1392. Lucretia B. daughter of C. B. & Rachel Rogers, died Sept. 15, 1836, aged 20.
Our dear Lucretia now is dead
Her cold & lifeless clay,
Has made in dust its silent bed
And here it must decay.
Farewell, dear child, a long farewell,
For we shall meet no more,
Till we are raised with thee to dwell
On Zion's happier shore.

1393. Mrs Hannah, the beloved wife of Mr Shubael Smith, died Sept. ye 19, 1719.

1394. Albert F. son of Albert and Lucy Smith, died in July, 1835.

1395.
Erected to the Memory of
Rev. John Sterry; for
23 years Pastor of the Baptist Church
in this place, who died Nov. 7,
1823, aged 57.
Blessed are the dead who die in the Lord.

1396. Charles Stephen, son of John B. and Elizabeth Tilden, died April 27, 1844, 7 years, 8 months.

1397.
SACRED
to the memory
OF
ELISHA TRACY,
Who died
March 10,
1842,
Aged 75.

"God will redeem my
soul from the power
of the grave: for he
shall receive me."

(Removed to Tracy lot,
Yantic Cemetery, Norwich.)

1398.
LUCY C. TRACY,
Wife of
Elisha Tracy,
died
May 9, 1846,
Aged 68.

Shed not for me the bitter tear,
Nor waste one sigh in vain regret,
Tis but the casket that lies here,
The gem that filled it sparkles yet.

(Removed to Tracy lot,
Yantic Cemetery, Norwich.)

1399.
SACRED
TO
the memory of
MARY G. TRACY
Child of
Elisha & Lucy C. Tracy,
WHO DIED
Sept. 15, 1835
Aged 19 years.

Forgive, blest shade, the tributary tear,
That mourns thy exit, from a world
like this.
Forgive the wish that would have kept
thee here
And stayed thy progress to the scenes
of bliss.

(Removed to Tracy lot,
Yantic Cemetery, Norwich.)

1400. TRACY MONUMENT.

(First Side).
Winslow Tracy,
son of
E. & L. C. Tracy,
died May 11, 1823, aged 23.
Thy noble heart is done,
The towering form
Where brilliant talent
Energy of thought;
Where height of Soul
And generous friendship dwelt.
Now fill the solemn shroud:
Thy flowing grief
Thy fate untimely
All thy kindred mourn.

(Second Side).
Blessed be the memory
& peace to the remains of
Stephen Decatur,
the much lamented son of
E. & L. C. Tracy,
who was removed to
Heaven through a
watery grave June 21,
1817, aged 4 years.

(Third Side).
Sacred
to the memory of
Hannah P. Tracy,
the lovely & beloved child of
E. & L. C. Tracy,
who died
Feb. 13, 1810,
aged 1 year
& 10 months.

(Fourth Side).
Elisha D. Tracy,
son of
E. & L. C. Tracy,
died June 17, 1823,
aged 13.
With friends long lov'd thou
shalt remember'd be,
Thy virtues cherish'd 'till
we meet with thee.

1401. Dothea, wife of Seth Wadhams, died April 5, 1851. 64.

1402. Marcia A., daughter of Oliver & Eunice Wattles, died Dec. 8, 1849. 8 years, 8 days.

1403. Thomas T. Wilcox died July 30, 1833. 24.

1404. Harriet M. wife of Luther S. Yerrington, died Feb. 3, 1842. 20.

1405. George F. son of Joseph H. and Ellen F. Yerrington, died April 30, 1855. 16.

MEMORIAL GATES ON EAST TOWN STREET
Erected by Faith Trumbull Chapter, D. A. R.

INDEX

A

Abel—Abell
Abel, Ann — 13
Abel, Bethiah, Mrs. — 68
Abel, Caleb — 32
Abel, Elizabeth, Mrs. — 33
Abel, Hannah — 81
Abel, Isaac, Capt. — 39, 81
Abel, Jerusha, Mrs. — 33
Abel, Joshua, Mr. — 33, 68
Abel, Lucretia — 81
Abel, Lydia — 33
Abel, Lydia, Mrs. — 33
Abel, Rufus Backus, Mr. — 106
Abel, Samuel — 33
Abel, Theophilus — 32
Abbott, Daniel, Mr. — 88
Abbott, Sarah, Mrs. — 88
Adgate—Adget
Adgate, Abiah, Mrs. — 76
Adgate, Abigail — 76
Adgate, Abigail, Mrs. — 76, 80
Adgate, Andrew — 76
Adgate, Elijah, Mr. — 76
Adgate, Eunice, Mrs. — 75
Adgate, Hannah — 76
Adgate, Jabez — 76
Adgate, Lucy — 75, 76
Adgate, Mary, Mrs. — 75
Adgate, Martha — 63
Adgate, Matthew, Mr. — 76, 80
Adgate, Matthew, Mr., Jr. — 76
Adgate, Phile, Miss — 76
Adgate, Philip — 75
Adgate, Rebecca, Miss — 71
Adgate, Ruth, Mrs. — 63, 71, 73, 75
Adgate, Thomas, Mr., Jr. — 73
Adgate, Thomas, Dea. — 63, 71, 73, 74, 75
Adgate, Thomas, 3d — 75
Adgate, William, Mr. — 75
Allen, Benjamin, Mr. — 75
Allen, Elizabeth — 26
Allen, Hezekiah, Mr. — 59
Allen, John, Mr. — 26
Allen, Maria — 165
Allen, Mary, Mrs. — 59
Allen, Nancy — 150, 151
Allen, Rebecca, Mrs. — 75
Allen, Sarah G. — 150
Allen, Stephen — 150, 151, 165
Allen, Theo. E. — 165
Allen, Tuzah, Mrs. — 26
Allyn, Robert — 9
Ames, Erasmus D. — 121, 122
Ames, Sarah Ann — 122
Anderson, Elizabeth — 122
Andrews, Mary — 9
Arms, Hiram P. — 165
Arms, Lucy Ann — 165
Armstrong, Ace — 162
Armstrong, Anna — 107
Armstrong, Balsheba, Mrs. — 73
Armstrong, Catharine H. — 162
Armstrong, Edward — 162
Armstrong, George A. — 162
Armstrong, George S. — 162
Armstrong, Henry H. — 162
Armstrong, Jabez — 107
Armstrong, Lucy — 158
Armstrong, Mary — 163
Armstrong, Nancy — 107
Armstrong, Olive, Mrs. — 162
Armstrong, Peleg — 158
Armstrong, Silas, Mr. — 73, 84
Armstrong, Thomas — 162
Arnold, Absalom King — 18
Arnold, Benedict, Capt. — 18
Arnold, Elizabeth — 18
Arnold, Hannah — 18
Arnold, Mary — 18
Arnold, Oliver, Capt. — 38
Austin, Rev. David — 105
Austin, Lydia, Mrs. — 105
Austin, Willis R. — 137
Avery, Candace, Mrs. — 43, 107
Avery, Charles, Mr. — 43
Avery, Elizabeth, Mrs. — 40
Avery, Elizabeth — 23, 45
Avery, Eunice, Mrs. — 43, 45
A H — 40
Avery, Henry — 43
Avery, Jabez, Mr. — 35, 36, 45
Avery, Jonathan, Mr. — 40
Avery, Lucy, Mrs. — 35, 36
Avery, Lydia — 35
Avery, Samuel — 23, 107
Avery, Samuel, Mr. — 43

B

Babcock, Mary (Cook) — 147
Babcock, Silas — 147
Backus, Abigail — 44
Backus, Absalom — 41
Backus, Ann — 41
Backus, Asa, Mr. — 143
Backus, Asa — 143
Backus, Caroline — 143
Backus, Dorothy C. — 22
Backus, Eber, Esq. — 143, 144
Backus, Ebenezer, Esq. — 44, 58
Backus, Elijah, Esq. — 22
Backus, Elizabeth — 95
Backus, Eunice — 144
Backus, Eunice, Mrs. — 32
Backus, Jabez, Mr. — 32
Backus, James — 22
Backus, John — 165
Backus, John, Dea. — 22
Backus, Josiah — 40, 41
Backus, Love, Mrs. — 40, 41
Backus, Lucy, Mrs. — 22
Backus, Lydia — 40
Backus, Margaret, Mrs. — 22
Backus, Nancy — 22
Backus, Ozias — 40
Backus, Parthena, Mrs. — 143
Backus, Samuel, Lieut. — 22
Backus, Sarah Jane — 143
Backus, Simeon, Mr. — 40
Backus, Simon, Mr. — 22, 143
Backus, Stephen — 9
Backus, William, Sr. — 9
Backus, William, Lieut. — 9

Bailey—see Bayley
Bailey, Catherine, Mrs. — 53
Bailey, Cynthia, Mrs. — 52
Bailey, Eunice, Mrs. — 52
Bailey, Samuel, Mr. — 52, 53
Baldwin, Abigail, Mrs. — 59, 100
Baldwin, Alice, Mrs. — 111
Baldwin, Bethiah — 100
Baldwin, Bethiah, Mrs. — 60, 64, 100
Baldwin, Ebenezer, Capt. — 60, 64, 100
Baldwin, Elijah — 64
Baldwin, Jabis, Mr. — 59
Baldwin, Jabez — 100
Baldwin, John, 1st — 9
Baldwin, John — 100
Baldwin, Luce — 100
Baldwin, Margaret — 111
Baldwin, Rhoda — 60
Baldwin, Thomas, Mr. — 59, 100
Baldwin, William, Mr. — 111
Barnes, Isaac — 154
Barnes, Mercy, Mrs. — 154
Barrett, Ezekiel — 54, 55
Barrett, Sarah — 54, 55
Bassett, Abner — 149
Bassett, Harriet S. — 149
Bassett, Harriet S., Jr. — 149
Bassett, John, Mr. (of Boston) — 73
Bayley, Mary Ann — 157
Bayley, Sally — 157
Bayley, William — 157
Beebe, Cushing — 42
Beebe, David — 42
Beebe, David, Jr. — 42
Beebe, Eunice — 42
Bennet, Celinda Cordelia — 157
Bennet, Mary — 157
Bennet, Zeph — 157
Bill, Beriah, Mr. — 11
Bill, Chester — 130
Bill, Ephraim, Mr. — 94
Bill, Gorden — 94
Bill, Judith, Mrs. — 11
Bill, Lydia, Mrs. — 94
Bill, Lynde — 94
Bill, Mira, Mrs. — 130
Bill, Orrin H. — 130
Bill, Silvester — 94
Billings, Abigail — 93
Billings, Charles — 93, 94
Billings, David A. — 141
Billings, Henry, Capt. — 93
Billings, Julia Ann — 141, 165
Billings, Lucretia, Mrs. — 93
Billings, Lucretia, Jr. — 93
Billings, Mary — 88, 93, 165
Billings, Mary, Mrs. — 93
Billings, Mary Ann, Miss — 111
Billings, Mary Ann, Miss — 165
Billings, Richard — 165
Billings, Ricard Leffingwell — 93
Billings, Thomas — 141, 165
Billings, William — 88, 93, 165
Bingham, Mary — 112
Bingham, Thomas — 9, 30
Bingham, William — 112

Name	Page
Birchard—Burchard	
Birchard, Asa H.	146
Birchard, Elisha	33
Birchard, Emily	146
Birchard, Eunice	33, 146
Birchard, Eunice, Mrs.	32
Birchard, Gideon, Mr.	32, 33
Birchard, John	9
Birchard, John W.	146
Birchard, John, Mr.	37, 146, 165
Birchard, Joseph W., Mr.	146
Birchard, Lois, Miss	32
Birchard, Sarah, Mrs.	37
Birchard, Thankful	33
Birchard, William H.	33
Bliss, Abby W.	137
Bliss, Anna L., Miss	127
Bliss, Elias	101
Bliss, George	137
Bliss, John, Mr.	50, 126, 127, 137
Bliss, Lydia L.	137
Bliss, Sarah	50, 127, 137
Bliss, Sarah	50, 137
Bliss, Temperance, Mrs.	137
Bliss, Thomas, Jr.	9
Bliss, Thomas, Sr.	9
Bliss, William	101
Bliss, William H.	101
Bliss, Zephaniah, Mr.	137
Bolles, John, Capt.	46
Bowers, Morgan	9
Bradbury, Thomas	122
Bradford, John	9
Brooks, Delia A.	152
Brooks, Elizabeth A.	152
Brooks, Harriet A.	152
Brooks, Jonathan W.	152
Brooks, Jonathan, Dr.	152
Brown, Ann	41
Brown, Anne, Mrs.	41, 42
Brown, Betsey	41
Brown, James, Mr.	41, 42
Brown, James, Mr., Jr.	42
Brown, James Noyce, Mr.	43
Brown, Jesse, Mr.	41
Brown, John	84
Brown, Mary	41
Brown, Philena, Miss	41
Brown, Russel, Mr.	41
Brown, Sarah Ann	162
Brown, Temperance, Mrs.	84
Brown, William A.	162
Buck, Daniel, Mr.	90
Buck, Hannah	90
Burdick, Emeline	122
Burdick, Jane E.	122
Burdick, John A.	122
Burnham, James, Mr.	84
Burnham, Sarah, Mrs.	84
Burnham, Zebulon P.	115
Bushnell, Abishai	77
Bushnell, Benaiah, Capt.	77
Bushnell, Caleb, Capt.	82
Bushnell, David, Mr.	91, 94
Bushnell, Eunice, Mrs.	92, 94
Bushnell, Fanny	125
Bushnell, Hannah, Miss	132
Bushnell, Jabez, Mr.	132
Bushnell, James	126
Bushnell, John, Mr.	125, 126
Bushnell, John	126
Bushnell, Joseph, Mr.	89
Bushnell, Lucinda	126
Bushnell, Lucy, Mrs.	125, 126
Bushnell, Lucy, Miss	125, 126
Bushnell, Mary Ann	126
Bushnell, Mary, Mrs.	89, 94
Bushnell, Richard, Capt., Esq.	82
Bushnell, Sinda	126
Bushnell, Zeruiah, Mrs.	77
Butler, Benjamin, Mr.	12, 13
Butler, Diadama, Mrs.	12
Butler, Minerva, Miss	12
Butler, Rosamund, Miss	12

C

Name	Page
Cady, Asa, Mr.	9
Calkins, Daniel	38
Calkins, Hugh, Serj.	30
Calkins, Hugh, Deac.	9
Calkins, John	9
Calkins, Samuel	100
Calkins, Sally	100
Calkins, Sary	18
Campbell, Mary B.	123
Carew, Abigail, Mrs.	44, 97
Carew, Azor, Dr.	118, 119
Carew, Charles	139
Carew, Diadema	97
Carew, Daniel	41, 43, 117, 119
Carew, Daniel, Mr.	117
Carew, Ebenezer, Mr.	69, 74, 139
Carew, Eliphalet, Mr.	43, 109, 119
Carew, Eliphalet, Jr.	118
Carew, Elizabeth Lathrop	74
Carew, Eunice	165
Carew, Eunice, Mrs.	69, 74, 88
Carew, Gardiner	69
Carew, Joseph, Mr.	88
Carew, Joseph, Capt.	88
Carew, Lucy	41, 117
Carew, Lucy, Mrs.	117
Carew, Lucretia	41, 97, 109
Carew, Maria	69
Carew, Maria Gardiner	74
Carew, Mary	41, 43, 154
Carew, Mary, Mrs.	22, 119
Carew, Mehitable, Mrs.	69, 74, 139
Carew, Nancy, Mrs.	119, 139
Carew, Palmer, Mr.	39
Carew, Richard, Mr.	26
Carew, Thomas, Mr.	44, 97, 139
Carew, William M.	154
Carpenter, Anne	136
Carpenter, Daniel	139
Carpenter, Eunice, Mrs.	53, 136
Carpenter, Gardner, Mr.	110
Carpenter, Gerard F.	136
Carpenter, Joseph, Mr.	53, 136, 140
Carpenter, Mary, Mrs.	110
Carpenter, Mary Ann	140
Carpenter, Rebecca E.	136
Case, Asahel	51
Case, John, Mr.	48
Case, Louisa	51
Case, Mehitabel, Mrs.	48
Case, Rosanah	51
Case, Samuel	55
Case, Simeon, Mr.	48
Case, Susan	55
Case, Susanna	55
Caswell, Sally R.	162
Chapel—Chappel	
Chapel, Nathan, Mr., Jr.	38
Chapel, Susannah, Mrs.	38
Chapel, Infant	38
Chapman, Rebecca, Mrs.	58
Chapman, Simon, Mr.	58
Charlton, Charles, Mr.	109
Charlton, Dolly	122, 123
Charlton, Dwight	123
Charlton, Eliza Ann	123
Charlton, Howard	123
Charlton, Maria	123
Charlton, Samuel	122, 123
Charlton, Sarah, Mrs.	109
Chester, Freelove, Mrs.	63
Childs, Timothy, M. D.	124
Choate, Hannah, Miss	71
Choate, John, Esq.	71
Choate, Mary, Mrs.	71
Christophers, Joanna	93
Christophers, Hon. Richard	93
Claghorn, Caroline Philura S.	153
Claghorn, Fedinand C.	153
Claghorn, Philura P.	153
Claghorn, Samuel	153
Claghorn, Wm. Quinby	153
Clark, Elisha, Mr.	10
Clark, Hannah	10
Clark, Lydia, Mrs.	10
Clegg, Eunice	101
Clegg, Philip	101
Clegg, William	101
Clement, Elizabeth	165
Clement, Peabody	165
Cleveland—Cleaveland	
Cleveland, Abiah	9, 10
Cleveland, Aaron, Mr.	10
Cleveland, Aaron Porter	10
Cleveland, David	11
Cleveland, Eunice	11
Cleveland, Francis	101
Cleveland, Harriet S.	101
Cleveland, Jerusha, Mrs.	11
Cleveland, John, Mr.	11
Cleveland, Margaret	101
Cleveland, Marcy, Mrs.	11, 27
Cleveland, Samuel, Mr.	11, 27
Cleveland, Samuel	11
Cleveland, Samuel	27
Cleveland, Sarah	10
Cleveland, Susan	101
Cleveland, Walter hous	11
Cleveland, William	101
Coats, Lucy	161
Coats, Matilda	162
Coats, Oliver	161
Coats, Oliver C.	162
Cobb, Katharine, Mrs.	48
Cobb, Mary	48
Cobb, Nathan, Mr.	48
Coggeshall, William, Esq.	129
Coit, Abigail	85
Coit, Benjamin, Esq.	85
Coit, Daniel L.	152
Coit, Elizabeth	63, 152
Coit, Joseph, Dr.	62
Coit, Joseph, Esq.	63, 106
Coit, Joseph, Mr.	117
Coit, Lucy	95
Coit, Lydia, Mrs.	63, 106
Collier, Benjamin, Mr.	30
Collier, Lucy	30
Collier, Mary, Mrs.	30
Collier, Richard, Mr.	30
Collins, Benjamin	21, 28, 96
Conoy, Edward, Mr.	9
Converse, Augustus	154
Converse, Emma, Mrs.	154
Cook, Mary	147
Cooley, Abby	125
Cooley, Erastus	125
Cooley, Frances T.	121
Cooley, George A.	125
Cooley, William H.	121

Name	Page
Cooley, William S.	121
Coolidge, Frances Jane	103
Coolidge, Henry Joseph	103
Coolidge, Lucy	103
Cotton, Lake, Mr.	59
Cotton, Thomas, Deacon	59
Cottrell, Jesse	163
Cottrell, Mary (Armstrong)	163
Crocker, Amy, Mrs.	150
Crocker, Catharine	118
Crocker, Jonathan	118
Crocker, Lucy, Mrs.	30
Crocker, Samuel, Mr.	30
Cryer, John	120
Culver, Hannah, Mrs.	26
Culver, Henry, Mr.	130
Culver, Jonathan, Mr.	26
Culver, Jonathan, Capt.	26
Culver, Mary, Mrs.	26

D

Name	Page
Danforth, Elizabeth, Mrs.	49
Danforth, Harri	56
Danforth, John, Dr.	49
Danforth, John, Mr.	49
Danforth, Mercy	56
Danforth, Samuel, Mr.	56
Danforth, Sarah, Mrs.	48
Danforth, Six children of Mr. Thomas & Sarah	48
Danforth, Thomas, Mr.	48
Darby, Blancher, Mr.	43
Darby, Henry	111
Darby, Mary	111
Darby, Mary, Mrs.	111
Darby, Rufus	111
Davis, Elizabeth	115
Davis, Stephen	115
Deolph, Mark Anthony	110
Deolph, Priscilla, Mrs.	110
Doane, Betsie H.	120
Doane, Emily C.	120
Doane, Eunice Howes	119
Doane, Eunice H.	119
Doane, John, Capt.	119
Doane, John G.	119
Douglass, Daniel, Mr.	36
Douglass, Hezekiah, Mr.	37
Douglass, Lois, Mrs.	36
Douglass, Polly	108
Dumont, Claudius Monsr	58
Dunn, Ann	42
Dunn, Cary	42
Dunn, Cary, Jr.	42
Durkee, Barre	29
Durkee, Eliphalet, Mr.	29
Durkee, John, Col.	47
Durkee, Martha, Mrs.	47
Durkee, Parker H.	29
Durkee, Sally, Mrs.	29
Durr, J. & M.	120
Durr, John M.	120
Dyar, John, Col.	93
Dyar, Joanna	93

E

Name	Page
Edgerton, Benjamin, Capt.	39
Edgerton, Elisha, Capt.	78, 79
Edgerton, Elisha	115
Edgerton, Elizabeth, Mrs.	78, 79
Edgerton, Eunice	88
Edgerton, Gurdon	117
Edgerton, Three infants of Gurdon	117
Edgerton, John, Lieut.	71
Edgerton, John, Mr.	79, 88
Edgerton, Laura	117
Edgerton, Lucy	132
Edgerton, Lucy, Mrs.	114, 115
Edgerton, Lucy Griswold	115
Edgerton, Lurah	117
Edgerton, Phebe, Mrs.	79
Edgerton, Richard	9
Edgerton, Richard, Mr.	87
Edgerton, Ruth	71
Edgerton, Sally	39
Edgerton, Samuel	78
Edgerton, Simon	114, 115
Edgerton, Susanna, Mrs.	39
Edwards, Abel	119, 120
Edwards, Anna	120
Edwards, John H.	119
Edwards, Lois	119
Edwards, Lois Mix	120
Edwards, William	120, 121
Emes, Joseph, Mr.	44
Emes, Lidia	44
Elderkin, John	9
Ellsworth, Chloe	46
Ellsworth, Daniel, Esq.	46
Ellsworth, Mary, Mrs.	46

F

Name	Page
Fanning, Abigail	24
Fanning, Anne, Mrs.	17
Fanning, E.	25
Fanning, George E.	24
Fanning, Infant son	25
Fanning, Jane T.	165
Fanning, Jane Abby	24
Fanning, John	24
Fanning, John, Capt.	24
Fanning, John H.	25
Fanning, Lucretia	25
Fanning, Lydia	25
Fanning, Lydia, Mrs.	25
Fanning, Nancy	25
Fanning, Thomas, Esq.	24, 25
Fanning, Thomas, Capt.	17, 19
Fanning, Thomas T.	24
Fanning, Thomas, Mr.	25
Fanning, Infant son	25
Fargo, Aaron, Mr.	31
Fargo, Sarah, Mrs.	31
Farlin, Lucretia F. Richards	152
Farlin, William B.	152
Fellows, Prudence	107
Fitch, Ebenezer	87
Fitch, Eunice	87
Fitch, James, Rev.	9
Fitch, Mary	87
Ford, Origin, Mr.	165
Fosdick, Alvan, Mr.	137
Fosdick, Lydia, Mrs.	137
Foster, Daniel, Capt.	51
Foster, Welthea, Mrs.	51
Fox, Eunice C.	133
Fox, Ezekiel, Mr.	133
Fox, Lydia, Mrs.	133
Fuller, Anna Havens	125
Fuller, Cynthia	156
Fuller, Daniel Havens	125
Fuller, George D.	124, 125
Fuller, Hannah M. Havens	124, 125
Fuller, John M.	156
Fuller, Milton	156
Fuller, Susan Sophia	125

G

Name	Page
Gager, John	9
Gager, Samuel	9
Gardiner, Abigail, Miss	139
Gardiner, David, Mr.	62
Gardiner, Hannah	62
Gifford, Anne, Mrs.	29
Gifford, Daniel	165
Gifford, Daniel D.	165
Gifford, Experience	32
Gifford, Experience, Mrs.	32
Gifford, Hannah, Mrs.	11
Gifford, James, Mr.	29, 30, 44
Gifford, James	30
Gifford, John, Mr.	11
Gifford, John, Mr., Jr.	11
Gifford, Samuel, Mr.	29, 30, 32
Gifford, Samuel, 3d	29
Gifford, Sarah, Mrs.	108
Gifford, Stephen, Mr.	11, 108
Gifford, Susan	30
Gifford, Susan H.	108
Goodell—Godell	
Goodell, Anne	135
Goodell, Sarah	136
Goodell, Sarah, Mrs.	43, 136
Goodell, Silas	136
Goodell, Silas, Capt.	43, 136
Goodell, William	43, 136
Gorton, Benjamin	156
Gorton, Benjamin F.	156
Gorton, Eliza Ann, Miss	156
Gookin, Sarah A., Mrs.	67
Gookin, Anne, Miss	58
Gookin, Daniel	67
Gookin, Edmond, Mr.	67
Gookin, Elizabeth, Mrs.	67
Gookin, Sarah, Mrs.	67
Grant, Hannah, Mrs.	108
Grant, James, Capt.	108
Grant, Sarah, Miss	108
Green, Sarah	138
Green, William	138
Greenslit, Zerviah, Miss	157
Griffin, Elizabeth	105
Griffin, Jeremiah	105
Griswold—Griswould	
Griswold, Abel, Mr.	28, 136
Griswold, Abigail, Mrs.	28
Griswold, Anna	104
Griswold, Andrew	104
Griswold, Esther, Mrs.	136
Griswold, Experience	165
Griswold, Francis	25
Griswold, Francis, Mr.	28, 165
Griswold, Francis, Lieut.	9
Griswold, Hannah, Mrs.	31
Griswold, John, Esq.	22
Griswold, Joseph, Deacon	29
Griswold, Lucy	22
Griswold, Lucy	115
Griswold, Lydia, Mrs.	29
Griswold, Patience, Mrs.	28
Griswold, Ruth, Mrs.	28
Griswold, Samuel, Capt.	27, 31

H

Name	Page
Hall, Parker, Mr.	29
Hallam, Amos, Mr.	14
Hallam, Sarah, Mrs.	14
Harland, Edward	116
Harland, Fanny	116
Harland, Hally	116
Harland, Hannah	10, 116
Harland, Harriet	116
Harland, Henry, Mr.	116
Harland, Mary	116
Harland, Thomas	116
Harland, Thomas, Jr.	116

Harris, Elizabeth	92	
Harris, Henry B.	134	
Harris, John, Mr.	92	
Hart, Levi, Dr.	80	
Hart, Lydia, Mrs.	80	
Havens, Antoinette H.	124	
Havens, Daniel	124	
Havens, Daniel, Capt.	124	
Havens, Desire (Howes)	124	
Havens, Etta	124	
Havens, Fanny	165	
Havens, Hannah M.	124	
Havens, Harriet D.	124	
Havens, Jonathan C.	125	
Havens, Jonathan Collins, Jr.	125	
Havens, Julia E.	124	
Havens, Maria Antoinette	125	
Havens, Patia	125	
Havens, Philemon	165	
Havens, Philemon, Jr.	165	
Havens, Washington H.	124	
Hazard, Almira J.	129	
Hazard, Carder, Jr.	129	
Hazard, Carder, Mr.	129	
Hazard, George Carder	129	
Hazard, Julia	129	
Hazard, Sarah	129	
Hazard, Sarah Eliza	129	
Hazard, Sarah, Mrs.	129	
Hazard, William Coggeshall	129	
Hazen, Abigail	39	
Hazen, Clarissa	39	
Hazen, Frederick, Mr.	39	
Hazen, Jacob, Capt.	39	
Hazen, Sarah, Mrs.	39	
Hazen, Sophia	39	
Hendy, Richard	9	
Hewlett, Edwin, Mr.	122	
Hewlett, Edwin R.	122	
Hewlett, Eliza	122	
Hibbard, Mehitable, Mrs.	37	
Hibbard, Nathan, Mr.	37	
Hide—see Hyde		
Hogan, Andrew	122	
Hogan, Isabella, Jr.	122	
Hogan, Isabella, Mrs.	122	
Holt, Harriet	137	
Holt, Henry	137	
Hopkins, Catherine C.	150	
Hopkins, Charles A.	150	
Hopkins, Charles T.	150	
Hosford, Caroline	100	
Hosford, Dudley	100	
Hosford, Charles	100	
Hosmer, Joseph, Capt.	130	
Howard, Thomas	9	
Howes, Desire	124	
Howes, Dorcas	120	
Howes, Eunice	119	
Howes, Gustavus Adolphus	120	
Howes, Mulford	120	
Hoxie, Charlotte B. Pitcher	160	
Hoxie, Eunice C. Pitcher	160	
Hoxie, James	160	
Hubbard, Joseph	106	
Hubbard, Lydia	73, 106	
Hubbard, Lydia	106	
Hubbard, Lucretia	73, 106	
Hubbard, Mary, Mrs.	57	
Hubbard, Russell, Mr.	57	
Hubbard, Thomas	57	
Hubbard, William	57, 73, 106	
Hubbard, William	106	
Hughes, Hannah	99	
Hughes, Hannah	45	
Hughes, John	45	
Hughes, John, Capt.	99	
Hughes, Ziporah, Mrs.	45, 99	
Hunn, Betsy, Mrs.	31	
Hunn, David, Mr.	31	
Hunn, Hannah, Miss	31	
Hunn, Jonathan, Mr.	31, 165	
Hunn, Phebe, Miss	28	
Hunter, Henry	104	
Huntington, Abigail, Mrs.	32, 33, 97, 107	
Huntington, Abby Lathrop	165	
Huntington, Anna, Mrs.	142	
Huntington, Anne	48, 86, 95, 96, 97, 98, 113	
Huntington, Annie	113	
Huntington, Andrew, Mr.	57, 95, 98	
Huntington, A.	127	
Huntington, Benjamin, Jr., Esq.	54, 95, 97	
Huntington, Benjamin Franklin	165	
Huntington, Caleb	48	
Huntington, Four infant children of Caleb and Anne	48	
Huntington, Caleb, Dea.	142	
Huntington, Charles	53	
Huntington, Charles E.	99	
Huntington, Charles L.	127	
Huntington, Charles Ellsworth	165	
Huntington, Charles Stuart	165	
Huntington, Charlotte	98, 113	
Huntington, Charlotte Lathrop	165	
Huntington, Chester P.	99	
Huntington, Christopher, Mr.	9, 33	
Huntington, Christopher, Dea.	32, 87	
Huntington, Civil, Mrs.	89	
Huntington, Cornelia E.	158	
H. D.	96	
Huntington, Daniel	97	
Huntington, Daniel, Mr.	97, 98, 114, 122, 132, 165	
Huntington, Dorothy, Mrs.	61	
Huntington, E. and A.	127	
Huntington, Ebenezer	95, 158, 159	
Huntington, Ebenezer, Dea.	14, 53, 57	
Huntington, Edward	98	
Huntington, Eleanor Foster	158	
Huntington, Elias	78	
Huntington, Elijah, Esq.	84, 131	
Huntington, Elizabeth Backus	95	
Huntington, Elizabeth, Mrs.	32, 46, 53, 98	
Huntington, Ellen F.	157	
Huntington, Emily L.	95	
Huntington, Erastus, Esq.	127	
Huntington, Eunice	84	
Huntington, Eunice Carew	165	
Huntington, Eunice W.	158, 159	
Huntington, Ezra, Mr.	53	
Huntington, Felix, Mr.	98, 112, 113	
Huntington, Frederick	50	
Huntington, Frederick, Capt.	50	
Huntington, Freelove, Mrs.	98	
Huntington, George Frederick	165	
Huntington, George F.	157	
Huntington, George W., M. D.	123	
Huntington, George Washington	95	
Huntington, Gilbert	165	
Huntington, Gurdon, Mr.	61, 95, 96	
Huntington, Hannah	83, 95	
Huntington, Hannah, Mrs.	78, 83, 84, 87, 89, 97	
Huntington, Hannah Williams	95	
Huntington, Hannah (Phelps)	95	
Huntington, Harriet Lucretia	165	
Huntington, Hezekiah, Mr.	78, 84	
Huntington, Hezekiah, Hon.	61, 83, 86, 87	
Huntington, Isaac, Esq.	83, 90	
Huntington, Jabez	95, 98	
Huntington, Jabez W.	123	
Huntington, Jabez, Col.	95	
Huntington, James, Mr.	46, 98	
Huntington, James, Ensign	98	
Huntington, Jedediah	95, 97	
Huntington, Jeremiah, Mr.	88	
Huntington, Jesse	106	
Huntington, John	33, 50	
Huntington, John, Mr.	48, 89, 107	
Huntington, Joseph	165	
Huntington, Joseph H.	157, 158	
Huntington, Joseph S.	143	
Huntington, Joseph Ellsworth	165	
Huntington, Joshua	95, 97, 98	
Huntington, Joshua, Capt.	96	
Huntington, Louisa E.	142	
Huntington, Louisa M.	95	
Huntington, Lucretia	106, 134	
Huntington, Lucy	14, 165	
Huntington, Lucy, Mrs.	57	
Huntington, Lucy (Coit)	95	
Huntington, Lydia Coit	106, 165	
Huntington, Lydia Coit (2)	165	
Huntington, Lydia Coit (3)	165	
Huntington, Lydia	96	
Huntington, Lynde, Rev.	142	
Huntington, Martha	98	
Huntington, Martha, Mrs.	108	
Huntington, Mary, Mrs.	33, 48, 53, 54, 114	
Huntington, Mary Ann	159	
Huntington, Mary Ann (Strong)	139, 165	
Huntington, Mary B.	123	
Huntington, Mary Brown	113	
Huntington, Mary B. Campbell	123	
Huntington, Mary (McClellan)	95	
Huntington, Merial	122	
Huntington, Nancy L.	95	
Huntington, Nancy	143	
Huntington, Nabby, Mrs.	127	
Huntington, O. E.	139	
Huntington, Ozias, Mr.	48	
Huntington, Peter, Mr.	50	
Huntington, Peter, Mr.	98	
Huntington, Philip	131	
Huntington, Phila, Mrs.	131	
Huntington, Philura (Tracy)	134	
Huntington, Priscilla, Mrs.	98	
H. R.	96	
Huntington, Rebeckah	83, 131	
Huntington, Rebeckah, Mrs.	83	
Huntington, Richard	33	
Huntington, Robert	96	
Huntington, Roger, Mr.	54	
Huntington, Rufus	134	
Huntington, Ruth, Mrs.	50	
Huntington, Sally Ann	123	
Huntington, Samuel	83, 134	
Huntington, Samuel T.	159	
Huntington, Samuel, Esq., Governor of Conn.	108	
Huntington, Sarah	14, 50, 53, 57, 94	
Huntington, Sarah	88, 96	

Huntington, Sarah Isham	95	
Huntington, Sarah I.	95	
Huntington, Sibel, Mrs.	97	
Huntington, Silas	53	
Huntington, Simon, Dea. 53, 54, 57, 94, 95		
Huntington, Simon, Dea.	96, 114	
Huntington, Simon, Mr.	89, 95	
Huntington, Simeon, Capt.	98, 99	
Huntington, Sophia	142	
Huntington, Susannah, Mrs.	96	
Huntington, Thomas J.	147	
Huntington, Thomas M.	123	
Huntington, Thomas Z. B.	123	
Huntington, Wm. Stuart	165	
Huntington, Wm. L.	159	
Huntington, Zechariah, Mr. 94, 123		
Huntington, Zipporah, Mrs. 54, 57, 114		
Huntley, Ezekiel, Mr.	11	
Huntley, Lydia, Mrs.	11	
Hyde—Hide		
Hyde Abial	42	
Hyde, Abiel, Mr.	42, 127	
Hyde, Anne	64	
Hyde, Anne, Mrs.	36, 64, 73, 91	
Hyde, Betsey	46	
Hyde, Charles	46	
Hyde, Clara Eliza	159	
Hyde, Chloe, Mrs.	46	
Hyde Diadama	12	
Hyde, Ebenezer	46, 47, 50, 142	
Hyde, Eleazer, Mr.	37, 38, 165	
Hyde, Eliab, Mr.	38, 122, 141, 142	
Hyde, Elisha, Mr.	12, 14	
Hyde, Elisha, Esq.	115, 116	
Hyde, Eliza M.	128	
Hyde, Elizabeth	71	
Hyde, Elizabeth, Mrs.	50, 142	
Hyde, Erastus	128	
Hyde, Erastus N.	128	
Hyde, Experients, Mrs.	38	
Hyde, Ezra, Mr.	77	
Hyde, Fanny B.	128	
Hyde, Fanny B., Mrs.	128	
Hyde, Flavius	73	
Hyde, Isaacher, Mr.	37, 165	
Hyde, Jabez, Capt. Esq.	50	
Hyde, James	46, 47	
Hyde, James, 2nd	46	
Hyde, James, Capt.	46, 127	
Hyde, James Jarvis	40	
Hyde, James Jarvis, 2nd	40	
Hyde, James N.	159	
Hyde, Jane Lee	164	
Hyde, Jedediah, Mr.	12, 14	
Hyde, Jedediah, Capt.	34	
Hyde, Jerusha, Mrs.	12	
Hyde, Joseph, Mr.	127	
Hyde, John, Mr.	32	
Hyde, John	163, 164	
Hyde, Lewis	143	
Hyde, Lydia, Miss	12, 122	
Hyde, Lydia, Mrs.	12, 142	
Hyde, Lucy Ann	142, 143	
Hyde, Lucretia, Miss	36	
Hyde, Lucretia G.	158	
Hyde, Marey, Mrs.	34	
Hyde, Martha, Mrs.	46, 127	
Hyde, Mary, Mrs.	42, 127	
Hyde, Mary A.	159	
Hyde, Mary M.	163	
Hyde, Mary	143	
Hyde, Nabby, Miss	127	
Hyde, Nancy	116	
Hyde, Nancy, Miss	127	
Hyde, Nancy Maria	116	
Hyde, Peleg, Mr.	40	
Hyde, Phebe, Mrs.	50	
Hyde, Rachel T.	163	
Hyde, Richard, Capt.	91	
Hyde, Richard, Esq.	36	
Hyde, Samuel	9	
Hyde, Sarah	46	
Hyde, Sarah, Mrs.	37, 38, 47	
Hyde, Sarah R.	163, 164	
Hyde, Sarah R., Jr.	164	
Hyde, Silas, Mr.	39	
Hyde, Susannah, Mrs.	40	
Hyde, Theodore, Mr.	37	
Hyde, William, Mr.	9, 64, 71, 73	
Hyde, William, Capt., Esq., Jr.	82	
Hyde, Zebadiah, Mr.	37	

I

Ingraham, Be, Capt.	165
Isham, Sarah	95

J

Jarvis, Abigail, Mrs.	65
Jarvis, James, Capt.	65
Jenks, John	165
Jenks, Martha	165
Jenks, Martha, Mrs.	165
Johnson, Ann Maria	141
Johnson, Experience, Mrs.	32
Johnson, Isaac, Mr.	32
Johnson, Stephen D.	141
Jones, Ebenezer	103
Jones, Elizabeth	46
Jones, Elizabeth	103
Jones, Keziah, Mrs.	46
Jones, Parmenas	103
Jones, Rosana	103
Jones, Sylvanus, Mr.	46
Jones, Tryphena	46

K

Kahr, Jacob	159
Kahr, Sophia	159
Kehr, Jacob	159
Keeney, Edward, Mr.	108
Keeney, John, Mr.	108
Keeney, Patience, Mrs.	108
Kingsley, Cornelia J.	133
Kingsley, Eleazer, Mr.	10
Kingsley, Eunice, Mrs.	10, 74
Kingsley, Gurdon	10
Kingsley, Hannah	165
Kingsley, Jeremiah	165
Kingsley, Lydia	165
Kingsley, Mary P.	133
Kingsley, William L.	133
Kinsman, John	128
Kinsman, Joseph	128
Kinsman, Rebecca	128

L

L. D.	15
Lamb, David, Mrs.	164
Lamb, Esther, Mrs.	164
Lancaster, Anna	143
Larraza, Nancy E.	151, 152
Larraza, Yldefonso V.	151, 152
Larraza, Yldefonso S.	152
Lathrop—Lothrop	
Lathrop, Abby L.	134
Lathrop, Abby W.	109
Lathrop, Abigail, Mrs. 16, 50, 61, 76	
Lathrop, Ann M.	148
Lathrop, Anna, Mrs.	50
Lathrop, Araunah	84
Lathrop, Asa, Mr.	65, 111
Lathrop, Augustus, Capt.	109
Lathrop, Augustus Frederick	109
Lathrop, Azariah, Esq.	50, 51, 61
Lathrop, Azariah	120
Lathrop, Benjamin, Mr.	84
Lathrop, Betsey	134, 148
Lathrop, Betsey, Miss	130
Lathrop, Burrell, Mr.	65
Lathrop, Burrel	134, 166
Lathrop, Ca	58
Lathrop, Charles, Dea.	153
Lathrop, Charlotte	61
Lathrop, Civil, Mrs.	52, 61
Lathrop, D.	15
Lathrop, Daniel, Dr.	66
Lathrop, Daniel	65, 66, 148
Lathrop, Darious, Mr.	131
Lathrop, Ebenezer, Capt.	57
Lathrop, Ebenezer, Mr.	52
Lathrop, Eleazer L.	166
Lathrop, Elizabeth, Mrs. 65, 70, 82, 111	
Lathrop, Ezra, Mr.	131, 133
Lathrop, Frank T.	148
Lathrop, Gideon	84
Lathrop, Hannah, Mrs.	70, 104
Lathrop, Hannah 61, 62, 65, 105, 133	
Lathrop, Israel, Mr.	72
Lathrop, Jabez, Mr.	82
Lathrop, James	66
Lathrop, Jane E.	133
Lathrop, Jane Eliza	166
Lathrop, Jane F.	120
Lathrop, Jedediah, Mr.	52, 61
Lathrop, Jeremiah	133
Lathrop, Jerusha	66, 105
Lathrop, Jerusha T.	166
Lathrop, Joanna Leffingwell 93, 153	
Lathrop, John	76
Lathrop, John A.	163
Lathrop, John B.	165
Lathrop, Jonathan, Mr.	130
Lathrop, Joseph	66
Lathrop, Joshua, Dea.	62, 65, 105
Lathrop, Joshua	65
Lathrop, Levi, Mr.	104
Lathrop, Lucy L.	134, 163
Lathrop, Lydia	105
Lathrop, Lydia, Mrs. 58, 62, 106, 131, 133	
Lathrop, Lynde, Mr.	76
Lathrop, Margaret	65
Lathrop, Margaret F.	134
Lathrop, Martha, Mrs.	69, 70
Lathrop, Mary	65, 109, 133
Lathrop, Mary L.	166
Lathrop, Mary A.	120
Lathrop, Mary, Mrs.	84
Lathrop, Matthew	84
Lathrop, Mercy, Mrs.	62, 65, 105
Lathrop, Nabby, Mrs.	51
Lathrop, Nancy Louisa	163
Lathrop, Nathll Mr.	50, 51
Lathrop, Nathll, Mr., Jr.	65
Lathrop, Rebecca, Mrs. 72, 131, 133	
Lathrop, Roswell	61
Lathrop, Rufus	70
Lathrop, Sally	27
Lathrop, Samuel, Mr.	16
Lathrop, Sarah	55

Lathrop, Simon, Col. 69, 70	Leffingwell, Simeon 68	Manning, Samuel, Mr. 20, 21
Lathrop, Thede, Mrs. 130	Leffingwell, Thomas, Mr., Ens.	Mansfield, Hannah, Mrs. 12
Lathrop, Thomas, Mr.	9, 23, 78, 80, 83, 85, 92	Mansfield, Hannah Hyde 118
62, 65, 105, 106	Leffingwell, Thomas, Dea.	Mansfield, William, Mr. 12
Lathrop, William, Mr.	53, 87, 88	Manwaring, Deborah 113
54, 55, 65, 105	Leffingwell, Zerviah, Mrs. 92	Manwaring, Elizabeth, Mrs. 52
Lathrop, William, Mr., Jr. 55	Leonard, Hannah, Mrs. 48	Manwaring, Robert 52
Lathrop, Z. 27	Leonard, Jeams, Capt., 2nd 48	Manwaring, Robert, Deac. 52
Lathrop, Zachariah 102	Leonard, Sarah 48	Manwaring, Susan, Mrs. 52
Lathrop, Zerviah, Mrs. 70	Lester, Albert 59	Maples, Betsey 121
Lathrop, Zephaniah, Mr. 104	Lester, Alexander H. 159	Maples, Eleazor 121
Leach, Daniel, Jr. 105	Lester, Ann 140	Maples, Elisha 15
Leach, Eliza Ann 105	Lester, Ann G. 140	Maples, James 158
Leach, John, Mr. 51	Lester, Harriet 140	Maples, John 121
Leach, Lydia 105	Lester, Jane G. 159	Maples, Lucretia G. (Hyde) 158
Ledlie, Chloe, Mrs. 43	Lester, Joseph Carpenter 140	Marsh, Jonathan, Dr. 51
Ledlie, Hugh, Mr. 43	Lester, Margaret, Mrs. 59	Marshall, Abiel, Mr. 64
Lee, Asa Fitch 144	Lester, Mary 59	Marshall, Anne, Miss 45
Lee, George W. 144	Lester, Mary Ann 140	Marshall, Anne, Mrs. 45, 64
Lee, James E. 144	Lester, Peggy 59	Marshall, Freelove 126
Lee, Lyman W. 153	Lester, Sarah Eliza 140	Marshall, Lucretia, Miss 45
Lee, Martha T. 153	Lester, Timothy, Capt. 59	Marshall, Sally, Mrs. 39
Lee, Mary L. 153	Lester, Walter 140, 141	Marshall, Thomas, Mr. 39, 45, 126
Lee, Robert M. 144	Lester, Walter R. 140	Marshall, William 126
Lee, Susan 144	Levonian, Barckeve 151	Mason, Andrew 121
Lee, Susannah 144	Lewis, Cory K. 145, 146	Mason, Edwin H. 121
Lee, William D. 144	Lewis, Dinah Palmer 145	Mason, Emily F. (Ross) 121
Leffingwell, Abigail 23, 90	L'Hommedieu, Giles 155	Mason, John, Maj. 9
Leffingwell, Alice, Mrs. 117	L'Hommedieu, Abigail Reynolds	Mason, John, Capt. 9
Leffingwell, Allis 93	155	Mather, Eleazer, Mr. 85
Leffingwell, Andrew, Mr. 80	Lincoln, George S. 150	Mather, Lorinda, Mrs. 85
Leffingwell, Benajah, Mr.	Lincoln, Rachel 150	McClellan, Mary 95
68, 78, 83, 92, 93, 166	Lord, Abigail, Mrs. 77, 91, 92	Mead, Charlotte 94
Leffingwell, Benajah, Jr. 83	Lord, Anne, Mrs. 81	Mead, John 94
Leffingwell, Betsey 93	Lord, Asa 91	Meeker, Hannah, Mrs. 126
Leffingwell, Betsey, Mrs. 90	Lord, Benjamin, Mr. 77, 81, 85	Miller, Barb. 159
Leffingwell, Christopher, Esq.	Lord, Benjamin, Rev., D. D.	Miller, Caroline 159
63, 66, 67, 74, 92, 93	77, 80, 81, 111	Miller, Jacob 159
Leffingwell, Daniel, Mr., Jr. 90	Lord, Cyperon, Mr. 58	Miller, Lucretia, Mrs. 110
Leffingwell, Dyar 93	Lord, Ebenezer, Mr. 133	Miller, John Saniford 110
Leffingwell, Elisha, Mr.	Lord, Eleazer, Mr.	Miller, Thomas, Capt. 110
93, 117, 118	36, 91, 92, 111, 112	Miner, Anne, Mrs. 42
Leffingwell, Elizabeth	Lord, Elisha, Dr. 55	Miner, Charlotte 42
63, 67, 68, 74	Lord, Elizabeth 80	Miner, Cyrus 115
Leffingwell, Elizabeth 67, 85, 93	Lord, Elizabeth, Mrs. 58, 111	Miner, Lucy H. 115
Leffingwell, Elizabeth, Mrs.	Lord, Henry 146, 147	Miner, Nathan 107
80, 90, 92, 93	Lord, Henry Edwin 146	Miner, Prudence (Fellows) 107
Leffingwell, Eunice, Mrs. 74	Lord, Hez, Mr. 146	Miner, Sarah 42
Leffingwell, Frances M. 66, 117	Lord, Joseph, A. M. 81	Miner, Seth, Capt. 42
Leffingwell, Frances 117	Lord, Judith, Mrs. 146	Moore, Chloe 84
Leffingwell, Frances H. 117	Lord, Lydia 17	Morris, Sally of Colchester 125
Leffingwell, Hannah, Mrs. 90	Lord, Nabby 36	Morgan, Abigail, Mrs. 35
Leffingwell, Hart, Capt. 74	Lord, Richard, Esq. 17	Morgan, Anne, Mrs. 35
Leffingwell, Hezekiah, Mr. 85	Lord, Sarah B. 146, 147	Morgan, Ann H. 109
Leffingwell, Hezekiah 83	Lord, Temperance, Mrs. 133	Morgan, Elizabeth, Mrs. 26
Leffingwell, Jerusha 67	Lord, William 85	Morgan, Eunice, Mrs. 26
Leffingwell, Joanna, Mrs.	Lord, Zerviah, Mrs. 91, 92	Morgan, Hannah, Mrs. 35
78, 83, 93, 153, 166	Low, David 166	Morgan, Margaret, Mrs. 35
Leffingwell, Joanna 83		Morgan, Mary, Mrs. 42
Leffingwell, John, Capt. 67, 73	**M**	Morgan, Peter, Mr. 26, 166
Leffingwell, Joseph 166	M A 19	Morgan, Roswell 109
Leffingwell, Lucretia 117	M J 19	Morgan, William, Deacon 35
Leffingwell, Lydia, Mrs.	M L 20	Morgan, William, Mr. 42
74, 80, 83, 85, 87, 88, 92, 105	Mabrey, Anna 142	Morse, Avery 104
Leffingwell, Martin, Mr. 80	Mabrey, Orinell 142	Morse, Carpenter, Mr. 104
Leffingwell, Mary, Mrs. 23, 73, 87	Mabrey, Oramel 142	Morse, Daniel, Mr. 103
Leffingwell, Nathaniel 166	Mabrey, Orrimille 142	Morse, Elizabeth, Mrs. 102
Leffingwell, Oliver, Mr. 80	Mabrey, Thankful S., Mrs. 143	Morse, John, Mr. 102
Leffingwell, Phineas, Mr. 68	Mabrey, William Henry 142	Morse, Julia, Miss 102
Leffingwell, Richard 78	Manning, Anne 21	Morse, Sophia 103
Leffingwell, Richard, Capt. 92	Manning, Anne, Ye 2d 21	Morse, Susanna, Mrs. 102
Leffingwell, Ruth, Mrs. 63	Manning, Anne, Mrs. 21	Morse, Susanna Amanda, Miss 102
Leffingwell, Samuel, Esq. 90	Manning, Anna 20	Morse, Timothy, Capt. 104
Leffingwell, Samuel, Capt. 90	Manning, Diah, Mr. 20	Mumford, Abigail 91
Leffingwell, Sarah 53	Manning, Eunis 21	Mumford, Abigail, Mrs. 91
Leffingwell, Sarah, Mrs. 67, 68, 90	Manning, Josiah 54, 58	Mumford, Thomas, Mr. 91

N

Nevins, David	112
Nevins, David, Jr.	112
Nevins, Henry	112
Nevins, Lucretia	112
Nevins, Mary, Mrs.	112
Nevins, Mary, Jr.	112
Nevins, Mary	112
Nutter, John, Mr.	12
Nutter, Mary, Mrs.	12
Nutter, William	12
Nutter, Two infant brothers	12

O

Olmstead, John, Dr.	9

P

Parish, Andrew, Mr.	55
Parish, Andrew, Capt.	56
Parish, Ebenezer, Mr.	55
Parish, Elijah, Mr.	55
Parish, Susanna, Mrs.	56
Parkerson, Eleanor S.	51
Parkerson, James V.	51
Parkerson, Varney	51
Pease, John	9
Peck, Bela	130, 131
Peck, Betsey	131
Peck, Elizabeth	15
Peck, Joseph	15
Peck, Lydia	131
Pendleton, Amelia, Mrs.	60
Pendleton, Anna, Mrs.	60
Pendleton, Joshua, Deac.	60
Pendleton, Joshua, Mr., Jr.	60
Perit, Jerusha (Lathrop) Mrs.	105
Perit, P. of New York	105
Perkins, Abigail	44
Perkins, Adonijah	161
Perkins, Andrew	95
Perkins, Anne	95
Perkins, Betsey	161
Perkins, Betsey H.	147
Perkins, George F.	147
Perkins, George, Rev.	147
Perkins, George	148
Perkins, Hannah H.	148
Perkins, Jacob, Jr.	41
Perkins, Lucy Ann, Miss	161
Perkins, Marionette	148
Perkins, Mary	41
Perkins, Olive	128
Perkins, Simeon, Mr.	44
Perkins, Simon	128
Phelps, Hannah	95
Phillips, Harcoless, Mr.	110
Phillips, Hannah	110
Phillips, Hannah, Mrs.	110
Pierce, Abigail, Mrs.	148
Pierce, John, Mr.	148
Pitcher, Adelina	160
Pitcher, Asher	163
Pitcher, Bethiah	163
Pitcher, Charles	121
Pitcher, Charlotte B.	160
Pitcher, Clarissa E.	121
Pitcher, Cornelia Ann	163
Pitcher, David	160, 161, 162
Pitcher, Desire, Mrs.	160
Pitcher, Elijah	24
Pitcher, Emily	160
Pitcher, Ephraim, Mr.	160
Pitcher, Eunice C.	160
Pitcher, Francis	163
Pitcher, Hannah	24
Pitcher, Hannah, Mrs.	9, 24
Pitcher, Leverett B.	121
Pitcher, Louisa	163
Pitcher, Lucretia	163
Pitcher, Mary	160
Pitcher, Mary B.	161
Pitcher, Matilda, Mrs.	162
Pitcher, Oliver E.	160
Porter, Epaphras	106
Porter, George S., Address	1-6
Porter, Margaret, Mrs.	106
Porter, Lucretia (Huntington)	106
Post, Experience, Mrs.	16, 21
Post, Jabez, Mr.	21
Post, John, Mr.	20, 21
Post, Mary (Andrews)	9
Post, Nathaniel, Mr.	21
Post, Ruth, Mrs.	19, 21
Post, Samuel, Mr.	19, 20, 21
Post, Samuel, Jr.	19, 21
Post, Sarah	20
Post, Sarah, Mrs.	19, 20
Post, Stephen, Mr.	19
Post, Susannah, Mrs.	21
Post, Thomas	9
Potter, George W.	150
Potts, Christopher, Mr.	11
Potts, John Cunningham	11
Potts, Susannah, Mrs.	11
Pratt, Nathan	27
Pratt, Sarah E.	27
Prior—Prier	
Prior, Abigail	47
Prior, Joshua, Mr.	47
Prior, Lucy	47
Prior, Sarah, Mrs.	47

R

R D	14
Randal, Abiah, Mrs.	47
Randal, Amos, Mr.	47
Raymond, Ebenezer	115
Raymond, Ebenezer, Mr.	115
Raymond, Phebe, Mrs.	115
Read, Josiah	9
Reeve, Abigail, Mrs.	10
Reeve, Bethiah, Mrs.	10
Reeve, Ebenezer, Mr.	10
Remington, Mary	105
Remington, Mary Ann	105
Remington, Stephen	105
Reynolds—Raynolds—Renels—Renells—Renold—Renalls	
Reynolds, Abigail	155
Reynolds, Anne, Miss	18
Reynolds, Charles	154
Reynolds, Elisha Lee	17
Reynolds, John	9
Reynolds, John, Mr.	16, 17
Reynolds, Joseph, Mr.	16, 17, 18, 19
Reynolds, Lidya, Mrs.	16, 17
Reynolds, Mary	154
Reynolds, Phebe	18
Reynolds, Phebe, Mrs.	18, 19
Reynolds, Ruth	16
Reynolds, Sarah, Mrs.	16, 17
Reynolds, Sarah, Miss	154
Reynolds, Stephen	17
Richards, Ann T.	148, 149
Richards, Elizabeth T.	149
Richards, George	43
Richards, James T.	148, 149
Richards, John, Mr.	43
Richards, Lucretia F.	152
Richards, Martha	43
Richards, Thomas Tracy	149
Richmond, Coral E.	110
Roath, Abiel, Mr.	156
Roath, Anna, Mrs.	44
Roath, Lidia	44
Roath, Lydia, Mrs.	45
Roath, Mary, Mrs.	156
Roath, Peter, Mr.	44
Roath, Robert, Mr.	44, 45
Robertson, Amy, Mrs.	25
Robertson, James, Mr.	25
Robinson, Charles	166
Rogers, Anne	77
Rogers, C. B.	166
Rogers, David, Mr.	44, 137
Rogers, Denison	113
Rogers, Eleazer, Esq.	132
Rogers, Elizabeth	31
Rogers, Elizabeth, Mrs.	44, 71, 74, 78
Rogers, Ezekiel, Dr.	74
Rogers, Frances	78
Rogers, Hannah	132
Rogers, Henry C.	133
Rogers, James, Mr.	132, 166
Rogers, Lucy	132
Rogers, Lucy, Miss	132
Rogers, Lucy Edgerton	132
Rogers, Lucretia	71
Rogers, Lucretia B.	166
Rogers, Lydia, Mrs.	9
Rogers, Maria	133
Rogers, Maria, Jr.	133
Rogers, Nancy	113
Rogers, Penelope, Mrs.	71, 77
Rogers, Rachel	166
Rogers, Sally	71
Rogers, Sarah	132
Rogers, Sophia	31
Rogers, Theophilus, Dr.	71, 74, 77
Rogers, Thomas Jefferson	132
Rogers, Zabdial, Col.	9
Rogers, Zabdiel, Capt.	31, 71, 78
Rogers, Zilpah, Mrs.	132, 166
Ross, Alice, Mrs.	154
Ross, David M., Mr.	154
Ross, Ellen A., Miss	153
Ross, Emily F.	121
Royce, Jonathan	9
Russell, Joseph, Esq., of Bristol	90
Russell, Sarah	90

S

Sanger, Anne	164
Sanger, Anne, Mrs.	82
Sanger, Iriger, Mr.	82
Savage, Rebecca, Mrs.	23
Shapley, Joseph, Mr.	44
Shapley, Mary, Mrs.	44
Shepard, Almira	138
Shepard, Elias Van Buren	138
Shepard, Elias, Mr.	138
Shepard, Harriet K., Miss	138
Shepard, Henry H.	138
Shepard, Sally G., Miss	138
Shepard, Sally, Mrs.	138
Sherman, Abiel B.	128, 129
Sherman, Joanna R.	129
Sherman, Julia (Hazard)	129
Sherman, Julia S.	129
Shipman, Abigail	85
Shipman, Elizabeth, Mrs.	85
Shipman, Lydia L.	85
Shipman, Nathaniel	17
Shipman, Nathaniel, Mr.	16, 17, 85

Name	Page
Shipman, Nathaniel, Deacon	85
Shipman, Nathaniel, Junr.	85
Shipman, Ruth, Mrs.	16, 17
Slocum, Ashahel	164
Slocum, Asenath, Mrs.	164
Slocum, Edward, Capt.	164
Smith, Abner	67
Smith, Albert	166
Smith, Albert F.	166
Smith, Anna	164
Smith, Hannah	166
Smith, Hannah, Mrs.	10
Smith, James	67
Smith, Lemuel	162
Smith, Lucy	166
Smith, Martha, Mrs.	67
Smith, Matilda (Coats)	162
Smith, Nehemiah	9
Smith, Obadiah, Capt.	63, 67
Smith, Potter	164
Smith, Shubael, Mr.	166
Snow, Benjamin, Mr.	71, 72
Snow, Charles Knox	72
Snow, Sally, Mrs.	71, 72
Spalding, Asa, Esq.	113, 114
Spalding, Eliza Ann	157
Spalding, George	157
Spalding, Luther	157
Spalding, Lydia	114, 157
Spalding, Mary	157
Spalding, Maria Elizabeth, Miss	114
Spalding, Rufus, Dr.	153
Starr, Christopher	128
Starr, Jonathan, Mr.	68
Starr, Mary L.	128
Starr, Olive	128
Starr, Sarah, Mrs.	68
Starr, Sarah L.	128
Stark, Jerusha, Mrs.	12
Starkweather, Esther, Mrs.	101
Starkweather, Henry B.	101
Starkweather, Henry, Mr.	101
Sterry, Consider	109
Sterry, John, Rev.	166
Stevens, Aaron	156
Stevens, Adaline	156
Stevens, Charles	156
Stevens, Edward L.	156
Stoughton, Chloe	43
Stoughton, Dan, Mr.	43
Stoughton, Joanna, Mrs.	43
Strong, Charles H.	135
Strong, Eunice	87
Strong, George A.	135
Strong, Harriet L.	135
Strong, Joseph, Rev., D. D.	135, 136
Strong, Joseph H.	135, 139
Strong, Lucretia	135, 139
Strong, Mary	165
Strong, Mary, Mrs.	135
Strong, Mary Ann	139
Stroud, Mary, Miss	55

T

Name	Page
Talcott, Gov.	66
Talcott, Jerusha	66
Tanner, Gilbert H.	151
Tanner, Hannah	151
Tanner, Harriet E.	151
Tanner, Margaret	151
Taylor, Anne	81
Taylor, Edward, Rev.	81
Thomas, Annie	135
Thomas, Caroline	135
Thomas, Caroline Eunice	135
Thomas, Charles	56, 134, 139
Thomas, Chloe, Mrs.	56
Thomas, Clarina, Miss	160
Thomas, Deborah, Mrs.	49
Thomas, Ebenezer, Mr.	49, 56, 138
Thomas, Elizabeth	160
Thomas, Elizabeth, Mrs.	49
Thomas, Eunice	33
Thomas, Eunice, Mrs.	56
Thomas, Fanny	56
Thomas, George	138
Thomas, Gurdon	56, 134
Thomas, Hannah, Mrs.	49, 56
Thomas, Harriet D.	159
Thomas, Henry	56
Thomas, Jerusha	56
Thomas, John Austin	135
Thomas, Joseph, Dr.	138, 139
Thomas, Lucretia, Miss	49
Thomas, Lucretia, Mrs.	160
Thomas, Mary	134, 135
Thomas, Phebe	139
Thomas, Simeon, Esq.	159, 160
Thomas, Thomas, Mr.	134, 135
Thomas, Thomas L., Mr.	33, 135
Thomas, Thomas L., Capt.	56
Thompson, Mary, Miss	59
Throop, Elizabeth	155
Throop, Cary, Jr.	155
Throop, Cary, Mr.	155
Throop, Sarah Maria	155
Throop, Selah E.	155
Throop, Sophronia H.	155
Throop, Sophronia A.	155
Throop, Sophronia S.	155
Throop, Thomas L.	155
Throop, William C.	155
Tilden, Charles Stephen	166
Tilden, Elizabeth	166
Tilden, John B.	166
Touzin, Dominic, Doct.	47
Townsend, Fanny	99
Townsend, Hannah, Mrs.	99
Townsend, John H.	99
Townsend, Nathaniel, Mr.	99
Tracy, A., Mrs.	114, 144
Tracy, Abigail	86
Tracy, Abigail, Mrs.	23, 35, 74, 86, 89, 145
Tracy, Alice, Mrs.	149
Tracy, Andrew, Esq.	29, 30
Tracy, Anna, Mrs.	15
Tracy, Anne, Miss	107, 141
Tracy, Augustus C.	118
Tracy, Benjamin, Esq.	108
Tracy, Betsey, Mrs.	41
Tracy, Carolina, Mrs.	35, 36
Tracy, Charlotte M.	114
Tracy, Clarina	35
Tracy, Daniel, Mr.	23, 24, 78, 86, 89
Tracy, Daniel, Jr.	23
Tracy, Daniel	86
Tracy, Deborah	107, 149
Tracy, Deborah D.	114
Tracy, Dorastus, Mr.	36, 100, 101
Tracy, Elisha	14, 166, 167
Tracy, Elisha D.	167
Tracy, Elisha, M. D.	13, 14, 114
Tracy, Elizabeth	23, 31, 50, 78, 89, 149
Tracy, Elizabeth	14, 114
Tracy, Elizabeth, Mrs.	57
Tracy, Francis, Master	114
Tracy, Francis C.	149
Tracy, Frederick	107, 149
Tracy, Hannah	89
Tracy, Hannah Hyde	118
Tracy, Hannah, Mrs.	27, 79, 108
Tracy, Hannah P.	167
Tracy, Harriet F.	144
Tracy, Henry	149
Tracy, Isaac, Mr.	31, 91
Tracy, Jabez, Mr.	34, 79
Tracy, Jabin	36
Tracy, Jared, Esq.	22, 96, 145
Tracy, John	9
Tracy, John, Mr.	89
Tracy, Joseph, Capt.	14
Tracy, Joseph, Mr.	15
Tracy, Joseph W.	145
Tracy, Joshua	118
Tracy, Joshua P.	118
Tracy, Juliet	118
Tracy, Lois, Miss	141
Tracy, Lovisa	36, 100
Tracy, Lucretia	12
Tracy, Lucretia, Mrs.	24
Tracy, Lucy	14
Tracy, Lucy C.	166, 167
Tracy, Lydia	25
Tracy, Margaret	22, 145, 149
Tracy, Mary, Mrs.	14
Tracy, Mary	114
Tracy, Mary E.	149
Tracy, Mary G.	166
Tracy, Molly, Mrs.	29, 30
Tracy, Mundator, Mr.	35, 36
Tracy, Nabby, Mrs.	36
Tracy, P., Dr.	114, 144
Tracy, Peleg, Mr.	41
Tracy, Philemon, Dr.	145
Tracy, Philura	134
Tracy, Polly	30
Tracy, Richard P., Dr.	144
Tracy, Samuel, Esq.	23, 24, 25
Tracy, Samuel	78, 86
Tracy, Sarah	145
Tracy, Sarah G.	145
Tracy, Sidney	39
Tracy, Simon, Mr.	35, 50
Tracy, Simon, Dea.	35, 36
Tracy, Solomon, Mr.	86
Tracy, Stephen Decatur	167
Tracy, Susannah	96
Tracy, Sybel, Mrs.	23, 24, 25, 86
Tracy, Thomas, Lieut.	9
Tracy, Thomas, Major	23
Tracy, Uriah	141
Tracy, Wealthy	145
Tracy, Winslow	167
Tracy, Wm. George	141
Tracy, Zeporah, Mrs.	34
Trapp, Caleb, Capt.	164
Trapp, Charles W.	164
Trapp, Esther, Mrs.	164
Trott, Lydia	145
Trowtrow, Boston	94
Trumbull, John, Mr.	25
Trumbull, John, Jr.	25
Trumbull, Lucy	25
Trumbull, Timothy	25
Turner, Ann Abell, Mrs.	13
Turner, Anne, Mrs.	14
Turner, Betsey H.	147
Turner, Charles William	13
Turner, Elizabeth, Mrs.	88
Turner, George Frederick	13
Turner, Hannah	148
Turner, John, Dr.	147, 148

Turner, Joseph, Mr.	88	
Turner, Joseph, Jr.	88	
Turner, Philip, Esq.	13	

W

Wade, Robert	9
Wadhams, Dothea	167
Wadhams, Seth	167
Wadsworth, Abigail, Mrs.	66
Wadsworth, Daniel, Rev., Mr.	66
Walden, John	25
Walsworth, Justin, Dr.	121
Wallis, Richard	9
Waterman, Anne	78
Waterman, Anne, Mrs.	78
Waterman, Asa, Mr.	34, 76
Waterman, Asa, Capt.	34
Waterman, Eleazer, Mr.	63
Waterman, Elisha	40
Waterman, Eliza	16
Waterman, Elizabeth	18
Waterman, Elizabeth, Mrs.	19, 77
Waterman, Erastus	143
Waterman, Eunice	15
Waterman, Eunice, Mrs.	20, 34
Waterman, Hannah	18
Waterman, Hannah, Mrs.	54
Waterman, John, Mr.	16, 18, 20, 77, 78
Waterman, Lucy, Mrs.	34, 76
Waterman, Lucy, Miss	76
Waterman, Lydia	40
Waterman, Margaret, Mrs.	16
Waterman, Martha, Mrs.	63
Waterman, Mary	77
Waterman, Nehemiah, Esq.	16
Waterman, Nehemiah, Mr.	15
Waterman, Nehemiah, Capt.	15
Waterman, Sarah, Mrs.	15, 40
Waterman, Simoen's wife and child	54
Waterman, Susannah, Mrs.	15, 16
Waterman, Thomas, Mr.	34
Waterman, Thomas, Ensign	19
Waterman, Thomas, Sergt.	16
Waterman, William, Mr.	16
Wattles, Andrew L.	118
Wattles, Eunice	167
Wattles, Louisa M.	118
Wattles, Marcia A.	167
Wattles, Margery, Mrs.	118
Wattles, Oliver	167
Webster, Ruth	63
Webster, Palatiah	63
Wedge, Abigail	40
Wedge, Joshua, Mr.	40
Wedge, Rebecca, Mrs.	40
Wedge, Rebecca, Mrs.	40
Welch, Deborah E., Mrs.	118
Welch, Hannah, Mrs.	118
Welch, Henry, Mr.	118
Wentworth, E. and E.	158
Wentworth, Abigail	39
Wentworth, Cynthia States	158
Wentworth, Cynthia States, 2d	158
Wentworth, E. and E.	158
Wentworth, Esther	158
Wentworth, Erastus	158
Wentworth, Elizabeth	158
Wentworth, Jared, Mr.	39
Wentworth, John Harkness	39
Weston, Amaziah, Mr.	88
Weston, Betsey, Mrs.	88
Wetherell, Jeremiah	85
Wetherell, Joseph, Dr.	85
Wetherell, Lydia	85
Wetmore, Anne, Mrs.	86
Wetmore, Prosper, Mr.	86
Wheat—Wheate	
Wheat, Anne, Mrs.	72
Wheat, Benjamin, Mr.	72
Wheat, Benjamin, Dr.	64
Wheat, Elizabeth	72
Wheat, John Deshon	64
Wheat, Mary	72
Wheat, Mary, Mrs.	72
Wheat, Nathan	72
Wheat, Samuel, Capt.	64
Wheat, Sarah	64
Wheat, Sarah, Mrs.	64
Wheat, Susanna	72
Whipple, Joanna Starr	64
Whipple, Joshua, Mr.	64
Whipple, Sarah	64
Whipple, Sarah, Mrs.	64
White, Samuel, Mr.	26
Whiting, Abigail	44
Whiting, Anne	65
Whiting, Anne, Mrs.	64, 65
Whiting, Bernice, Miss	64
Whiting, Charles, Capt.	65
Whiting, Charlotte, Miss	64
Whiting, Ebenezer, Capt.	65
Whiting, Ebenezer, Major	64
Whiting, Frances M.	66
Whiting, John, Col.	65
Whiting, Nabby, Mrs.	51
Whiting, Phebe, Mrs.	115
Whiting, Philena, Mrs.	65
Whiting, Samuel	66
Whiting, William Bradford, Mr.	44, 51
Whiting, Zenas L.	115
Whiting, Zenas, Capt.	115
Whitley, Abel P.	107
Whitley, Mary	107
Willcox—Wilcox	
Willcox, Adaline J.	146
Willcox, Amy E.	119
Willcox, Amy	119
Willcox, Emily T., Mrs.	146
Willcox, Hannah	119
Willcox, Stephen	119
Willcox, Thomas T.	146, 167
Williams, Dorothy H.	60
Williams, Eunice, Mrs.	61
Williams, Eunice C.	152
Williams, Hannah	27, 95
Williams, Harriet	131
Williams, Hezekiah	60
Williams, Hezekiah H.	60
Williams, John	60
Williams, John, Mr.	61
Williams, Mary, Miss	150
Williams, Mary, Mrs.	150
Williams, Sally	27
Williams, Sally, Mrs.	27
Williams, Solomon, Mr.	27
Williams, Thomas S.	152
Williams, Vashti	150
Williams, William	131
Williams, William Peck	131
Willis, Cornelia S.	148
Winship, Elizabeth, Mrs.	82
Winship, Joseph	104
Winship, Joseph, Capt.	82
Winship, Joseph, Jr.	82
Winship, Joseph, 3rd	82
Winship, Lucy, Mrs.	104
Winship, Sally, Miss	104
Witter, Jacob, Mr.	60
Witter, Rhoda, Mrs.	60
Wood, Betsey	51
Wood, Charles T.	51
Wood, Mary B.	51
Woodbridge, Elizabeth, Mrs.	164
Woodbridge, Harriet, 1st	164
Woodbridge, Harriet, 2nd	164
Woodbridge, Samuel, Mr.	164
Woodbridge Tomb	9
Woodword, Joshua, Mr.	11, 26
Woodworth, Asa, Mr.	28
Woodworth, Dyar	28
Woodworth, Elizabeth, Mrs.	28
Wright, David, Esq.	151
Wright, Martha	151
Wright, Mary Ann	151
Wright, Russell H.	151
Wright, William H.	151
Wyman, Edward W.	103
Wyman, Eliza C., Mrs.	103

Y

Yeomans, Joshua	161
Yerrington, Ellen F.	167
Yerrington, George F.	167
Yerrington, Harriet M.	167
Yerrington, Joseph H.	167
Yerrington, Luther S.	167

Z

Zibbero, Dezenah	94
Zibbero, Rodisa	92, 94

www.ingramcontent.com/pod-product-compliance
Lightning Source LLC
Chambersburg PA
CBHW062129160426
43191CB00013B/2245